V. RAYMOND EDMAN:

In the Presence of the King

by

EARLE E. CAIRNS

with

A Tribute

by

BILLY GRAHAM

*with appreciation for
your generous support of
our alma mater,*

Cl Cairns

MOODY PRESS ● CHICAGO

© 1972 by
THE MOODY BIBLE INSTITUTE
OF CHICAGO

ISBN: 0-8024-9180-4

Library of Congress Catalog Card Number: 72-77948

To
Edith Edman,
faithful and loving wife
of V. Raymond Edman

Printed in the United States of America

Contents

A Tribute

IN THE SPRING of 1940 I met Dr. Edman's mother and his brother at the little Bible school I was attending in Florida, while they were vacationing. They came to hear me preach and urged me to go to Wheaton for my college training. I took their advice.

When I arrived at Wheaton in September, Dr. Edman just recently had been installed as the president.

The first time I saw him was as we passed each other between Blanchard and the old Stupe. He said, "Hi, Bill," and kept on going. I stopped in amazement. I had no idea he knew who I was. Over at the Stupe I remarked to other students about the incident; and they laughingly said, "He knows everybody."

The second encounter was a day or two later at a prayer meeting in a private home. It was attended largely by Christian and Missionary Alliance students. Since I had been closely identified with the C. & M.A. in Florida, I went. Dr. Edman came to me almost immediately and said, "Bill, how are things going?"

I replied, "Very well, sir."

He said both his mother and brother had told him quite a bit about me, that he hoped I soon would find my way around Wheaton, and that if there was anything he could do for me please not to hesitate to call on him.

This was the type of man he was. I never dreamed this was the beginning of one of the warmest, most enduring and important friendships of my entire life. Here was a man deep in the things of God, his life saturated with Scripture

5

and prayer. Here was a man of courage and integrity — but most of all, of compassion. He knew and understood the problems of the students in those days. Anyone could go in to see him and talk over personal problems. He was a marvelous listener. His counseling and his prayers were usually brief but to the point.

I remember him also as a professor. I took first-year history under him. The class was the largest in the school, and he knew his subject from A to Z. He made the classes interesting. No student could stump him.

Another early impression was of his chapel talks. At Wheaton we had many world-famous speakers from every area of Christian life; but students always preferred to hear "Prexy." He left us with something to chew on intellectually, but most of all he spoke to our hearts. If the alumni of those years were polled, I am sure they would be unanimous in saying his chapel talks were the highlight of their experiences at Wheaton.

Ruth and I had been dating with fair regularity for about three months when Prexy passed me on campus one day with this comment: "Bill, Ruth's one in a million." That's all he said, but it was enough to help confirm what I already knew — she was the one to be my life companion.

When Dr. Edman decided his college responsibilities were too great for him to carry on the pastorate of the Tabernacle — a church made up largely of students, that met in the old Masonic Temple — I was among those he recommended as his successor. In the summer of 1941 I received a letter from Dr. Edman, stating that the board at the Tabernacle wanted me to succeed him. After a great deal of agonizing and prayer I accepted, and for the next two years I served as student pastor.

During this entire time Dr. Edman encouraged me. On several occasions he called me to his office for prayer. Periodically he would come to the "Tab" and worship. Often he

gave me little gospel outlines because he knew I was strug-
gling to prepare new sermons while taking a full school
load. I always was amazed at how much time he seemed to
have for everyone. He never appeared to be in a hurry,
though the load he carried and the pressures he felt must
have been enormous.

In my senior year, when I received a call to be pastor of
the Western Springs Baptist Church, I went to Dr. Edman
for counsel. He did not give any direct advice except to say
he would pray with me about the matter. Eventually I accepted the call without further consultation with him.

I had been pastor there only a few weeks when I began to
get invitations to speak in other parts of the country, largely
on the recommendation of Dr. Edman. A number of these
places originally had wanted him; and because he was not
available, he suggested me. I accepted several of these engagements, and my ministry spread far beyond Western
Springs.

When Torrey Johnson invited me to become the first full-
time worker and evangelist in Youth for Christ International,
I consulted with Dr. Edman. Again he gave no direct advice one way or the other except to say, "Do what the Lord
tells you to do." We then had prayer. I felt peace about
accepting, and so did Ruth.

During all the years of my involvement with Youth for
Christ, Dr. Edman was a source of constant encouragement
and inspiration. He was one of the top advisers to Youth for
Christ International in its early days. In many a tense situation his humor, sincerity, and devotional approach helped us
to solve the problem. He always held before us the world-
wide outreach and evangelization mission of the church.

During the early days of my own ministry as an evangelist, he encouraged me at every level. I rarely made a major
decision without discussing it with him, usually by telephone. In the controversies in which I found myself during

the early 1950s, he publicly took my side because he thought
I was right. When there was no letup of criticism, neither
by the extreme right nor the extreme left, he would always
smile, give me a word of encouragement, and then say,
"Billy, pay no attention. You have only one Person to
please, and that's the Lord."

I constantly consulted him concerning the building of
the Billy Graham Evangelistic Association. He was a charter
member of our board of directors. He personally handled
many knotty problems for us; his counsel and advice were
absolutely invaluable. He always brought a business meeting around to a spiritual framework.

One of the things I remember about those many board
meetings was that he always went to bed early! He would
say, "You cannot accomplish anything after nine o'clock."
We would laugh and adjourn. He was an early riser and
usually would gather some of the business men and team
members on the board for an early morning prayer meeting
and Bible study.

Not only his prayer ministry and counsel but his writing
had a great impact on me and my family; I suppose I have
read everything he had published. One of the reasons I was
always interested in his writing is that I knew the life behind it.

Wherever I go in the world, there are men and women
who come and tell me they were touched in some way by
the ministry of V. Raymond Edman. We will never know
the full evaluation of his life and ministry until we stand at
the judgment seat of Christ, but still I have to say that he
was *the most unforgettable Christian I ever met.*

Billy Graham

1.

A Goodly Heritage

VICTOR RAYMOND EDMAN's lineage from both parents lay in Sweden. He thought fondly of his parents' homeland often — its "pine forests of deep green, reflected in its many lakes, its cottages of red and white, its hills of grey granite. . . ."

Grandfather Carl Edman hammered out a living as a blacksmith in Smoland. But his son Anders, born in Smoland on February 7, 1870, left the old world at nineteen and in 1894 proudly became a citizen of the United States.

On May 9, 1900, soon after the sturdy young father left the steel mills to clerk in a Swedish grocer's store in Chicago Heights, his second son, Victor Raymond Edman, was born. That same spring Anders had accumulated enough capital to open his own grocery business at 15 Illinois Street in Chicago Heights. As the Edman children became old enough, each helped in the grocery store after school and on Saturday. Young Ray's regular task was to look after the three horses which pulled the delivery wagons in the summer and the sleighs in winter. The boys also were required to mow the lawn around their big house at 1654 Euclid in Chicago Heights.

Anders Edman was a devout Christian as well as a businessman of rectitude. He faithfully attended the local Swedish Missionary Church affiliated with what later became the Mission Covenant denomination. Not only was he in his pew for two services on Sunday — one in Swedish and the other in English — and the midweek prayer meeting, but he also fulfilled his function as Sunday school superintendent for twenty-five years. Frequently he kept store until 7:00 P.M., and went directly to the prayer meeting. Dr. Edman described Pastor Karl A. Anderson, who had been reared in Sweden and converted there in his teens, as "a kindly, genial, jolly and rotund" individual.

His father practiced his religion in the home as well as in the church or at business. Dr. Edman in a 1942 Wheaton College chapel talk recalled how he and his sister Myrtle talked about the room with its well-worn rug where his father had knelt in prayer.

Proverbs 14:26 in Anders' Swedish Bible was well underlined and the page worn as he reviewed the biblical promise, "In the fear of the LORD is strong confidence: and his children shall have a place of refuge."

Family prayers were an important part of the homelife, and in them each of the children was faithfully named individually. When the senior Edman took long walks with the boys in the woods near their home on the edge of town, he taught them of God and man in unobtrusive ways.

The Sunday paper was not permitted in the home, and Walter Hoeppner, who lived nearby, remembered how the boys would often come to his less strict home on Sunday afternoons to read the comics.[1]

The Edmans used to go to the Cedar Lake Conference in what was one of the first automobiles in Chicago Heights. Here one person was impressed with Anders Edman's "kindly encouraging comments."[2] After his retirement he regularly visited Cook County Infirmary in Oak Forest to serve his fellow Scandinavians there. He brought them old suits he had gathered from friends, and boxes of cube sugar for their coffee. His wife would play the piano for lay services he held for the old county wards.[3]

This upright and godly father often found it hard to realize in later years that his family had grown up and were without need of his paternalism. When his son Raymond became engaged to Edith Olson, he took it upon himself to purchase an engagement ring for them.

After Raymond became a teacher at Wheaton, his father often told him that if he were ever asked to be president he should decline the position.[4]

Anders never encouraged his three sons to follow him in his business. He may have been strict and dominated his family but his sextet of youngsters — three boys, three girls — never rebelled under it. They readily accepted strict family rules. Dr. Edman's son David had a strong impression that V. Raymond Edman loved his father completely and considered his pattern of life as his ideal.[5]

Alma Tolf, Dr. Edman's mother, also was born in Sweden — arriving in the home of Algot and Emma Tolf on December 2, 1876. Her parents brought her to Batavia, Illinois, in 1878, when she was two. They joined cousins who had migrated there earlier to work in an iron foundry. Thence the family moved to Chicago's South Side where Algot took work in a steel foundry. His enormous physical strength was a matter of family pride. In a carnival concession he wielded the sledgehammer so effectively that his blow rang the bell and garnered the prize.[6]

Perhaps this was the time when Anders Edman took Alma to the Chicago World Fair of 1893. Shortly thereafter she became his wife, supported her husband submissively, and was a good mother to their large family. When he died in 1939, Alma Edman had a set of chimes installed in the tower of Blanchard Hall in his memory. The chimes' dedication was a part of her son Raymond's inauguration ceremonies as president of Wheaton College in 1941.

Elner, the oldest of the family, was educated in business at Northwestern University, worked as an accountant, and was associated for years with a wholesale coal company as an executive. Myrtle, the only one to attend Wheaton College, did so with the class of 1925 and became a teacher in an elementary school in Chicago Heights. She later entered the Wheaton school system and made her home with her mother until Mrs. Edman died.

Merrill, the youngest son, was associated with the Illinois Bell Telephone Company until his death in 1964. Another daughter, Evelyn, died in 1932 a short time after her marriage to Norton White.

The youngest sister, Florence, married Leslie Ferry, a businessman, and moved to California. Only she and Elner are still living. Because she was the youngest and often was ill, Florence needed much care. The boys had to be her nursemaids. Unlike many boys of that day who resented wheeling a baby carriage, they gladly looked after the baby sister whom they adored.[7]

Young Raymond Edman, who never used the Victor in his name except in the army,[8] was always nearsighted and wore thick glasses from the time he was in grade school. When her family was young, Alma Edman recalled, "We'd look at Ray always reading, always a book in his hand, and we knew that one must have an education."[9] She told another friend that, after talking with their father or hearing him read *Pilgrim's Progress*, Elner and Ray would debate spiritedly in their room on what they had heard.[10]

Ray's grandmother on his mother's side had also been noted for her clever wit.[11] Perhaps these were the reasons for his later ability to think and speak on his feet so well and to engage in clever and witty repartee with others.

Walter Hoeppner, who lived only a few doors away and attended the same elementary and high school, said that he was always a good student but was modest about his accomplishments. Always honest, reliable and truthful, he was admired by his classmates and tagged a "solid citizen."

His record reveals no scrapes, but he was still a "regular boy."[12]

He did resent the slur, "You big Swedes," which was often hurled at him and his brother Elner. He later wrote that this "epithet puzzled and angered me." As he began to study history and saw that there were indeed great Swedes, such as the soldier-king Gustavus Adolphus and the botanist Linnaeus, this heritage comforted him.[13] His mother later told a friend that she thought the nickname drew the boys closer together and encouraged them to find companionship in the home.

2.

Growing Up

BOYHOOD WAS NOT altogether limited to school and work in the store. In 1907 the parents took seven-year-old Ray and Elner with them to England and Sweden to help celebrate the golden wedding anniversary of their grandfather, Carl, and his wife. The grandfather died two weeks before the anniversary and instead they attended his funeral, which young Ray remembered vividly.

Back home again in America, the boys enjoyed the normal activities of their age. Their home was on the edge of town near a woods, which is now a part of Illinois forest preserves. The house still stands near Thorn Creek. "Colley's Bend," as they called it, was a curve in the creek which provided an ideal swimming hole with its clear, deep, quiet water. The Edman boys often slept in a tent during the summer and in the morning they would slosh through a swampy area infested with garter snakes to the pool for their morning swim. The boys hauled in bullheads, sunfish, crappies and crayfish in their creek. Muskrats had homes in holes in the bank, and Walter Hoeppner remembered how one winter he trapped several for their pelts.

Boys of the neighborhood McEldowney family had a metal canoe, and the boys took turns riding the small rapids in the creek at high water with little concern for an occasional collision with tree or rock. They spied on each other in mock summer wars and staged "battles" in the woods and fields. Fortunately there never were any casualties.

As the Edman boys became older they were given the pleasure of using the family car with some strict regulations. Young Ray often played tennis on the family court of the nearby Fair home. During the winter he would skate on the ice of the creek, often going a mile upstream. If he fell through the ice, he would build a fire, take off his shoes, dry them, and proceed on his way with never a worry about catching cold. Building snowhouses and forts consumed many an afternoon, and many a mock war was fought with snowballs between the Hickory Street and Euclid Avenue gangs of Chicago Heights.[1]

On June 19, 1914, he was given the large diploma of the grammar school, signed by the president of the board of education, the superintendent of schools, and his principal, Mabel E. Pingry. He kept it with his valuable papers all through the many moves of his life.

V. Raymond Edman went on to the relatively small high school of Bloom township, located in the building which is now the City Hall and Municipal Building of Chicago Heights. Only thirty-one were in his class by the time they became seniors. Mrs. K. B. Tiffany recounted how she had met his English teacher, Miss McDowney, who described his work in English as "always on time and interesting."[2]

Although he was more of a student than a top athlete in high school, young Edman tried every possible athletic activity. He liked to run simply for his own pleasure and was on the school track team in 1915 and 1916. Changing to basketball in 1916, he played each year until his graduation. He impressed Fred W. Landsea, later a banker who bought the Edman family home, as a "good athlete, playing basketball and football."[3] He was forward on the Heavyweights, the championship basketball team in 1918.

He enjoyed musical, forensic and literary activities. He

sang in the glee club in 1917 and 1918 and was second bass in the Bloom Male Quartette of 1918. Joining the Forum, the public speaking organization of the school in 1915, he became its secretary in 1916, and chairman of its program committee in 1918. In 1917 he had the honor of being its president. He indulged his literary bent on the staff of the yearbook, serving as advertising manager and junior associate editor in 1917 and editor-in-chief in 1918.[4] His hobby listed under his biography was *The Bloom*, the high school yearbook, and his "hereafter" was said to be "journalism."[5] These activities helped to elect him as president of his class in 1917 and 1918.

He was included in the makeup of the "Ideal Boy" because of his clear, easily heard, quiet voice which was so effective an instrument of public speaking then and later.[6] Perhaps this helped him to persuade his father to put an ad for the grocery business in *The Bloom*. The class prophecy described his future in these words:

> Ray Edman, our Prexy so stately
> In Congress will hold a place
> His eloquence, wit, and his learning
> To the Bloom and the Forum we trace.[7]

E. L. Boyer, Ray's high school principal, had a high opinion of him. He described him as "a leader in athletics, public speaking, and in other laudable school enterprises."[8]

This ability in and love of athletics help to explain why at Wheaton he was always present at football and basketball games and sat on the bench with the players. His forensic ability in high school and participation in the Forum were prophetic of his ability as a Bible conference speaker and as presiding officer of Wheaton College in its faculty meetings. The tide of writings that issued from his pen since 1947 would not have been possible without the well-laid literary foundations of high school literature courses and work in the Forum.

Dr. Edman had an enduring love of adventure and wanted to try new things. One summer he and his brothers went off on their bikes for several days, eating and sleeping on the road wherever it was convenient. During the summer of 1917 before his senior year he went to Saskatchewan, Canada, with two friends whose parents owned land there. The boys, who spent the summer clearing land of trees and breaking it with a plow, slept and batched in a one-room shack on wheels. Here Ray came to love the limitless flat prairie.[9]

During his final high school year he crystallized his religious experience by accepting Christ as his Saviour in a series of union evangelistic services sponsored by the Mission Covenant, Baptist, Presbyterian and Methodist churches of the community. The evangelist was Dr. I. E. Honeywell. A large wooden tabernacle was built for the meetings.

Dr. Honeywell's party conducted a high school assembly on Wednesday, May 27, at the invitation of the school board. During the assembly, D. L. Spooner, who conducted the choir during the meetings, sang "Never Let the Old Flag Fall" and a war song, "While We Are Canning the Kaiser," to the tune of "Marching Through Georgia." Dr. Honeywell spoke on "How to Win in the Battle of Life" with an "inspiring and instructive three points: Shun evil companions. Be honest in school and life. Avoid the use of cigarettes." The assembly ended with songs by a quartet, the McCombs, Miss Ferries and Mr. Spooner.[10]

When asked in 1950 to name the happiest moment of his life, Dr. Edman wrote of the 1950 Wheaton revival, the promise of money for the present library, the *Tower* dedication to him in 1940, his invitation to come to Wheaton in 1936, and his call to the mission field. But he concluded,

". . . perhaps the happiest moment was on a summer's night when there came assurance of salvation."[11]

In a chapel talk on September 28, 1942, he described that meeting in June, 1918. The large tabernacle had been filled to capacity. The large response to the invitation to come forward made it necessary for personal workers to give those who had come forward a little card to sign. The card indicated whether they were coming forward for consecration of life to God or to accept Christ as Saviour.

Dr. Edman said, "There was no question in my heart as to which of these statements was true in my life, despite the fact that I had an earnest Christian home for which I thank God. So after I had written my name on it, it seemed perfectly obvious that I came to accept Christ as my Savior."

Thus the boy just turned eighteen found a "quiet assurance of acceptance and rest of heart."[12] He also described his experience to Carl M. Vining in these words: "When I received the Lord Jesus as my Savior, I realized the forgiveness of sins and knew that only God could forgive sin."[13]

High school commencement finally came at 8:30 p.m. June 19, 1918. Thirty-two graduates were listed. Music and an address by Attorney Henry R. Rathbone preceded the presentation of the diplomas by the principal, E. L. Boyer. The class motto *Qui Non Praeficit, Deficit* (He who does not excel fails) was not to be true of that class. In 1947 Edman was asked to speak at the high school's Parent Teachers Association on founder's day.[14] When a community college was set up in 1960, he was invited to the dedication exercises of the new Bloom Community Township College on Sunday, January 17, but was unable to go.[15]

3.

To Arms!

FOUR MONTHS before World War I ended, Ray Edman and his friend Walter Hoeppner enlisted in the U.S. Army and were sent that month — July, 1918 — to Jefferson Barracks in Missouri. Because of his age, young Edman had to have his father's consent to enlist.

Many years later he recalled the day he left for camp when his eldest son, Charles, departed from the Edman home for the armed services. In 1918 he had thought mainly of the travel, adventure and even possible danger. Not until Charles left did Dr. Edman fully appreciate why his father had said so little as they walked to the station to take the train for the city.[1]

Upon his arrival at camp two days after his enlistment, the rosy glow of army life faded abruptly when he was ordered to peel potatoes, wash pots and pans, and set tables for two weeks. Walter had been assigned to a medical unit.

A month after Edman's enlistment a colonel appeared, the young soldier thought, to pick out men for service in France. Edman fervently asked God to give the right answers so he could be immediately dispatched overseas to the war theater.

"Why are you in the army?" the colonel asked him.

Ramrod straight, Private Edman answered, "To be of service, sir!"

19

The colonel said nothing, and young Edman afterward felt stupid at giving such an obvious answer. But two days later he was relieved to find that those he was certain had given correct answers were assigned to permanent duty at the barracks and did not go overseas.[2]

A letter to Victorine Stolberg, the woman who later married his brother Elner, describes the doughboy's occasional longing for home. In thanking her for a box of food, he wrote:

> Folks in civilian life who are accustomed to get home-cooked grub three times a day, and sit at a table with a tablecloth, real silverware, and manners, cannot appreciate what a box of real home-made Swedish goodies mean to a soldier, who has to march to a board table, and grab all the chow near at hand, and holler for what he can't reach. Army chow is wholesome and healthful, but it isn't cooked with the same individual care as at home. Except for some days when all we get is beans, beans, beans, pork & beans, & more beans, then lima beans, and finally brown beans. Wowie!

He added that after such food when the mail brings a box of food that "doesn't have to be chewed for 45 minutes — Oh Boy!" It also shows that "folks at home are thinking of a fellow, and that puts all the pep and ambition in a soldier."

He closed the letter by telling Victorine of his excitement about rumors that a shipment of men overseas would take place. By this time in August he had been in the army two months. In a postscript he added that he had found that the rumor was true and that they would leave the following Thursday for Camp Crane near Allentown, Pennsylvania. This was an overseas training camp. He had "asked the Lord every day to put me on shipment, and if He wants me to go, I have entrusted my future to Him, and I know that He will do the best for me."[3] Within a short time after that he was on his way to Brest, France, on the "old cattle boat," the S. S. *St. Louis.*

Unlike many enlisted men, he did not neglect his Christian life while in the army. Through his father's influence he joined the Pocket Testament League, promising to read a portion of Scripture each day. He used the New Testament given to him by his Sunday school class after he had enlisted. The soldier also knelt for his evening prayer, even though an occasional shoe was thrown at him for so doing. He relished Christian fellowship as well as coffee and doughnuts in a Salvation Army canteen.[4]

In France he heard much of the Baptist chaplain, Dan Poling, later editor of the *Christian Herald,* who was a "great help to the troops in France."[5]

Shortly before Christmas in 1918 he and a few medics of Company B completed the long march after the November 11 Armistice through the Argonne Forest to Verdun, then through Luxemburg, along the Moselle River valley, and across the Rhine to the Westerwald. Upon their arrival on December 23 they were housed in a lice-laden shelter that had been the barracks for Russian prisoners of war. The weather was frigid and the snow lay deep. Their bed was the floor. Some windows were missing, but the men managed to coax a warm fire in an old stove.

Just when Edman thought he would be warm and comfortable, a runner arrived with orders to transfer five men to C Company located some distance away. The tough Kansas sergeant barked an order: "Edman, you're in charge of this detail."

A throat ailment of the previous winter was recurring because of his sore throat and fever. This new task seemed to be too much. He slipped out to a side room, knelt in prayer and cast himself on God for strength to complete his assignment. During this crisis he became deeply aware of the presence of Christ and went out to lead the unit through the snow to Boden.

When they arrived, their billet was not an abandoned prison camp but a comfortable German home. The Frau, who was preparing a meal when he arrived, sensed that Edman was ill. Rather than put him in a cold room, she arranged his quarters in a snug attic room with her brother and gave him a mammoth feather tick for his bed. Then he realized why the presence of God had been so real and why he had been forced to move. This story was frequently repeated in chapel talks, in the college *Bulletin,* in magazine articles and in his books.[6]

Several letters to Victorine Stolberg tell of his feelings and experiences in 1919 with the army of occupation. Letters came infrequently because of slow mail service. After receiving two letters from home which were several weeks in arriving, he wrote to her in February: "Yesterday I was the happiest bird. . . . If the folks in 'God's country' only realized with what joy and anticipation a lonely doughboy — way across the Rhine — receives a letter from the States, I think I should receive more letters. Letters are so few and far between that I prize each most highly," especially when they were often four months in coming.[7] He asked her to notice "the 9½ hob-nailed clodhoppers" and the divisional insignia in the picture that accompanied the letter. He explained that the red "1" meant:

> 1st in war
> 1st in peace
> 1st in the hands of the Military Police.

Because he was "a Regular Army man," he expected to be with the last outfit to get home.

Another letter to Victorine in April demonstrated the young man's pride in being a part of the regular army and of the famous fighting First Division. Speaking of a boy at home who was now in college and who had talked much of joining the army but never did, young Edman wrote, "I'd like to see him soldiering in a hardboiled outfit like this first Division. . . . It's the Regular Army, and the only place to be in the U.S. Army." He spoke fondly of his companions, some of whom had been in the army for thirty-eight years, as "soldiers by *choice* and profession."

From February until June, 1919, Edman was in training at the Army Medical School of the Twenty-eighth Infantry at Meudt, Germany. This training was to serve him well some years later when he practiced simple medicine to heal the ailments of the Quechua Indians in Ecuador's towering Andes.

He soon became proficient in German and was attached to the Headquarters Company. Here he served as an interpreter for the headquarters staff under Lt. Colonel Heubner. During this time he told Victorine that he was "carefully studying these people [Germans], and my knowledge of their language helps me wonderfully."[8]

A 1962 letter to James E. Smith, Jr., who was writing a paper on the military occupation of the Rhineland for a class at Northern Illinois University, reveals how carefully Edman had observed during this period and also shows quite a mastery of the political situation in Germany for a boy of nineteen.[9]

He was soon made a private first class, his highest rank. His service with the army of occupation was recognized in 1947 when, along with others, he received an army of occupation medal on March 21, 1947, "for honorable service in Germany during the occupation period between 12 November 1918 and 11 July 1923."

Periods of leave lessened the drudgery of routine army life. One leave was spent in the lovely French Alps at Aix-les-Baines. Eight of them were crowded into a third-class railroad compartment for the long trip back to camp. Because he was so tired, he climbed up to the "little baggage rack 16 inches wide at the most, and six feet long and slept" on that precarious perch on a swaying train.[10]

He reassured Victorine in the same letter that his friends at home need not worry lest he get a German sweetheart because German girls "cannot begin to compare with real United States women — in looks, intellectuality (?) or anything else." Because he had not talked to an American woman for nearly a year, he admitted that he was so bashful he was afraid to speak to the YMCA women at Aix-les-Baines. He "felt crude and vulgar after soldiering so long with men."

He highly respected the Salvation Army for its work in France. In the month of May he attended a Saturday night party in Meudt put on by that group. He wrote home ecstatically about the "real ice cream and cake" and added that "The S.A. is the grandest outfit, and most popular with the fighting units." He thought this was because of their interest in the spiritual as well as material welfare of the men. At the party an officer called for silence and prayed fervently "for us boys and the folks back home."[11]

By August of 1919, rumors that they were soon to go to the port of embarkation for the United States in a "boxcar special *Homeward Bound*" were confirmed. The American soldiers began to pack "in preparation to start for the dear old U.S.A." so they would be home in September of 1919. The letter is alive with joy at the start for home after a year's absence.[12]

The glorious day of August 20, 1919, arrived when the transport *Orizaba* sailed from Brest toward the United States. When it docked at Hoboken, New Jersey, on August 30, Pfc. Edman sent a card to his brother Elner with this enthusiastic message: "Back in a white man's country!! Great life!" That same day he sent a telegram to his father telling of his arrival at New Jersey's Camp Merritt. He participated in the September 3rd Victory parade down New York's Fifth Avenue, marching behind General Pershing. Edman also marched in the Washington, D.C., parade. He was mustered out of the army at Camp Sterling in Illinois where he joyfully dropped his serial number and the name Victor by which he had been known in the army.

While it was a joy to be home, he was glad that he had had the experience of army service. Over forty years later he summed up his impression of the value of his army career in these words: "I have never regretted the time of service in the Army that I had between high school and college. Many of the earliest lessons in Christian life I learned in the service."[13]

Upon his return to his home he purchased a large scrapbook and pasted snapshots and other mementos of army life in it. The inscription in it reveals his sense of history: "To perpetuate the memory of the days when the schoolboys of America laid aside their books to cross the seas and drive back the Hun that this world might be a decent place to live in, this book of my military collections has been made." This sense of patriotic obligation remained with him all his life.

Although he was late for the opening classes, the ex-soldier enrolled at the University of Illinois in September. He joined the social fraternity of the Pi Pi Rho[14] and began his studies.

4.

That Girl

COLLEGE IS A WORLD REMOVED from the grimy front lines of war. Civilian Edman confessed that his studies at the University of Illinois were difficult for a restless doughboy, but he applied himself to his courses — English composition, literature, speech, European history, psychology, chemistry, and physiography — and won. Algebra offered the toughest stand because he had been poorly advised to enroll in an advanced section with engineering students. He had one failing exam during the course, but he regrouped mentally and fought back to finish the semester with a high grade.[1]

As he began to consider the challenge of the mission field, Edman added French to his roster of studies at Illinois. Spanish and French made up almost one-third of the seventy-seven hours of credit he received at Boston University, from which he finally graduated. On October 3, 1921, he was awarded a certificate of preliminary honors. This honor was given to Illinois freshmen and sophomores who earned a grade of A in half their work and no grade below C in 15 percent of their work. He achieved this record without studying on Sunday, a plan he frequently urged upon his Wheaton "lads and lassies" in chapel. The promise in Isaiah 58:13-14 that the Lord would prosper those who delighted themselves in Him and properly observed the day of rest, he found to be true.

His editorial experience on *The Bloom* helped him to se-

cure the position of sophomore assistant on *The Illio,* the
university annual for 1922.[2] He hoped that in his junior
year he might become the editor of the 1923 edition, a position that would bring financial aid, society membership, and
campus leadership which Edman felt could be used for God's
glory.

The publications board met on a Tuesday to pick an editor. Edman played a softball game that afternoon with
another team in intramural competition, and his team lost.
A second disappointment came after the game when he met
members of the board coming out of University Hall after
their meeting. He asked about their decision and was told
that students named Henry and Green had been chosen as
editor and business manager for the next year. The choices
surprised him. Henry had been made editor when he had
been only the business manager the previous year. Later he
found out that campus and fraternity politics had been involved in the decision. Going to his room after the evening
meal to pray about this disappointment, he slowly began to
realize that the rejection might be God's way of showing
him that he should do something else.[3]

Back home again that spring, he saw in his father's love
for him a picture of God's care for him. Through the plate-
glass section of the front door of the family home he could
see the stairs and the hallway. When he rang the bell he
knew his father's shadow would soon be cast on the hall
landing by the light which burned each night, and he knew
also that his father would warmly welcome him and talk
with him.

The previous summer had been good spiritual preparation.
He had gone to a youth Bible conference at Cedar Lake,
Indiana, where Paul Rader, pastor of Chicago's Moody
Memorial Church, was the speaker. One evening the popu-
lar evangelist took the text, "Where there is no vision, the
people perish."[4] Young Edman dedicated himself in that

meeting to full-time service for God and felt an initial calling to missionary work in South America.[5]

After the death in 1882 of A. B. Simpson, founder of the
Missionary Training Institute, Paul Rader became chairman
of the board of trustees and president of the institute which
had been moved to Nyack in 1887. When young Edman
sought his advice, he urged him to teach Spanish at Nyack
and to take Bible training to prepare for missionary service.
Edman agreed upon the plan.

The institute stressed Bible training, spiritual life, practical service, and a disciplined devotional life. The last involved half an hour of devotions before breakfast, chapel,
prayer in classes, a noon prayer meeting, and after-dinner
devotions in the dining hall where missionaries were frequently asked to speak. The cost was $100 a term for board
and room, $10 for tuition per term, and $1 for each registration fee and the diploma. Each student was required to do
three hours of chores per week.

Edman listed the name of Paul Rader for one of his refer-
ences on his application. He also listed high school, first-aid
school in the army, and the University of Illinois as places
of earlier accomplishment. His editorial service on *The
Bloom* and *The Illio* and a stretch as a salesman constituted
his work experience. He also declared that he could teach
and that he was called to be a missionary in South America.[6]

On registration day, September 13, 1921, he enrolled in
the one-year Junior Institute course at Nyack. His thirty-
four hours of work that year included twenty-two hours of
biblical studies. This was to be his only formal training in
Bible. The course was not as demanding as his studies at
the University of Illinois, and he received A's in every course
in addition to serving well as a student teacher of Spanish.
Miss Agnes Brown, a former missionary to South America,
recollects that as a teacher of Spanish and a student himself "he was highly thought of as a student and a friend."[7]

In a Wheaton chapel message on Nehemiah 8:8 on October 26, 1943, he spoke of himself and several Nyack friends who organized themselves as "The Terrible Ten." With the help of Robert Ekvall, who had come to Nyack from Wheaton, they organized a group to meet one hour and a half each Tuesday with a faculty member as their critic to develop facility in public speaking. Ekvall would assign a poem, a portion of Scripture, or some other work upon which each would recite.

Sometime during that fall of 1921 Edman visited Boston, where he met two people who would have a most important place in his life. Paul Rader speaking at a missionary conference in the Park Street Church drew the fledgling missionary. During the meeting he took note of the alert red-haired man who was leading the meeting. When he spoke to Dr. Rader after the service, the preacher introduced him to E. Joseph Evans, the colorful Welshman he had noticed earlier. Evans, converted during the historic Welsh revival at the beginning of the century, had been widely used by God. The Welshman, serving as superintendent of the New England district of the Christian and Missionary Alliance, asked him what he was going to do after the service. Edman explained that he was headed for the station to catch a train back to Nyack. Dr. Evans invited him instead to stay overnight in his home and to enjoy the balance of the conference. Thus began a lifelong friendship with "Uncle Joe" for Mr. and Mrs. Edman. Dr. Edman described him later as the one "who brought up friend wife and me in the Gospel when we were young people in Boston."[8] Young Edman, Charles Shaw, and several others were tagged at Nyack as "Uncle Joe's boys."[9]

The Welshman remained a fast friend at various crises in Dr. Edman's life.

Edith Olson was at the same conference in Park Street Church. A dark-haired, vivacious girl, she was also of Swedish descent. Her grandparents were Johanna and Carl Peter Bergman. Carl was a carpenter in Sweden who migrated to the United States. Their daughter Elizabeth married Gustaf Olson, and the young couple settled in a home at 314 Columbia Street in Cambridge, Massachusetts. Dr. Edman's son David later described his grandfather as a "humble, quiet, sweet saint."[10]

Edith Marie Olson was born on September 29, 1899. She had two brothers: William Olson, who later became a Salvation Army officer, and Edwin G. Olson, a professor of history at New York University. (Both are deceased.) The family faithfully attended a Swedish Baptist Church.

Edith Olson became an earnest Christian at the age of fourteen. She attended a stenographic school for a year, training which opened up a position during World War I as a secretary in the Quartermaster Corps.

During the war she thought she detected a divine call to missionary service in Indo-China where the Christian and Missionary Alliance had a flourishing work. She enrolled at Nyack in September, 1919, and took the two-year Senior Institute course from which she graduated on May 17, 1921. She needed to earn half her expenses and did so as a secretary because of her previous experience.

After graduation she became a secretary in a Boston rescue mission. Her boss was Uncle Joe.

Throughout her early student experience at Nyack, Edith remained uncertain whether the Far East was indeed to be her future field of service and with what mission board. Walking alone into the woods near their summer home in Old Orchard, Maine, she knelt by an old pine stump to pray. Finally the girl was able to confess her willingness to do anything or go anywhere that God desired. Edith soon afterward met her future husband. Mrs. Edman spoke of the dramatic encounter with God when her husband was inaugurated as president of Wheaton in 1941.

Not long after Edith's big decision, the young student-teacher from Nyack stood at the back of Park Street Church looking for a seat. He noticed what looked like space in the front pew and took it. The man on his left whispered, "That's reserved for the pianist." When the piano player came, young Edman tried to make room for her. "I'm sorry," he said. "That's all the room I can make."

The following afternoon his friend Charles Shaw introduced him formally to the girl who had played the piano.[11] That evening they were both dinner guests in the home of the pastor. Edith Olson sat across from her future husband. "I thought he was older than I," she recalled, "and married."[12]

After that eventful week in which he met Uncle Joe and his future wife, young Edman returned to his studies and teaching at Nyack. His need for higher education increasingly occupied his mind. Nyack's curriculum of that day did not offer him enough intellectual challenge.

Before graduation on May 16, 1922, he and a Canadian student named Kirk Patrick decided to wait tables on a steamer going as far south as Chile that summer, in order to become acquainted with South America — their chosen field of Christian service. Edman told Charles Washburn, his hymnology teacher, on May 6 that he planned to take the ship on May 8 because he would have his examinations and grades completed by then.

"Uncle Charlie" warned that he was making a hasty decision. He quoted Isaiah 28:16, reminding the restless young man that the one who believes will not make haste. Edman's obligation to Nyack did not end until May 16. They prayed. Young Edman finally abandoned his impetuous plan. He let Kirk go on alone to the Canal Zone and Chile.[13]

His commencement address as a graduate from the one-year institute revealed his deep interest in missions. In it he outlined the immense needs of South America. He told how little the church was doing to meet that need and challenged his audience to rise and serve in that area.[14]

Uncle Joe was on campus before the commencement on Monday, May 9, and questioned his young friend about plans for the summer. When he learned the young man had none, he invited him to move to Boston and live with him. Young Edman was thankful he had "abandoned ship" and finished his term.

5.

Knees Down

ON ONE OCCASION that year Ray Edman expressed his restlessness to Uncle Joe who had begun to wonder when his young friend would finally settle down. The senior Edman also had been concerned as to when his son would begin his career, and on one occasion had plaintively inquired of Uncle Joe, "Do you think he will ever amount to anything?"

As Uncle Joe talked to his lad in the dining room of the Somerville home, surrounded by lovely antiques from all over the world, he quite seriously counseled, "Ray, God has a plan for your life. When you *abandon* yourself, God will reveal it."

Ray slid from his chair to his knees, stabbed by conviction. He prayed with deep emotion that he would "abandon himself to God and await His will." Dr. Evans and Mrs. Edman both agree that this experience was climactic. Until this point Edman's love of adventure, his energy, and his preference for "busy holiness" had withheld the sense of direction he now experienced.[1]

Summer school at Columbia University in New York was arranged. He took three hours of phonetics, three hours of Latin American history, and two hours of Spanish. He planned to graduate from Columbia but was told by the registrar's office that the eight hours of military credit in military drill recorded by the University of Illinois for his military service would cause difficulty in transfer.

He left Columbia perplexed that August of 1922. Landing in Boston with fifteen cents, he used five cents to phone Uncle Joe and ten for carfare to Somerville. He cast about in his mind fruitlessly as he rode through the darkness in the streetcar. Suddenly a vivid sense of the Lord's presence descended upon him. A clear inner conviction ordered that he remain in Boston that winter, help Uncle Joe in return for living in his home, attend Boston University until he got his degree, and then go to South America as a missionary. At last he felt he had clearly determined the Lord's will for his life.[2]

He worked hard at Boston University, stoked the furnace in the Somerville home, chauffeured Uncle Joe in his Model T Ford, and ran errands for Jennie Evans, Uncle Joe's sister. He treasured the golden hours of Bible study and prayer with the older man, often poring over the Scriptures far into the night.

His Boston University transcript reveals a heavy academic load: six hours of German, six hours of Latin, six hours of Romance languages, nine hours of social science, and four hours each in education and philosophy. He earned twelve hours of *A*, eighteen of *B*, and five of *C*.

He made time frequently to see Edith Olson. At the University of Illinois he had been "very timid about women," and spent little time in their company. Now Cambridge crept into his "nocturnal itinerary several times a week."[3]

One early experience stands out as memorable. Evidently Uncle Joe had needed secretarial help and merely directed, "Call Edith Olson, and she will do this work for me." He left without giving Edman his secretary's phone number.

The young man began perusing the long list of Olsons in the Boston phone directory until he remembered the girl lived in Cambridge. When he phoned the girl who would be his wife for forty-three years, he apologized for the tardy call, explaining that the delay had been caused by the abundance of Olsons in the phone book. "I suggest you change your name," he added.[4]

Because Edith was in his employ, she was not surprised when Uncle Joe invited her to his house one evening. When she arrived, he and the others had to leave shortly. She was alone with her young admirer.

They talked at length, and then he escorted her home. Would he like some day to see the famous glass flowers at Harvard? she inquired. He agreed, provided she would let him show her some locally displayed paintings.

On one occasion when he chauffeured Uncle Joe to a conference in Worcester, Dr. Evans took his secretary along. Other such occasions deepened their friendship. He was relieved to learn that her yearning to serve as a missionary in the Far East had been replaced with a call to serve the Lord anywhere. He told her of his call to South America. They prayed together and agreed to separate for a time to test the sincerity of their love and to determine the will of God fully. By spring, 1923, they were convinced it was God's will for them to become engaged, to get married later, and finally to serve together in South America.

Commencement day, graduation with his A.B., and the completion of a major in Spanish came on June 18, 1923. He described his feelings in this fashion:

> While there was the satisfaction at having completed a given prospect, there was no warm heart attachment to a large and relatively impersonal university. . . . Being employed at some distance from the university, which I attended only during class hours I came to know fairly few students. . . .[5]

Perhaps the impending separation from Edith Olson was on his mind. They announced their engagement on the day of his graduation. There was also the desire to get on with the work in Ecuador to which he had been called.

6.

Missions and Marriage

EVIDENTLY the young suitor's father approved of Edith Marie Olson, for he hurried downtown to the jewelry store and purchased an engagement ring for his son to give to her! The elder Edman was also pleased that his son finally was to have an occupation after all those years of preparation.

Somehow, within ten days of his graduation, Edman drew all the loose ends of preparation together, boarded the Grace Liner *Santa Teresa* on June 28 at Pier No. 33 in Brooklyn, and was on his way to Ecuador to begin a missionary career. With the exception of an enforced residence in the United States due to ill health in 1926 and 1927, the experience occupied his life from 1923 until 1928. His Spanish major and historical studies provided the historical background and the language to work well with the people. His salary for services rendered was $1,500 a year.

His companions on the southbound voyage were George P. Simmonds, who had been on the field since 1916, and H. P. Dinwiddie of the Pioneer Missionary Agency. The pain of separation from Edith Olson was lessened by the presence of many friends who came to give him a Christian send-off. A black male quartet from Cleveland was present to sing several songs. Among their selections were "Goodbye, Pharaoh" and "No Goodbye in Heaven."

Seasickness troubled the young missionary until the ship reached the smoother waters of the warm Caribbean. The passengers celebrated the Fourth of July at the Canal Zone. After transferring to the *Silver Spray* at Manta, they arrived at Guayaquil at 5:30 P.M. on Sunday, July 9. The new arrivals were requested to speak briefly in the evening service and did so to the edification of the missionaries and the nationals in the Ecuadorian congregation.

Simmonds and Dinwiddie prepared at once to survey part of the Amazon Valley to find out if missionary work was feasible there. They resisted an impulse to take young Edman with them, to his disappointment, because they decided it was best that he begin his language study immediately.

Work with mountain Indians interested Edman most, so leaders of the mission decided their new recruit should spend the summer in Quito studying the Quechua language of the tribes to which he would be assigned.[1] He wrote his brother Elner in August that "the climate in Quito is agreeable and refreshing, and the only drawback is the utter lack of good Swedish grub. When I am inhaling a lot of this tough stuff, I shall be thinking of you and the little precious wifey at Kaffee Kalas, if that is the way you spell it." He added that his health was "very good because the Lord hath promised to care for that. . . ."[2]

He enjoyed a respite from language study when mission leader H. G. Crisman invited him on a trip on August 31 with several other missionaries to Agato. A stray dog ate a dozen of their sandwiches out of an unguarded saddlebag on the trail, causing uncomfortable hunger pangs for the party. At the end of the long Saturday trek they were glad to have a swim in a lake on their arrival at their stopping place in the evening.[3]

He described a later trip in a letter to Victorine Stolberg in this fashion:

Lately I have been on the jump a good deal of the time. Last week I covered considerably over two hundred miles on horseback, some days covering sixty miles from three A.M. to five-thirty P.M. over long, dusty, hot, rough trails. At one place we crossed a great canyon, a miniature Grand Canyon of Colorado. The trail zigzagged down a steep cliff of volcanic origin; at places a slip by the horse would have meant a slide of half a mile into the river; at other places the pony would set his four feet and slide in the volcanic dust and sand. On the other side was the long, long climb; and all the while the merciless tropical sun beat down upon us. Then we went over the Mojanda, and crossed a range of the Andes at close to fourteen thousand feet elevation, and there the heavy woolen Indian poncho was a great boon. For about five hours we descended along an old Inca trail; in places the old road of stone, about five feet wide, was in good repair, but in most places it had been washed away, and had left a faint trail for us. Billy, my pony, would stand trembling, with his four feet together before some washout, or narrow, deep stream; and a kind word or two in Spanish, a patting on his neck, and a gentle application of the spurs would send him leaping across like a jack rabbit.[4]

Edman was not always tactful with colleagues at Quito. When Mr. Crisman was to be absent on one occasion, he asked young Edman to take his place at the head of the table and lead breakfast prayers in the mission home. After the meal Edman got out his Bible and said he would have morning prayers there. Mrs. Crisman asked if they were not going as usual to the living room to sing. He replied that he thought their morning worship was a farce. Mrs. Crisman immediately excused herself, and an awkward constraint was present in prayers that morning.[5]

After his summer in language study at Quito, young Edman was assigned to Agato with the Carlsons to work among the Quechua Indians. He bought a horse for $50 to ride the eighty miles to Agato and then to use there. His main task in the time with the Carlsons was to perfect his knowledge of Quechua and Spanish because Ecuadorian Spanish differed so much from his college Spanish that he had difficulty communicating. He studied language in the mornings and went for long walks in the afternoon. Saturdays he often spent in Otavalo with his six foot four inch host, Carl Carlson, and his wife, Clara, who had come from Montana. They preached and handed out tracts in the marketplace.

Menial tasks such as felling and cutting up trees for firewood he took in stride. His friendliness won Spanish and Indian esteem and affection.[6] World War I training in army medical school enabled him to help Clara, a nurse, in her healing ministry to the Indians. Mr. Carlson handled the teeth pulling assignments.

The valley was alive with Indians who lived in their thatched homes with mud walls on their farms of an acre or a little more. Edman described the Indian men as wearing "broad heavy felt hats shaped like a mixing bowl, woolen ponchoes of red or blue, jackets and trousers of native homespun wool, uncolored, and are barefooted."

The women had hats and ponchos like the men, but their blouses were of uncolored wool and their dresses were blue with a girdle of red. They carried babies on their backs. Sometimes when coming to market with a bundle they would place the bundle on their back, and the baby would be perched on top of the bundle. Boys and girls dressed in junior-sized versions of their fathers' and mothers' outfits.[7]

In addition to language study, gospel work in the markets, and activities around the mission station, young Edman wrote his older brother that God was good to him in keeping him in "exuberant health and spirits" and giving him "ability to teach Sunday School in Spanish, play the organ for the songs, and in many ways to tell the Sweet Story of Redeeming Grace."[8] The children did not understand his Spanish too well, and since they were animists they had no background for understanding Bible concepts. Edman spanned the communications gap with object lessons. He washed a small dirty stone in a brook to show how Christ could cleanse from sin. When he dropped it in the dust and it became dirty, he explained how even Christians needed daily cleansing from sin. The children thought it best that the stone remain in the brook to keep clean. He commented, "That is good theology and very practical."

Every Indian family kept sheep which the children tended, so it was easy to tell them of the good Shepherd.[9] He also did a little work in an evening school where he tried to teach the Indian boys and girls to read.

Glad that the Lord had helped him in the languages, he wrote to Elner, "I have no difficulty in expressing myself in Spanish, and I enjoy very much the study of the Quechua." He was fascinated by those proud, distant and independent Indian descendants of the original Indians who had been conquered by the Incas about a century before the Spanish came. He saw them on the road to the Otavalo market on Saturdays and again on the way home from the market in the afternoon. Too often the men would be drunk with too much *Aguardiente* (literally "firewater"). Many of them had a veneer of Roman Catholicism which made them submit their children for baptism, but they were basically animistic, worshiping the spirits in things. They genuinely feared their witch doctors.[10]

He and the Carlsons prayed and fasted each Wednesday to ask God to help them achieve a breakthrough for the gospel. One Wednesday an old Indian came to ask help for his son who had been ill for three years and had an open sore on his back. When they arrived at the house, young Edman thought of the word, "Today is salvation come to this house." The boy, lying on his face, had a large ulcer on his back and was in the terminal stages of tuberculosis. Edman explained that they might not be able to help the boy but would come back the next day with more medicine. He returned the next day with Rosa, an Indian girl, as an interpreter. Through Rosa he told them of the parable of the lost sheep in "God's Book." The boy said he understood that his dirty heart would keep him from going to heaven. Later the boy said that he had asked Christ to wash his heart and was no longer afraid to die. He did die, but as a Christian.[11]

Stolid indifference, ridicule and even hatred discouraged Edman at times. He wrote to Elner in December, 1923, that on a long trip to Southern Colombia he thought upon the need of the Indians:

> As I rode hour after hour through those bleak uninviting mountains of mud and lava — the very ground was under the curse of God, and thot of the immortal souls in the wretched little villages who have not one chance of hope of heaven unless *I* tell them, of the fifty five thousand Indians in the Imbabura valley — the parish of us four young missionaries; I commenced to sing a Nyack chorus "Hallelujah, Hallelujah, Hallelujah for the Cross; Hallelujah, Hallelujah, It shall NEVER suffer loss," and the hot tears came trickling down my cheeks. It seems so impossible, the field is so large, the workers are so few and so poorly equipped; all around us they are dying, dying in utter darkness, going out into an eternity without God or hope. They fear death, they shrink, they scream; but they sink into utter blackness. . . .[12]

He was encouraged on a visit to Guayaquil when a fellow missionary reminded him that the Christian had to be an overcomer wherever he was.[13]

Edman stayed on in Agato the early part of 1924, but he interspersed his stay there with visits to Quito and to

Guayaquil. When he took the prayer meeting in Quito on Thursday, December 27, Mr. Crisman wrote in his diary that he "talked very well" and when he preached on the next night, "God helped him."[14]

The Indians loved him and came to have such confidence in him that they accepted him as one of themselves. This was because of his caring for the sick in their huts, his working knowledge of their language, his friendly, jovial nature, and his habit of playing with and teaching their children. They understood his simple clearly illustrated, and yet spiritually deep, messages. Some of these children are now leaders in the church at Agato.[15]

Letters to Elner reveal his anxiety to have his fiancée come to the field as soon as possible so they could get married and have their own home and mission station. In August, 1923, he wrote, "I have to exercise patience until a little Swedish cook comes along for me — and then — here is where words fail me."[16]

In later letters he reported that he had sent two trunks home to Boston for her use and asked Elner and his bride to buy for him a cedar chest about the size of a steamer trunk and send it to Edith Olson. It would come with her effects duty free and be ideal for keeping insects and moths out of her clothes which she would store in it.[17] He commented that a woman had to give up so much to come out to "this wilderness" that he wanted to do all in his power "to make a pleasant home" for her.[18]

These desires surfaced, despite field policy to permit no marriages of missionaries until the principals had been on the field for two years. Paul Young, in charge of the field, expressed disappointment in Edman as one who was letting his feelings run his life.[19]

Mr. Crisman was surprised when Edman arrived at Quito from Otavalo late in March of 1924 to leave on the morning train to go to Guayaquil to meet his fiancée because "he simply can't wait." Young Edman told Mr. Crisman, who was in charge of the Quito area, that there were often things he could not eat in mission quarters because of a stomach condition, and that a regular diet and home would help him. The more likely reason, in the opinion of Mr. Crisman, was that he was so deeply in love that he did not want to wait two years.[20] He asked Mr. Crisman to rescind the two-year rule in his case, but was told by Crisman that he had no authority to do so.

The young missionary wrote to his "Uncle Joe" asking him to take up the matter of permission with the board in New York. Evidently he did so, for in a few weeks a letter came to the field chairman authorizing young Edman to marry Edith Olson as an exception to the two-year rule.[21] When the letter came on June 14, 1924, Mr. Crisman dropped his opposition, even though he had said earlier that he could not give his consent to the exception "as much as I like him."[22]

In the meantime Edith Olson had sailed with the Reuben E. Larson family on a Pan American steamship to Panama where they had transferred to the Spanish steamer *Buenos Aires,* on which they arrived at Guayaquil on March 24, 1924. Her fiancé had gone there earlier to meet her. His letter describes the meeting in these words:

> How I thank God for bringing Edith safely too. I was in Guayaquil to meet her; and what I experienced as I watched that steamer coming up the river I shall never be able to put in words. It seemed an eternity from the time the boat cast anchor until it was received and we were allowed to go on board. . . . It was after nightfall before our launch came alongside, and Paul Young and I went up the ladder in jigtime — and such a meeting on the deck. Now I am getting things ready for the wedding, which has no date yet, but I feel that the Lord would have us go soon to our own station. Edith remained in

Guayaquil a few weeks longer; and then she will come up to Ambato.[23]

He was the first person aboard after the ship cleared quarantine.

Shortly after his fiancée's arrival, Edman moved from Agato, where he was still in language study, to Quito which had better access to Ambato where Edith Olson was studying Spanish.[24] He went to Ambato a couple of weeks in late May to teach Spanish to the Larsons. His impatience evidently irked Mr. Crisman because he dryly wrote in his diary, "Well, he has lots to learn yet, even if he is from several colleges."[25] Even after the letter exempting them from the two-year rule had come on June 13, young Edman told Mr. Crisman he would wait until September as they had planned. But he came to him again the next day and said that he wanted to get married the next week.

In Quito at the missionary home, engaged couples were required to burn a light while sitting in the living room. One night Mr. Crisman heard voices in the dark living room as he passed by and reminded them of the rule. They replied that they were sorry they had violated it. When Mr. Crisman went by the next evening, he heard voices and went into what was apparently a dark room. They had put a tiny candle on the table and jokingly replied that they had a light in the room.[26]

Dr. Edman described their wedding ceremonies in these graphic terms:

> It is all over now but the shouting; and I nearly shouted from sheer delight when I saw my lovely bride coming toward me. . . . On Saturday morning, June 14, Mr. Crisman, field chairman, told me in Quito that the Board said we could be married at our earliest convenience. I took one sweeping glance at the calendar, and roared "Next week." Then I wired Edith in Ambato to get her dress ready;

went there myself on Monday's train, packed up her chattels, extracted a civil marriage according to the laws of the land, while she secured a stunning dress; and we were off early Thursday morning for Quito. We arrived there at six; and as all arrangements had been made by wire and letter, the preacher announced us man and wife before nine in the evening. Perhaps Edith could picture the ceremony better for you than I can. Anyway, the living room was quite filled with flowers; Reuben Larson, a colleague, and I did the waiting stunt; Mrs. Larson stood up for Edith, and she came with a Mr. Spahr, a dear, fatherly German Christian.[27]

This description of the wedding coincides with that of Grace Morrison who described them "as a radiant bride, and Ray a very happy bridegroom" in a "solemn and beautiful ceremony."[28]

Thus they were married by the necessary legal ceremony in Ambato on June 18, 1924, and by a clerical marriage on June 19 in the Crisman's second-floor living room in the mission headquarters in Quito. The couple stood in an arch decorated with calla lillies. Two Indian boys from Agato, Daniel Amaguana and Nicholas Concha, and Dr. Edman's university student friend, Ripalda, were present as guests. Mr. Crisman performed the short ceremony in English, and his little daughter Edna was the flower girl. After the ceremony Mr. Crisman spoke briefly, and they sang " 'Tis So Sweet to Trust in Jesus" and "In Step with Jesus" in Spanish with Grace Morrison as the pianist. Mrs. Lettie Crisman had made a cake and put kewpies on it for decoration. This and ice cream made up the wedding refreshments.

Because the train from Ambato had been late, the wedding activities did not start until 8:45 P.M. and were concluded by 11:00 P.M. The next day, June 20, was dark and

raining, and when the photographer came at 9:00 A.M. for
the pictures, they had to move the wedding arch out into
the corridor to take the wedding pictures. Horses were then
brought for them and the Larsons to ride to Agato. One
horse was sick, so they decided to have lunch at 11:40, and
after securing another horse, got off on the two-day, eighty-
mile ride to Agato at 1:00 P.M. The couple went there for
a few days because the young missionary wanted to show
his wife an Indian festival and his area of missionary activity before she came to the field.[29]

When Mrs. Edman was asked in later years what her
most unusual wedding gift was, she replied, "How many
get this for a wedding gift — a beautiful bay horse? I did
— and that from my brand new husband."[30]

Robert Bartel, one of his student friends, heard Dr. Edman later describe how he had purchased this horse for his
wife's wedding gift. One day Edman had heard hoofbeats
on the street that indicated to him a high-spirited horse.
He hunted up its owner, bought the horse, and broke it for
her.[31]

His report of their short time at Agato indicates how he
enjoyed it: "Well, Friday morning we four, Larsons and Edmans, mounted the ponies, and were off for the Imbabaura.
We arrived here Saturday afternoon, after a dandy trip over
the mountains; and now we are enjoying a most novel honeymoon among the Indians. Some speed, no?" During their
stay they had a picnic by the lovely lake.[32]

After the Agato honeymoon the Edmans were stationed
in Quito. The groom believed it would be easier for his
wife to learn Spanish there than among the Indians. Again
he manifested his impatience with established procedures.
When the Crismans volunteered for work in southern Colombia, young Edman asked that the Larsons be assigned to
work with them at Quito. Crisman said that he would take
the matter up with the committee, and that, if no one ob-

jected, he would not oppose it. Young Edman asked one member of the committee if he had any objections. When he replied, "No," Edman remarked that this meant that two out of three had no objection and that the majority ruled. On his own he dispatched a wire asking the Larsons to leave Agato and come to Quito. The unconsulted member did object later but to no avail.

They conducted open-air meetings, worked among students, and held services and Sunday school in a church building for Spanish people. Edman worked out a proposal with the head of the Quito Tramways Company to display Scripture verses and to advertise Bibles for sale on placards placed in the trams. He actually caught a robber in their house and afterward wryly remarked, "Now he is inside looking out."[33]

When the prayer conference met in Guayaquil in November, 1924, the Edmans were assigned to Riobamba and the Larsons to Ambato. The new couple lived there until Edman was taken to Guayaquil with typhus fever. Mrs. Edman did go to Ambato about the time they were expecting the birth of their first child. Charles was born there on May 15, 1925. She returned home when he was three weeks old.[34]

Riobamba was in a mountain valley 9,000 feet high between the two ranges of the Andes and halfway between Quito and Guayaquil. Mrs. Edman proved to be an excellent housewife and hostess. The boards of the adobe brick home were always scrubbed white, and she made the plain home attractive.[35]

Etelvina Jara, now Mrs. E. Peto in Arlington, Virginia, was at the time a little thirteen-year-old Indian orphan who lived with them and helped them in the home. She recalls how on market days the Edmans would distribute tracts and converse with the people in the large and picturesque

Indian market. Each Sunday they held services in their
home.

Miss Jara described how they would rise early in the cold
morning, take an ice-cold shower, and have breakfast which
she would prepare. She said Dr. Edman read the Bible to
her as she sat by his desk. She described herself as having
"the feeling of what St. Paul says, 'In the heavenly places,' "
and added, "For me he was like a father." He taught her
to read and write English. She remained with them until he
had to leave Ecuador after his first illness.[36]

It was also at Riobamba that Edman believed he had a
heavenly visitant. Their home was surrounded by a protec-
tive fence, iron grillwork, and a locked gate. He heard the
bell ring one day in the spring of 1925 and hurried to the
gate. An unusually attractive Indian woman was there and
spoke to him in commendation of his work and assured him
of God's blessing upon it. She left, and when he quickly
went out to catch her so that he could invite her to stay with
them, she was nowhere to be seen. He could see the only
way she could have gone in any direction, and there was
no side street or building she could have entered. He concluded an angel had visited him, as stated in Hebrews 13:2.
He often told this story and used it in periodicals and in
one of his books.[37]

V. Raymond Edman. "That's what it says," Dr. Edman often remarked of God's Word in conversational tones.

IN CHILDHOOD HOME. Baby Ray in rocking chair poses with elder brother, Elner.

BROTHERS AND SISTERS. Standing, *left to right,* are Elner, V. Raymond, Myrtle, Merrill, Evelyn, and Florence.

SOUTH AMERICAN PRAYER BAND. At Nyack in 1922, Ray Edman, *third row, sixth from left,* was one of the group.

ENGAGEMENT ANNOUNCED. Ray Edman and Edith Olson are the happy couple, Boston, 1923.

WEDDING DAY ON THE MISSION FIELD. Ray and Edith Edman were attended by Reuben and Grace Larson, June 19, 1924. Flower girl was Edna Crisman.

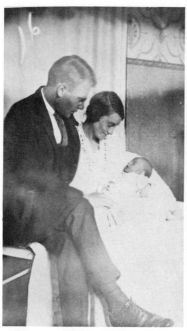

YOUNG MISSIONARY PAR-
ENTS. Ray and Edith ad-
mire their first son, Charles
Victor.

IN ECUADOR. Missionary
Ray captioned this photo,
"Imbabura for Jesus!"

WITH QUECHUA INDIANS. After language study in Quito,
Ray was assigned to the Agato mission station.

ON VACATION BY WINONA LAKE. Professor Edman relaxes at Bethany Camp, 1939, with his family: *left to right,* Roland, Prof. Edman, Norris (on lap), Charles, Edith, and David.

HOMECOMING 1940. Wheaton alumni are greeted by "Brown Dog," Norrie, and Acting-President Edman.

STILL A HAPPY COUPLE. "Prexy" vacations with "Friend Wife" in Arkansas, 1951.

ON THE GRANDSTAND. Dr. and Mrs. Edman and a grandson welcome Vice-President and Mrs. Richard M. Nixon to the Wheaton campus.

IN NATAL, BRAZIL. Dr. Edman and industrialist R. G. LeTourneau took many trips together (1956).

AT BILLY'S BOSTON CRUSADE. Prexy chats with Billy Graham and "Uncle Joe" Evans, Wheaton trustee, just after the prayer session, September 24, 1964.

OPENING OF NEW LIBRARY BUILDING. Miss Julia Blanchard, daughter of Wheaton's second president and librarian of the college for many years, assists President Edman by cutting ribbon. The library was the generous gift of Trustee and Mrs. R. E. Nicholas, standing in center.

COMMENCEMENT, 1961. President Edman marches in the processional.

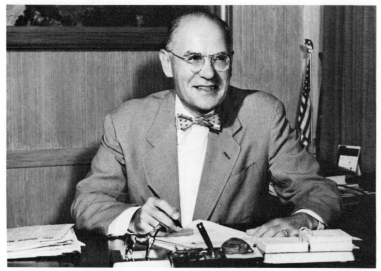

BUSY AUTHOR. A prolific writer, Dr. Edman works on another manuscript.

IN MEMORIAM. Dr. Billy Graham presents the sermon at memorial services for Dr. V. Raymond Edman. Other participants in the program are, *left to right,* Raymond McAfee, soloist; Dr. Hudson T. Armerding, Wheaton president; Dr. E. Joseph Evans, Wheaton College trustee; Dr. Malcolm Cronk, pastor of Wheaton Bible Church; and Dr. Nathan Bailey, president of the Christian and Missionary Alliance.

7.

Empty Black Coffin

In 1925 Ray had his first encounter with death. He had gone in June to an Indian mountain village to check on the security of property belonging to the Gospel Missionary Union. A thief had preceded him and dug a hole through the adobe bricks to enter the house. Some of the Indians were ill with typhus fever in homes where Edman searched for goods stolen from the mission home.

General pain quickly gripped him on the homeward road that Saturday afternoon. He had to dismount occasionally and lie by the side of the road until he felt strong enough to go on. He reached home safely, but chills and high fever returned as he was playing the tiny folding organ in their home on Sunday morning before the usual morning service. Appropriately he was playing the hymn, "Anywhere with Jesus I Can Safely Go," when he almost collapsed. Suspecting typhus, he asked Mrs. Edman to isolate him in a room removed from the household. She took that Sunday service on June 21 by herself despite her fears.

Edith tried to get her husband on the train to Guayaquil the following day and again on Wednesday, but all seats were reserved. Had she asked one of the American conductors, all of whom liked him, they would have helped her.

That Friday, June 26, George P. Simmonds with whom he had sailed to South America, arrived on the train and prepared to stay with the Edmans. He was at that time on loan to the American Bible Society. One look at his friend and a knowledge of his high fever told him that Edman could not last long at that altitude.

He talked to the stationmaster who told him again the train was full and that he could do nothing. Remembering the traffic manager at Huigra farther down the line, Simmonds made contact at 6:00 P.M. The manager persuaded the stationmaster to provide space in the baggage car. Later the manager called back to say the car was loaded with perishable fruit which would be a loss if held over until Tuesday when the next train would go through. Simmonds reminded him that an American life was at stake and that the railway was an American-owned railway manned by Americans. If the missionary were left to die for a small amount of fruit and vegetables, it would not look good for the railway. The manager again talked to the stationmaster and ordered him to unload enough freight to make room for the sick man.

Simmonds wired missionaries in Guayaquil, "Have a launch ready at Durán" to carry Edman across the river to the hospital in Guayaquil. He flashed other messages to stations farther on to pack ice to help keep the patient comfortable as the train moved into the lower hot tropical zone. He arranged for four men to carry him to the station on Saturday morning.

Mrs. Edman spent most of the night squeezing oranges to make juice for her husband. Tender hands carried him to the train on Saturday morning, June 27. Simmonds accompanied him on the twelve-hour train trip over 120 miles.

Mrs. Edman returned dejectedly to the house to discover some of the Indians who had carried him to the station had stolen their pet dog. But she was comforted when baby Charles curled his little hand around her finger.[1]

The party was met at Durán that evening by fellow missionaries Will E. Reed, John D. Clark, and Roscoe O. Stull.

They carried their colleague through the streets of Guayaquil to Dr. Herbert Parker's clinic. The physician was convinced that twenty-four more hours away from the hospital would have meant death. Without treatment so long at that high altitude, his chances of living were only about six in a hundred. Dr. Parker, a specialist in tropical diseases and a warm friend of the mission, worked hard but had little hope for Edman's recovery.

Early the following week telegrams requested Mrs. Edman to come down on the next train. Muriel Owen and Grace Morrison were asked to go to Riobamba to take over the work while the Edmans were absent. The missionaries prayed and also cabled New York, asking the people at home to join them in prayer.

When Mrs. Edman and Etelvina arrived at the hospital, Dr. Parker told Mrs. Edman that her husband's feet were already cold and that he would likely die soon. Mr. Reed ordered a black cloth-covered board coffin to be made because in that hot tropical climate, burial had to be made quickly. Because Mrs. Edman had no black dress, Etelvina was told to dye the wedding dress black. Mr. Reed arranged for a funeral service at 3:00 P.M. on that sad Saturday of July 4.

Far away that very Saturday Uncle Joe Evans at the Alliance Camp Hebron at Attleboro, Massachusetts, felt an unusual sense of need for prayer on behalf of his young missionary protégé. He asked the congregation of some two hundred persons to pray earnestly with him for the young man's deliverance because he sensed that he was facing some desperate crisis. More than two hours of agonizing prayer were followed by a sense of divine intervention.[2]

In Guayaquil, Dr. Parker, who had been sure that Dr. Edman could not live, said that if he could last a few hours more there was hope of recovery.[3] Dr. Edman remembered sorting out the words of a national nurse who said, "Today is Dr. Parker's day" — a quaint reference to July 4. Scene by scene, Dr. Edman's life from childhood seemed to unroll before him. He was outwardly unconscious but inwardly aware of imminent death. A sense of God's presence came into the room, enveloped his cot, and spread its protecting aura over him. He sensed "the overwhelming love of God in such a manner that death lost any terror." As in Germany and on the Boston streetcar, he knew that God's presence was with him.[4]

A week later he recognized his wife, but not until July 14 did his mind clear fully. He was moved to the mission home after a few weeks, and for another month he could do no more than read his Bible and walk for a few minutes each day. But it was progress from July 4 when he was sure he would die and looked forward with rapturous joy to seeing Christ. They remained in Guayaquil until February of 1926 when Will Reed, chairman of the mission, advised them to return to the United States to speed his return to health. Dr. Edman later looked back on this period of serious illness as his "most serious adventure" in South America when he engaged in "personal hand to hand conflict with death."[5]

Home again in the United States, the Edmans took a train to Simi Valley near Los Angeles, both to recuperate and to be near the bedside of Mrs. Edman's mother who was dying of heart disease.

In late summer of 1926, six months after the Edmans' arrival from Ecuador, Mrs. Olson died. Ray and Edith remained with Father Olson in Simi until the following May when they took him along to Boston. Uncle Joe was on the spot again to help. He rented an apartment for them in Jamaica Plains and secured a teaching position for the young missionary in a Bible school the Welshman had organized in Roxbury and which he served as president for a decade.

Edman taught in that school for the full term of their second year of recuperation in 1926-1927. In Jamaica

Plains their second son, Roland, was born on October 1, 1926.

The drama of living by faith followed them to New England. In the autumn of 1926 they were traveling to their apartment in Jamaica Plains. He had spent his last eight cents for graham crackers which they gave to Charles. When the old Model T Ford ran out of gas three miles from home, Edman walked to the nearby Bible school to see if he could borrow a dollar to buy gas. The house mother gave him his mail but shut the door before he could get around to requesting a loan. When he opened one letter with no return address he found inside a note with encouraging Scripture verses and two ten-dollar bills.[6]

They returned to Ecuador after school in May of 1927 with a party of seven missionaries. During the voyage Dr. Edman taught Spanish to the new recruits as a prelude to their formal language study. The circle met on the upper deck on the first day at sea and each day thereafter except Sunday during the entire voyage.

Professor Edman drilled them in grammar, sentence structure, vocabulary and composition. One older person had difficulty so Edman coached him privately in the afternoons. The man later became proficient in Spanish in later years and credited his mentor for the fine start. To Miss Mildred Peterson, Mrs. Edman's cousin, Dr. Edman was "an excellent teacher."[7]

The intensive language study was continued even after their arrival in Guayaquil. They met from 8:00 to 10:00 A.M. each day for grammar and vocabulary drill and from 10:30 to 12:00 with a national who listened to their reading and conversation and corrected their sentence structure and punctuation.

Edman strongly advised their taking a siesta each afternoon, a custom which he kept during his life. He spoke of it as a "delightful South American custom." The rest of the day was given to vocabulary drill and written assignments. Missionary Edman sprang tests unexpectedly so that they had to keep up daily. He suggested that they keep their evenings free for games, services, or fellowship.

After six weeks of lessons, male members of the class accompanied him to preach in the villages while women carried out visitation work in the city. These experiences whetted their appetites for more study because they realized the value of fluency in the language. Eight months passed and then came final examinations. Most of the class passed the first-year test, thanks to their hard-driving but tactful and thoughtful teacher.[8]

Mornings were occupied in teaching Spanish to new arrivals; evenings kept him busy teaching selected nationals. Out of that small beginning grew a Bible institute. Dr. Will E. Reed earlier had begun evening classes in a rented meeting hall for promising young Christian Ecuadorians. A new church building erected in 1927 provided space for day classes and for the students who lived there. Built of concrete, the structure had a high-ceilinged auditorium. Kitchen and dining rooms were on the first floor, and on the third floor and back of the balcony were rooms for the dean of the institute and students.[9] The institute was formally opened in 1927.[10]

Dr. Edman became director of the school and dean of students. He engaged national teachers to handle certain secular subjects, and fellow missionaries to teach biblical and theological subjects. A three-year course was planned for Ecuadorians with a high-school education, and a five-year course for those with only a grade-school education. Students paid thirty *sucres* a month for board and room. Their tuition was free, but each student worked in the class and dormitory rooms.

The classes met from 8:00 to 12:00 Tuesday through Friday mornings so students could work in the afternoons to earn money. Evenings were given over to supervised study under the teachers. On weekends the students traveled to neighboring villages to witness to their faith.[11]

Mr. Edman taught doctrine, church history, and Christian discipline. Mr. Reed designed the course to be simple and practical so that the graduates would be good *testigos* (witnesses). Ecuador's school year began in December and ended in May to coincide with the warm rainy season when work outside is curtailed. It also coincided with the schedule of the Ecuadorian public school system. Emanuel Prentice, who became director when Dr. Edman had to return to the States in 1928, taught biblical subjects. There were nine students the first year and eleven or twelve students the second year.

Both colleagues and friends generously praise Dr. Edman's work and friendship. Mr. Prentice recalled his "Christian love and humility." When he came back to Ecuador in 1927, Dr. Edman brought a new mohair suit for him, an appreciated luxury in the tropics. When the Prentices had their fourth child, complications during the pregnancy ran up a large hospital bill. Dr. Edman called on all the missionaries in Guayaquil for financial help and collected enough to take care of nearly the entire bill.[12]

Reuben Larson agreed with those who had worked with Dr. Edman in the institute that "his Christian spirit and leadership were dominant."[13] Mr. Crisman wrote: "He had a real gift for teaching, spoke Spanish fluently, and had a kindly, practical interest in the lives of the students." Pupils as well as national believers remember him "with great affection." Mr. Reed told Paul Young enthusiastically, "Ray Edman was the greatest teacher we ever had."[14]

José A. Lopez, a student who admitted he hated history in the secular school, found that Dr. Edman presented the events of church history "in a very fine and simple way that made them the most pleasant." José became "one of the best students on the subject." Edman had the courage to advise Lopez and his friend to leave the institute to become Christian businessmen. He told them that "the Lord needs Christian business men, Christian physicians, Christian lawyers, Christian store employees, and so forth; to testify for His Word." They took his advice and became successful businessmen. Lopez, who also has a lay preaching ministry to a small congregation, was happy when his son entered seminary.[15]

Manuel Orbe, another Edman protégé, ranked his instructor as a great teacher because he made things so simple that everybody could understand. He supplied material appropriate for each stage of their development. His mastery of Spanish and the Bible astonished them.[16]

This small beginning through him and Mr. Reed has developed into the present institution located in the beautiful Cuidadela "Urdesa" area of Guayaquil. The Seminario Biblico Alianza now enrolls nearly forty students a year and has several graduates in each class. Three nationals and five missionaries are full-time instructors, while several others teach one or two subjects.

Teaching Spanish to missionaries and Bible to nationals, as well as engaging in evangelism, did not exhaust Dr. Edman's energies. He also did work as an interpreter for German businessmen in the city.[17]

But soon his foreign missionary career was to be cut off again. Sometime in the latter half of the rainy season early in the spring of 1928, he made an itinerating evangelistic and colportage trip forty miles out to the coast from Guayaquil. Somewhere he became infected with amoebic dysentery. The doctor prescribed turpentine capsules which freed him of dysentery but left him with bowels so weak he could eat nothing but lemon cornstarch pudding. He became weak and quite thin. When he spoke he put his hands on the table to keep from falling. During the last

classes of the school year he had to teach the students from
his bed. When his weight dropped from 165 to 120 pounds,
the doctors advised, "Go home or die."[18] Mr. Reed and
Mrs. Edman strongly seconded the doctor's suggestion.

Emanuel Prentice recalled that when Edman delivered
his last message in the church he was so weak that he had
to speak while sitting in a chair. He used Zechariah 13:9
to show how the Lord in love would put one through the
crucible of trial to purge all dross from the soul. Mrs.
Edman listened to him from the balcony onto which their
apartment opened. She had an inner feeling that this was
his last day on the field, but she rejoiced as she looked out
on those he had won to Christ.[19]

When the time came to take the launch to the Dutch
steamer *Boskoop* in August, 1928, Edman insisted that no
one take time to see him off. Emanuel Prentice did ac-
company him and Charles to the boat and on the deck
commended them to the Lord. Prentice was saddened by
his leaving because he loved him for his love of Christ, his
fluency in Spanish, and his cheery optimism. Prentice succeeded Edman as dean after he left and drew up the diplomas for the first graduating class. When it became clear
that Dr. Edman could not return to the tropics, Mrs. Edman
and Roland followed him to the United States in November,
1928.[20] They were not to be in Ecuador together again
until November, 1965, when they both visited the mission
and Dr. Edman spoke at chapel. There was also a dinner
at which several of his former students were present. He
was also able to visit at Agato and to hold the first Bible
conference for the Aucas.[21]

During the 1928 voyage home he perused the Bible constantly and prayed. He prepared lessons for his classes in
the gospels and on the life and letters of Paul which he
hoped to use when he returned to teach in his beloved
institute. As they neared Panama, he was outlining 2 Co-

rinthians. The phrase in 2:14 — "always leadeth us to triumph in Christ" — particularly impressed him. As he read
it in the American Standard Version, the Holy Spirit
seemed to ask him whether he would be willing to go anywhere for God. He felt he was willing to go anywhere in
Ecuador, but a voice seemed to say, "I did not say 'in Ecuador.' I said, 'Anywhere.'" Finally he said he would go
anywhere the Lord would command him to go, and again
he had a deep sense of the presence of the Lord in his
life.[22]

This experience, he believed, was corroborated when he
returned to New York. He had prayed that he would find
Gonzalo, a Christian who had abandoned his love for the
Lord in Ecuador and come to New York. One evening
Gonzalo actually came to his apartment where Dr. Edman
led him back to faith in Christ. Gonzalo had been working
in a nightclub and on his evening off had gone to the Tabernacle at Sixth Avenue and Forty-Fourth Street. He heard
a request for prayer for a sick missionary from his own
country and felt impelled to find him. He had come to the
missionary home where he found Dr. Edman in bed, still
weak and ill.[23]

Edman's father was deeply concerned that he and Charles
had returned home alone. The family drove to Mr. Evans'
home in Boston where he and Charles were staying. When
he went to the doctors of the Department of Tropical Disease
at Harvard Medical School, they informed him that he could
not under any circumstances return to the tropics to live.
When Mrs. Edman and Roland arrived in November, 1928,
the Edmans went to Chicago where the family helped them
find an apartment. They remained there until early in 1929
when he went to Massachusetts to take a pastorate in
Worcester.

The move, he often insisted, "demoted" him from missionary work to serve in the United States because of his

poor health.[24] He was, however, in the providence of God to do more for the cause of missions at home than he could ever have done in Ecuador. All things did "work together for good" because he loved God.

8.

A Pastorate and a Doctorate

WHEN DR. AND MRS. JOHN E. GRAHAM, missionaries from China, decided that their work with the Alliance Tabernacle in Worcester, Massachusetts, was completed, Uncle Joe offered his "Ray" the pastorate.

This little church on the edge of Worcester had begun in a schoolhouse in 1910 and two years later joined the Alliance. The sanctuary was not yet complete because the small congregation had been wracked by divisions. The bitterly cold New England winter and the tiny flock made the prospect unpromising for the Edmans.

But the challenge brought Edman once more to a crisis, and once more he had an overwhelming sense of the presence of the Lord. He felt strangely moved to take this little church and later wrote a friend, "Often we think of that good promise in Joel 2:21 with which we went to Worcester."[1] He was assured by it, convinced that the Lord would do great things for them, and that they could go rejoicing without fear.

In February of 1929 Pastor V. Raymond Edman began his work in what he termed a period of obscurity. But before this hiatus was past, the congregation would be enlarged, a radio program started, and a Ph.D. degree awarded him.

To this date he had not been ordained. The service of ordination took place in Boston in February with Uncle Joe and the Reverend Fred Hayes participating. Andrew Hyndman, a missionary to West Africa, was ordained at the same service. The ordination certificate was "a small typewritten statement by the committee of the New England district."[2]

An invitation to teach part time in the growing Bible School at Roxbury some fifty miles away promised to ease the load on its small faculty and give the Edmans badly needed funds in that depression year of 1929.

During the winter the pastor hopefully began to make preparation for the coming classes. He planned to spend two or three days a week at the school as the little church only took up part of his time.

The Edmans experienced both cold and poverty that first Massachusetts winter. Their little apartment on the second floor of the clapboarded house at 102 Wildwood Avenue faced a pond swept by cold winds. The apartment was sparsely furnished and not properly insulated against the cold winter winds. A washcloth dampened in the evening would freeze solid by morning.

The great depression that year struck the United States. Gifts of money in a shower honoring their arrival had to go for the rent. Years later Dr. Edman wrote, "I had four years of graduate school during the depth of the depression. Not infrequently there was not enough food for all my family, and I would miss the meals so that friend wife and the little fellows had something for themselves."[3]

But prayer and generous friends helped to bridge hard times. Mr. and Mrs. Charles Walcott next door became quite fond of the Edmans. Charles and Roland spent much time at the Walcott home, often drawn by freshly baked cookies, cake or bread. Visits to the Walcott farm charmed the boys and strengthened their muscles. They never forgot the Walcotts. In later years they kept in touch with cards and letters. When each was in the army, visits were frequent when they were in that vicinity. Mrs. Walcott attended her neighbor's inauguration as president of Wheaton College in 1941.

He confided to his professor friend at Clark, Guy Burnham, that the weekly giving at the church averaged only
$20 and that only $7 or $8 of that amount was given to the
pastor for weekly food, rent, utilities and other expenses.
On one occasion when they had no money for food, Edman
slipped into All Saints Episcopal Church and spent half an
hour in prayer. When he came home, the boys jubilantly
announced to him that a former member of the Tabernacle,
now in Vermont, had sent them a chicken.

Mrs. Edman's father, a former cabinetmaker, lived with
them and shared his annuity.[4]

Henri Eckhardt, one of the Wheaton College fieldmen,
years later called on an elderly Baptist lady in Worcester.
She said she would often attend the Tabernacle. One day
she felt impelled to cook a ham and take it to the Edmans.
She explained her acute embarrassment but felt divinely
led to do it. She did not know that the Edmans had only
twenty-five cents to buy bananas and nothing else for supper. They had prayed for food that day.[5]

Sometime later the pastor learned that a brown-shingled
house with yellow trim up the street at 144 Wildwood was
for rent. The family soon had a whole house to themselves
with plenty of trees and a lovely view across the little valley
behind the house. From there they moved to 27 Wyola
Drive into a rectangular two-story white clapboarded house
with a two-story porch across two-thirds of the front of the
house. They lived there during the greater part of their
stay in Worcester until their departure in 1935.

There was often little gasoline money for the decrepit
secondhand Model T Ford which they owned. Edman
walked many miles to and from the church and in visitation.
He rode a streetcar the longer distance to the university.
Church reports from those lean years show that even in 1935
with the growth of the church under his ministry he received only $1,261.75 as pastoral salary for the year ending

September 30, 1935. Even with the $200 to $400 a year which he received in fellowships from Clark University, the family had only an annual income that rarely exceeded $1,800 a year. By 1935 there were four hungry boys to feed and clothe.

Perhaps it was the need to trust in the Lord rather than in material wealth that inspired Ray and Edith early in their Worcester experience to decide that they, like the Levites of the Old Testament, would never own real estate. They kept that vow and owned only personal property, such as car and furniture.[6]

The outcome of austere living for so many years on so little made Dr. Edman extremely frugal. These experiences taught him the worth of a dollar. They were in large part the reason for his conservative stewardship of college assets in later years. Frugality, rather than miserliness and greed for money, characterized him. He was generous to Christian causes, in some years donating up to 30 percent of his income.

Dr. Edman's annual reports to the district superintendent reveal the progress of his first pastorate. His report of November 13, 1929, expressed pleasure concerning growth of the Sunday school, the summer Bible School, and the monthly fellowship meetings.

A third report, dated October 7, 1931, expressed gratitude for "the quickening of spiritual life . . . and increasing hunger for the things of God" as well as for the payment of all debts except a mortgage of $200, the beginning of his radio ministry, and the near completion of the auditorium so it could be used during the summer months.

The report of October 5, 1932, stressed the completion of the auditorium, the painting of the building, and the planting of the shrubbery. These material gains in his opinion were overshadowed by the fact that twelve had confessed Christ in baptism and many other young people had accepted Christ. He had also spoken to Salvation Army gatherings, Epworth League conventions and at the Swedish Methodist Conference at Asbury Grove.

The report of October 3, 1934, gave news of the completion of three Sunday school rooms. The average attendance at church was 107. The attendance at the summer Bible School averaged 70. More were coming to the young people's meetings, and an orchestra had been started. Special services in January had brought others into the church. His father wrote in 1935 that he was "very much impressed with your great mission-offering in these hard times but God is able to supply it."[7] Dr. Edman was also pleased to report that in that same year he had held a six-week training course for Sunday school teachers. One member, Mrs. Sadie Murphy, reported that by 1935 one had to come fifteen minutes early to get a seat.

The invitation to teach in the Bible School in Roxbury during the 1929-30 school year never materialized although the young minister had devoted much time during the spring and summer to preparation for his classes. As he drove with his family to a faculty retreat at Cape Cod, Mrs. Edman confided to her husband that she had a persistent feeling that he would not get the teaching position. She and the boys had a long walk in the woods on that early September day following Labor Day while Edman attended the meeting. The faculty discussed the possibility that the anticipated increased enrollment might not materialize. Some did not want to surrender their classes to Dr. Edman. Courses were reassigned and at the close of the meeting there were none left for him. After a picnic dinner the Edmans spent the night in a cabin, and he drove home with a perplexed and discouraged heart to a cupboard with nothing in it but cereal.

At dawn the next day, September 12, 1929, he told his wife that the Lord had made it clear during family devotions that he was to begin graduate work at Clark University. When he checked their resources, he found they had fifty-six cents for food. But there was some gas in the car so he drove to the university.

The registrar, Carey Melville, received him graciously. When he heard that Dr. Edman had been in South America, he sent him to talk with Clarence Jones, the professor of economic geography and secretary of the graduate committee. Jones asked for pictures he might use in his forthcoming text on the economic geography of South America. He also inquired whether Dr. Edman had a scholarship and had him fill out an application for the committee which was to meet that afternoon. He phoned the Edmans in the evening to tell the pastor-student that a full-tuition scholarship had been granted to him for that school year and that he should decide on his fields of study.[8]

Dr. Edman had planned to make geography his main field of study but switched to colonial American history for the M.A. and international relations for the Ph.D. He once explained to Rowena Carr, his executive secretary at Wheaton, that he was forced into the switch because the geography lab fees were too heavy for him to pay.[9] He reasoned that graduate work would fit him to be a better teacher at the Bible institute in Guayaquil. In his application for financial aid in 1930 he wrote that he regarded "teaching as my life work in South America if my health permits my return there."[10]

He was allowed to attend classes even though much paper work had to be completed before he was properly enrolled in the graduate school. His high school principal, E. L. Boyer, in his letter of reference expressed his view that Dr. Edman was "a man of unblemished character, of exceptional mental ability, and of outstanding energy." He added that he was "an interesting speaker, a man of sound judgment," in short, "a versatile, well-balanced manly man" who was "a leader in athletics, public speaking. . . ."[11] In the reference from W. M. Trumbull, vice-president and foreign secretary of the Alliance, he was commended "in the highest terms" as "an exceptional man in his seriousness of purpose, application to the task in hand and intellectual ability."[12] He was formally accepted as a graduate student on September 19, 1930, and his tuition was remitted.

While looking after his church and taking the prescribed courses, V. Raymond Edman also completed his thesis for the M.A. degree. His topic was "The Boundary Dispute Between Ecuador and Peru" which he later expanded for his Ph.D. dissertation. He successfully passed his written comprehensive examinations over the year's work and sustained an excellent oral examination on his thesis May 31. His friend Dwight E. Lee was chairman of the examining committee. It was a happy day for the family when on June 16, 1930, Edman was awarded his M.A. degree in American colonial history at the university commencement.

He decided to work for the Ph.D. degree in Latin American history and international relations. He asked permission in December, 1930, to substitute Spanish and Quechua for French in the language requirement because his main sources for his dissertation were in Spanish.[13] This request was granted. He later made the point that "travel in Ecuadorean Amazonia has given me a firsthand acquaintance with the subject" of his proposed dissertation.[14]

Early in March, 1931, he received the third grant of a scholarship of $250 and remission of fees for the next school year. He was also made an assistant at $125 for the school year and given another $50 from a scholarship fund. Similar grants now bring students ten times the amount of his basic scholarship. This gives some idea of the impact of the depression upon the academic world.

During the 1930-31 school year he audited anthropogeography and took courses in American constitutional, Western and diplomatic history and international law. This gave him a load of eleven hours for the year. During the next year he continued his study of geography and American and South American history. He was admitted to candidacy for the Ph.D. degree on November 10, 1932. He passed his preliminary examinations for the doctorate with fields in American history and foreign policy, Latin American history (his special field), Latin American foreign policy and international law and geography which was his minor field. Again Dwight Lee was the chairman of the five-man committee, and his friend Jones examined him in geography.

The oral examination on his dissertation took place on May 17, 1933, at 2:00 P.M. with Dr. Blakeslee, who had supervised the writing of his dissertation, as chairman. Professors Clarence Jones, Walter Hunter, Dwight Lee, Jordan and Billington — all notable men in their fields — were the other members. He did well and passed. After fees of $25 for the diploma and $15 for the publication of his dissertation were paid, his work for the degree was complete. The boundary dispute between Peru and Ecuador, the subject of his thesis, was finally settled many years after the completion of his dissertation.

During the second semester of the school year 1930-31 he prepared a paper on the foreign policy of Secretary of State Charles E. Hughes in the course on international relations. When he gave it in seminar, he and some of the other students were disappointed by his dull performance. But the story doesn't end there.

During the oral examination in 1933 on his dissertation a professor he had not met before asked a question which Dr. Edman recognized as the crisis question of the oral. He asked who Edman thought was an outstanding secretary of state. Dr. Edman replied that, in his opinion, Charles E. Hughes was outstanding. When the professor asked the inevitable why, the paper Dr. Edman had prepared two years before came to his mind. He spoke on the main points of the paper for about fifteen minutes. He sensed that the committee was pleased with his answer, and he found the examination easier from that point. The dull task of two years before, which he had done well but unenthusiastically, helped him to do a good job at the climactic point of his examination.[15]

His brother Elner, Mrs. Charles Walcott and others in the church came to the commencement at Clark on June 5, 1933, to watch the colorful ceremony. He received his degree from the hand of President Wallace W. Atwood, himself a scholar of international reputation, and the hood of the doctorate was put on him. The president said to Dr. Edman as he awarded him his degree, "God bless you," so that Mrs. Walcott and Guy Burnham heard the words. This was one of the few remarks he made during the awarding of the degrees, and it indicated the high regard this scholar held for Dr. Edman.

He now faced the problem of God's will for the future, but no change seemed to be indicated. He wrote, "Thereafter we had two years of complete silence in which no one made inquiry as to what we were doing, or desired to have us help them in Christian work." He felt a little like Moses alone in the desert but took heart in the consciousness of God's presence with him.[16]

Because no other opening came, he decided to stay on at the church and continue with postdoctoral study at the university. He applied for another fellowship in the fall of 1933, stating that he wanted "to broaden my interests and information by regular school work" and "to have the stimulus of university work and associations."[17] That same day he was made an honorary fellow for the next school year to study in his field under the supervision of Dr. Blakeslee. This honorary fellowship was renewed for the 1934-35 school year.

Two other important events occurred early in his graduate career. Their third son, David, was added to the family on January 9, 1930, and Roland's illness caused him much concern. As he was undressing the boy on an October evening of that year, he noticed a lump on the child's side at the end of the scar from an earlier operation. He was alarmed because the seventh rib on the left side had been removed in 1928 just after their return to the United States because of a serious bone infection. He took Roland to the hospital and then went back to his office at the university with a heavy and concerned heart. He read Psalm 103:11, which told him of the measureless mercy of God. Again he had a vivid sense of the presence of God and an assurance that all would be well with his son. Surgery was successful, and the trouble did not recur.[18]

Responsibilities at the church, the new baby, Roland's illness, and his graduate work gave Dr. Edman enough to do. However, there was to be more. Ted Hill, manager of radio station WORC, in July, 1930, asked him to develop a religious broadcast to be called "The Church of the Air." This radio ministry brought him into contact with all segments of life in the city and "touched the hearts and souls of many people." The broadcast ran from 7:45 to 8:00 A.M.

The phone rang one day during the broadcast. A man in New Hampshire whose wife was dying asked Dr. Edman to come to see her. He did so immediately after the broadcast, read Psalm 23 and prayed with her. When the doctor came in, he said she was on the way to recovery. Later she was able to come to Worcester to see the Edman family.

On one occasion Edman told Professor Burnham, through whose office he had to pass to enter a little office where he did his work, that he was discouraged because nothing had seemed to happen during a series of talks at Oxford, Massachusetts. Burnham explained how one of his students, Lindsay Sands, had had his life straightened out by this very series of meetings. When Dr. Edman talked with Sands he felt amply repaid for his series at Oxford.[19]

The last of his "Four Horsemen" (as he fondly called his boys many times) was born during their last year at Worcester. Norman Elner was born at Fairlawn Hospital on April 21, 1935. The daily paper spoke of his birth as an eight-pound Easter gift to his parents.[20]

Dr. Edman was still uncertain of his future, but he sensed that his work at Worcester was drawing to a close. He evidently shared this concern with his father in April, 1935. The senior Edman wrote: "We hope that the Lord will lead you to where He can use you best."[21]

G. Vernon Brown, home secretary of the Alliance, on April 19 wrote inquiring if Edman would consider a position at Nyack as teacher. He added in the letter that H. M. Shuman, president of the Alliance and of the Missionary Training Institute, favored this invitation. Full-time teachers would receive $200 a month for twelve months. Except for vacation, one month of the teacher's time during the institute vacation period was to be at the disposal of the institute.

Edman evidently expressed interest in Brown's proposal for a letter from David Fant, secretary of the board of managers of the Alliance, on April 25 stated that Edman had been nominated as a teacher, and the doctrinal statement which he was to sign was enclosed. He also mentioned that in addition to the $200 monthly pay there would be allowances for the children of $11.40 per month for those under twelve and $15.20 for those from twelve to eighteen years of age.[22] He was formally elected as teacher for the school year of 1935-36 on June 5 by the board.

He notified the Worcester congregation of their imminent departure and resigned as pastor. Vernon Brown also wrote to the congregation, asking that they release their pastor to teach in Nyack beginning September 1.[23] Dr. Edman wrote a letter to the congregation on May 28. He stated that he knew that God had brought them to Worcester and in His providence was now calling them to "His glad service at the Missionary Training Institute of Nyack in New York." He had not anticipated such a call and requested their prayer that he might be worthy of it. The executive committee of the Tabernacle accepted his resignation because he had to make "a response to a divine call to duty."[24] In this manner the "two years of complete silence" after the doctorate from Clark in 1933 "in which no one made inquiry as to what we were doing or desired to have us help them in Christian work" were ended.[25]

9.

Winsome Teacher

THE CHURCH RESIGNATION and the move to Nyack occurred quickly that spring and summer of 1935, leaving Professor Edman little time to prepare for classes. Their departure from Worcester at the end of August put them in Nyack less than a month before his teaching began.

The transition from an industrial New England city with its large blue-collar worker population to the lovely little town on the scenic bluffs of the Hudson River involved a change of pace as well as scenery. The family was assigned a house which nestled against the foot of a hill behind the campus, not far from the grave of A. B. Simpson, the founder of the Alliance.

The children had to be started in school just after their arrival, and there were some anxious moments for both parents and children in this new environment. Mrs. Edman made arrangements with a salesman from the Dugan Bakery Company to buy groceries, and they continued to use Dugan products while in Nyack. Later Dr. Edman had the pleasure of having the Dugan children in Wheaton College.[1]

Now he plunged into preparation for his classes. The Nyack catalog for 1935-36 indicates that he had a heavy class load as professor of history, missions and Greek. He also had a sprinkling of courses in other areas for good measure.

Professor Edman taught ancient and medieval history for five hours a week each term as a background for understanding the Bible and the important role of religion in the Middle Ages. Four hours a week in the spring term were devoted to "The Preparation of Gospel Messages and the History of Preaching." Careful study of the lives and sermons of the great preachers of the ages was to be alternated with practice in the preparation and delivery of sermons and Bible readings during the course. A course in public speaking for two hours a week in each term also was assigned to him. He linked the preparation and delivery of speeches with the theory of public speaking.

Fortunately, he had some student secretarial help. Virginia Shuman was one of his students who through her roommate Vivian Showell became his secretary. She described herself as "a very excited (and an extremely nervous) first year student" who "took dictation from her teacher" whom she so strongly respected for his tremendous learning.[2]

One student wrote of "a most wonderful student-teacher relationship" because Dr. Edman created "a spirit of partnership in learning." In his ancient history classes "history came to life" with his witty, yet scholarly well-prepared lectures. The students considered his chapel talks a "high point" in the daily routine because "he always had some new insight to share."[3]

Dr. Louis L. King, who now directs the missionary program of the Alliance in the New York office, was one of his enthusiastic students. He said, "Nobody ever influenced me as much as Dr. Edman" in his classes on preaching and missions. Dr. Edman told them to write their sermons out beforehand and then speak without notes. King made this his life practice, and those who have heard his perceptive messages can testify to his effective practice of this principle which he learned from Dr. Edman.

Dr. King vividly remembered thirty years afterward Dr. Edman's chapel talk on "The Bulls of Bashan" when the professor had presented the sufferings of Christ from Psalm 22 with such depth of emotion in his voice and with tears.

Dr. Edman's study in his home was located diagonally across from King's room in the corner of the men's dormitory. When King arose at 5:30 A.M., he would notice that his teacher had already been up for some time and was busy with his devotions. He followed this practice consistently, even though he had a heavy load of classes and responsibility for the Sunday services in the Gospel Tabernacle in New York.

He always kept in touch with students by short notes of congratulations on a new step of triumph or of sorrow in their lives.

Each week Dr. Edman commuted to New York where he served as pastor of the Gospel Tabernacle at 692 Eighth Avenue which was without a regular minister. This church was intimately associated with the Alliance because it had been founded by A. B. Simpson and was linked organically to the Alliance which had its headquarters in the same building. Its pastor was also the pastor of the officials of the denomination in the headquarters who were either members or officials in the Tabernacle. It was an honor to be its pastor.

Dr. Edman taught a Bible class before the Sunday morning and evening services, and the Wednesday evening prayer meeting. At times the Rev. Thomas Williamson, who was the choir director, conducted the evening service for him. Edman's messages were practical and inspirational with their "very homely illustrations" and "down to earth" way of reaching people where they were. People liked his brevity and punctuality.[4] They were also pleased with Dr. Edman's willingness to go along on social outings with the young people. On two occasions boats were chartered for fishing trips, and girls were included on the second occa-

sion. Dr. Edman was the "life of the party" on these outings.[5]

This service to the Tabernacle increased his income so
that in this year he made over $3,600 — an amount that
went much further then in the days before inflation.

During this year of satisfying service in New York and in
Nyack, God began to work in Dr. Edman's heart about
teaching at Wheaton College. Revivals occurred at Wheaton in 1936, 1943, and 1950.

In 1910 when Charles Albert Blanchard, the president of
Wheaton, was seriously ill, he came to the conclusion that
the spiritual as well as intellectual growth of Wheaton students was important. Sometime between 1915 and 1920 he
began the practice of special services for a week early in
each semester with an emphasis on evangelism in the fall
and upon the spiritual development of the believer in the
winter. For several years college professors or local ministers were the speakers.[6]

A Wheaton gospel team visited Toronto during the fall of
1935 for evangelistic meetings. When the young men returned to campus they were concerned about the spiritual
state of the college and began to hold prayer meetings.[7]
Don Hillis, Robert Evans and Jack Murray were among the
student leaders who prayed for revival during the first term.
Robert C. McQuilkin, president of Columbia Bible College
in South Carolina, was to be the speaker from February 2-9,
1936. He had been the featured speaker also in 1932 and
1935. In 1935 he had emphasized the victorious Christian
life. He was accompanied by the same song leader, Homer
Hammontree; the pianist was Bill Thomas of the class of
1929. Dr. Howard A. Kelly, professor emeritus of gynecol-
ogy at Johns Hopkins, was to take the Wednesday morning
chapel when Dr. McQuilkin would be speaking in Founder's
Week services at Moody Bible Institute. Dr. Kelly was

scheduled also to bring afternoon messages on "Science and the Bible."[8]

This promising spiritual team disintegrated during the week. Dr. McQuilkin caught the flu just before the evening meeting on Tuesday, February 4, and was confined to the infirmary for the balance of the meetings. Dr. J. Oliver Buswell, Jr., the popular young president of the college, was on trial in Chicago before the Presbytery of Chicago of which he was a member because of his support of the Independent Board for Presbyterian Foreign Missions. Dr. Kelly left on Tuesday, and the song leader and the pianist also left for other engagements on Thursday night.

By Thursday, February 6, the situation seemed to be chaotic. Dr. Harold Laird, a Presbyterian minister of Wilmington, Delaware, who was present to defend Dr. Buswell in his trial, spoke on Tuesday and Wednesday. Dr. Walter Wilson, a medical doctor, and others helped out as well. Dr. Buswell remained in Chicago. The two vice-presidents, George Kirk (who was out West), and Dr. Enock Dyrness were both absent. Only Dean Wallace Emerson of the personnel office was left to take charge on Thursday.

After Dr. Walter Wilson's message in the Thursday morning chapel on February 6, Mr. Hammontree read an unsigned note. "I am a Christian student," the note read, "and I love the Lord. But I'm not satisfied and I want to know how to have a revival in my own heart."

Mr. Hammontree spoke briefly in answer to this question and led in closing prayer.

Senior Don Hillis, who had written the note, suddenly rose. He acknowledged his authorship of the note and desired to confess the sin of not letting God fully control his life. Hillis asked, "Why can't we have this [revival] now?"

Other campus leaders began one by one in an orderly, quiet manner to rise and confess their sins or their need of God. After many had spoken, a student in the gallery suggested, "Let's kneel in prayer," and the 1,000 students and faculty eagerly responded. Further testimony and confession followed.

About 5:00 P.M. Dr. Hammontree gave an invitation to those desiring to become Christians to come forward. More than twenty responded. He again closed in prayer, but no one moved. Many were still in the chapel when the evening meeting opened in which Dr. Laird spoke. The evening meeting was followed by an after meeting which went on into the night. Friday chapel went on for a long time, and on Saturday there was an all-day prayer meeting.[9]

News of the meeting stirred the townspeople. It also affected the Moody Bible Institute Founder's Week Conference and was widely proclaimed over Moody's radio station WMBI. Revival also occurred in the State Training Home for Girls in Geneva, Illinois, where the students had ministered from week to week. During the faculty prayer meeting, confessions were made and wrongs were righted.[10]

10.

Westward Ho!

JUST BEFORE this spiritual awakening at Wheaton, Dr. Edman in Nyack had awakened suddenly from a deep sleep on one cold night in January. It seemed that the Holy Spirit was saying to him, "What are you going to do about Wheaton College?" He prayed that if it were not the will of God for him to go there that no call from Wheaton would ever come to him. He immediately went back to sleep and said nothing of his experience, even to Mrs. Edman.

About mid-February he saw a notice on the bulletin board in the Tabernacle that Dr. Buswell, president of Wheaton, was preaching to a youth rally in Brooklyn the next Sunday afternoon. He was inclined to go and hear him but was afraid that he might meet him and be trying to answer his own feeling of that night in January. So he decided not to go.

Dr. Buswell wrote to him on March 5, stating that he was now in a position to offer him a place on the Wheaton faculty with the rank of associate professor in political science. His salary was to be $2,500, less the temporary 10 percent reduction that all faculty were taking in a period of financial stringency for the school. He asked him "to come to Wheaton at our expense at the earliest opportunity for conference in regards to courses and plans for the coming year."[1]

He shared with "friend wife" his experience in January and Dr. Buswell's invitation, and they prayed for guidance. He wrote an airmail letter to his faithful counselor and prayer helper, E. Joseph Evans in California, and another to Clarence Williams, a Christian carpenter, and his wife in Worcester, about the invitation. He asked them to pray with him and tell him what they believed was the Lord's will for him. Mr. Evans replied from San Mateo in a practical letter on March 9:

> I have prayerfully looked to the Lord and considered the proposition set before you. I cannot of course tell you what to do. But let me call your attention to the fact that you definitely prayed that "If it was not the will of God for you to go to Wheaton — that *no* call would come from Dr. Buswell," but the call has come. It seems to me that the path is plain. Your fleece is wet! !

Uncle Joe also reminded him that he would contact many who might be more spiritually needy at a liberal arts college than at the Bible School in Nyack, and that he could carry on a spiritual ministry on the weekends in the Chicago area. He concluded, "There are many reasons why I believe that this is an 'open door' for you. . . ."[2]

The Williams too believed that God had given them clear direction toward Wheaton. They put what they felt was the answer in a sealed envelope in their letter because they "thought best for you to get your answer yourself before you know what we got and then there would be no fear of your being influenced by our answer, but if we both hear from God our answer will agree, and ours will merely confirm yours."

The Williams prayed that God would provide the Edmans "a solid comfortable and enjoyable assurance that you have been made to know His will in this matter." The little enclosed note read, "After earnest prayer we received witness through and by which we are assured that it is God's will for you to accept the offer from Wheaton with joy. We will be glad to hear your experience but believe that it will agree with ours. God bless you."[3]

He decided to write Dr. Buswell for more information while awaiting these two letters. He enclosed the new faculty appointment questionnaire to supplement the one he had sent earlier with a photo. He wrote that he deeply appreciated "the honor, as well as the responsibility involved in your offer; and we have spread the matter before the Lord."

He alluded to salary at the institute where he was making $200 a month plus $12 for each of the children for a total of $248. This with the income from his interim pastorate at the Tabernacle was giving him about $3,750 a year, which was much more per year than Wheaton was offering. Money was not his main consideration, but he knew by experience that with four boys it would be hard to live on $2,250 a year.

Edman asked if it would be convenient for him to arrive by train on Monday so that he could get back to New York for the Wednesday evening prayer meeting. He also asked if the college would aid in moving expenses as Nyack had done.[4]

Aboard the Aurora and Elgin electric train going to Wheaton he once again felt God's presence in a deeply moving way. It seemed that God was saying to him, "Be a Shepherd to my people at Wheaton." He knew then that he was to go to Wheaton, and this experience was confirmed by the two letters from his trusted friends.

When he arrived, Dr. Buswell introduced him to the faculty and had him speak on his Christian experience, a practice which was regularly followed in the case of prospective faculty.[5]

Dr. Buswell again wrote to him on March 27, offering him a salary of $2,750, less the 10 percent reduction, but scratched out the $2,750 and in a postscript said that the trustees had decided on a basic salary of $2,800 less the 10 percent reduction.[6] Dr. Edman replied with an acceptance of the offer, thus opening the door to his major place of service for the remainder of his life.

Once he had made his mind up to go to Wheaton, he had to inform the institute and his denomination of his decision. A. C. Snead, the foreign secretary, after he found out that he was leaving, wrote to him of his concern that Nyack be a spiritual center but that it also needed "well-rounded scholarship which is spiritual, intellectual and practical." He believed that Dr. Edman's ministry was a "strong factor" in carrying out this purpose because there were so many "expressions of appreciation of your God-given capabilities and ministries." He was puzzled because God had seemed to lead so clearly in Edman's coming to Nyack "not only for teaching ministry but for true leadership, unofficial perhaps for a time. . . ." He also expressed concern over the cramped living quarters which they had had in the home on the hillside.[7]

Dr. Edman sent an official letter of resignation to the home secretary, G. Vernon Brown. In it he wrote that "after much prayer and waiting on the Lord" he felt free to resign to go to Wheaton even though they had been "very happy in the work and fellowship on the Hillside." If the Lord should lead, he had not shut the door to a later return to Nyack. He added that he would carry out the plans for his work in summer school and in the New York Tabernacle as long as he was needed.[8]

He hastened also to inform his father of the course of events. When he found out about it, Anders Edman was pleased and helped to locate the home at 330 East Franklin Street where the Edmans lived in Wheaton until he moved in 1940 to Westgate, the home of the president. Thus, Dr. Edman believed, was fulfilled the promise of Numbers 9:20 and 10:33 that he was promised a "resting place."

11.

History Plus at Wheaton

WHEATON WELCOMED the new professor heartily. In addition to picture stories in the *Wheaton Daily Journal* and the *Chicago Tribune*, he was welcomed editorially by the student *Record*, college *Bulletin*, and even the *Tower* yearbook for 1937.

Mrs. Mortenson of the registrar's office cheerfully signed as a property owner the necessary papers so the Edmans could have the water, gas and electricity turned on in their new home. Mrs. Mortenson became his ally some years later in launching the unofficial "Picker-upper Club." Members volunteered to keep the campus neat by picking up scraps of paper and other debris collected by wind, accidents and careless students.

The Edman's old Plymouth was beginning to show signs of trouble after its trip from the East with a heavy load of people and their necessities. Dr. Edman took it to Eddie Ruch's service station where began "not only the best of service for the succession of automobiles that we have had, but the finest of friendships."[1]

The matter of a church home in Wheaton was early business also. When he visited the Wheaton Bible Church, Dr. Edman was asked by the pastor to teach the college-age class in the church school. But he was surprised the following Sunday morning to learn that the chairman of the Bible department at the college was to be the teacher of the college-age class and that he was to conduct his class in the choir loft.

Half a dozen students followed him to a noisy, open choir loft. On the following Sunday this class was shifted to a smaller corner room. He went home, prayed about the matter, and decided there was no need for a second college class. He thus advised the Sunday school superintendent in a letter.

Russell Mixter, a teacher in the science department, asked him during the following week to take a college-age class at the Tabernacle in Wheaton. He started with "four guys and one gal" (a pianist), but the class soon filled the auditorium in the old Masonic Hall where the group met for services.[2] In the fall of 1938, Dr. Edman became the interim pastor, an office he filled until the fall of 1941. In later years Dr. Edman became a member of the Wheaton Bible Church and directed many of his gifts to Christian work through its treasurer.

Dr. Orrin E. Tiffany, his colleague and chairman of the department under whom he was to work, became a close friend. Dr. Edman recalled the friendship: "No one could have been more congenial and constructive to a beginner than you were to me when I came."[3]

When he began his work in the fall of 1936, construction was just being completed on the first section of what was then known as North Hall, a women's residence.[4] The first unit was completed by Christmas. He was to complete the other section of the building later, as well as many other buildings on the campus. The first mention of his name in faculty minutes for January, 1937, was in connection with his giving an opening prayer at the meeting.

His interests that fall were in academic matters rather than in physical facilities. The catalog of 1938 listed him as the teacher of History 103-104 — European History since 476. The Edman classes became popular courses. It was the author's responsibility in the fall of 1944 to take Dr. Edman's place in teaching this course when the responsibilities of the presidency made it impossible for him to teach any longer.

Dr. Edman also taught the diplomatic and political history of the United States. His main responsibility, however, was in the area of political science. At one time or another he taught American government, international law, comparative governments, international relations, American political theory and political literature. This was indeed an ambitious academic load, but he devoted himself to doing the best job he could.

He went to the classroom with definite ideas on the role of the teacher and the nature and methods of Christian liberal arts education. He expressed his convictions frequently in later years during talks to the faculty and through articles for periodicals.

In comparing secular and Christian colleges, he believed that while the secular college would prepare one physically and intellectually for life, the Christian college could do the same "plus the spiritual, not only in this life but for that which is to come. . . . The Christian college should provide true spiritual perspective by which to face realistically and understand the problems of our generation. Imagine trying to teach economics without an understanding of the selfishness of the natural heart, or biology without faith in the Creator."[5]

He told the Kiwanis Club of Evansville, Indiana, that students need accurate facts and that colleges should "give students faith in God and inculcate in students' hearts a fear and love of God."[6] In answer to a question as to the most important thing a student could learn at Wheaton, he wrote that it was "to learn to know the Lord Jesus for one's self and to learn how to study."[7] In his opinion any teacher who failed to be a "pastor" to his students to lead them to the Word and to Christ would not in a Christian college be properly fulfilling his function, however competent he was academically.

In an address to the faculty entitled "The Christian Teacher" he discussed the characteristics of a good teacher by indulging his popular penchant for alliteration. The good teacher, he said, is competent both in the secular and in the spiritual, is compassionate to his students, and is a consistent Christian in attitude, word, theology and action. He must also be contagious in every outlook, cooperative with others and, last but not least, creative, because teaching is an art as well as a science or discipline.[8] Character as well as grammar could, he believed, be taught by precept and example. For this reason he was to begin Christian character scholarship awards in the fall of 1954 which brought small sums of money to those who their supervisors believed showed development of character.

He thought that the Christian teacher could not be academically neutral but must relate the Saviour to his field of teaching because each area has its theological presuppositions. Because of this he must "give conflicting views in a disputed area" and then align his own position with the Scriptures.[9]

Good teaching involved, in his own words, "a source of sound information. A stimulus to intellectual curiosity. A steadiness of character. A smile."[10] He thought that one could stimulate thought and cut down memorizing by having "more of the discussion that makes one witty and wise."[11] He favored large classes for lecture sections, up to twenty-five for composition and language, and ten to fifteen for mathematics and discussion groups.[12] The study of a foreign language would be useful to develop the mind of the student, to free one from provincialism, to help one in travel "when he made his pile," or be useful in graduate work.[13]

Dr. Edman had clear-cut ideas as to the function of de-

votions at the beginning of each class. He believed that the
teacher should conduct them himself so that they could be
an integral part of the material for the day and "not a
perfunctory duty or something artificial." He wrote to one
teacher, "Rather the brief reading from the Scripture and a
little lesson drawn therefrom can be the very thing that
meets the spiritual need in the heart of some student. It
can create the desire of someone to come to you for counsel,
both academic and spiritual."[14]

He also had definite convictions concerning the role of the
student in the educational process. Students could better
their education by applying themselves to the great opportunities possible in the United States for education as com-
pared to Asia, Africa or South America. "Habits of careful
preparation and enthusiastic participation in the learning
process would carry over into life beneficially."[15] He wrote
the student body president of Grace College at Winona Lake,
Indiana, concerning what the student should learn in this
manner:

> A college student should learn the great essentials: the
> basic concept of our government and the American way of
> life and its contrast to slavery, old and new; the basic
> skills of reading accurately and rapidly and that of writing
> concisely and cogently; an acquaintanceship with good
> literature and appreciation thereof; an understanding of the
> scientific method of acquaintanceship through its use and
> also to know its limitations; and most of all, an under-
> standing of God's revelation, the Bible, and an acquaint-
> anceship with the Most High through Jesus Christ the
> Lord.[16]

Such were his theories of teaching. In many cases there
is a gap between theory and practice, but the universal
testimony of his students is that he put his theories into

daily practice in the classroom, though at times in an unorthodox but interesting manner. He had excellent rapport
with the students even when the work required lecturing
which might at times become dull.

He more often used the Socratic or inductive method in
his smaller classes for juniors and seniors. Through questions
he would draw the main points out of the students and
write them on the blackboard. A favorite question was,
"What do you allege?"[17]

Dr. Robert deVette, now a Wheaton professor, remembers
that in the introductory course in European history since
476 he integrated the material well in lectures and asked
demanding questions which involved trends, reasons, causes,
and the contemporary significance of past events. He related geography to history in order to show its influence
upon man.[18] Billy Graham thought that Dr. Edman knew
his subject well and presented many interesting sidelights
that "made history live."[19]

Dr. Edman's conservative political and economic views
surfaced in classes on American constitutional theory where
he insisted that government should be one of laws rather
than of men. He conscientiously tried to be objective in
the study of important Supreme Court cases.

Hudson Armerding, who became his successor as president, helped him by grading papers. He remembered that
Dr. Edman used mostly true-false questions and objective
completion questions that demanded much thought. Essay
questions were used also for analysis and integration. All
these questions were well worked out and incorporated the
main insights of the course.[20]

Mrs. Tiffany remembered some of his cleverer puns. When
she jokingly said one day that she would put her coat on
his hat, on that warm spring day his rejoinder was "That's
all right, it is a spring hat." Because he later signed some

letters to close friends with "Me," he enjoyed Mrs. Tiffany's notes to him as president which began with "Dear Me."

Dr. Buswell's secretary was not prone to humor. One day Dr. Edman came into Mrs. Tiffany's room holding his hip and limping. Asked what was wrong, he said, "Ella kicked me." Those who knew Ella knew that he had just experienced one of her quick and sometimes tart remarks.

On another occasion when he gave his report as chairman of the social committee, of which he happened to be the sole member at that time, he solemnly arose in the faculty meeting and said, "The Social Committee arises to make its report."[21] He was chairman of that committee for some time after June, 1937.[22] Needless to say, the social committee provided interesting programs for the faculty. In 1937 he had the faculty substitute a prayer and praise service followed by refreshments for their usual Thanksgiving dinner. He ably arranged the faculty, staff and trustee dinner and program in January, 1938, at a cost of seventy-five cents a plate.[23]

When Dr. Buswell sent a memo asking new faculty members to speak in chapel, Dr. Edman replied, "With timidity I respond to the circular of this morning in regard to chapel talks by new members of the faculty. I checked over the letter to make sure it was genuine and not a forgery." He said he would like to talk on either a Lenten series from the last week of Christ's ministry or give a devotional based on an Old Testament biography.[24]

His contacts with the Robert G. LeTourneau family brought an invitation to be the dean and director of their Bethany Camp at Winona Lake for the summer of 1937. Mrs. LeTourneau opened the camp that year and wanted good leadership. He went there again in the summers of 1938 and 1939, to the dismay of his boys who sometimes wanted a little more variation in their vacations.[25]

Another honor came to the new professor in the spring of

1937 when Carl Henry was chosen editor of the *Tower* of 1939 and he and his staff asked the popular new professor to become the faculty adviser of that publication. They developed a warm relationship and when Henry became editor of *Christianity Today*, he often turned to his former adviser for an article. When the *Tower* of 1939 appeared in the spring of 1939, Dr. Edman's picture not only appeared in it as adviser[26] but also as sponsor of the Naitermian Literary Association and as faculty adviser for the International Relations Club which he helped to organize in the fall of 1937.[27]

His work in political science and his desire to awaken people to their political responsibility led him in the winter of 1937-38, with the consent of the department, to give a series of six popular lectures on the decay of democracy. This series met with a good deal of public approval. He addressed the faculty on March 2, 1937, on "Trends in Political Philosophy."[28]

He was very much interested in the International Relations Club which he helped to bring into being. It was inaugurated, according to the *Tower* of 1939, "to supplement the course in political science" and it "has awakened a new interest in foreign affairs on the campus. With a background of South American life, Dr. Edman has been able to lead many a lively discussion as the organization's founder and promoter."[29] Howard Moffet, who now directs a large Presbyterian hospital in Taegu, Korea, was elected as president.[30] In one of their Friday morning meetings, Dr. Edman led a discussion after a paper presented by Clara Owen on "American Foreign Policy."[31]

He proposed at the Friday, October 15, 1937, meeting of the club that he plan a ten-day trip during the spring vacation to Washington and Philadelphia to see historic sites and to visit Congress and the Supreme Court as they were in session. The tour was to leave Grand Central Station in

Chicago on Sunday, April 10, and return on Friday, April 15. About twenty students took the trip, and it was so popular that a second tour was conducted in 1939.

A less ambitious tour involved a two-day auto trip to Springfield, Illinois, for "all the college family" to visit Lincoln country in that city and New Salem. It occurred in the semester break between the first and second semester in January, 1939.

In the midst of busy work at Wheaton he received a letter in November, 1937, concerning an opening as dean at Nyack. The letter intimated that there was desire to change leadership "for the sake of the school itself, to say nothing of its effect on the entire society." The writer asked him to give serious prayer and thought to the possibility.[32] During the summer of 1939 he had an invitation to become president of Nyack, but again he declined the honor.[33]

With all these tasks he still had time to pursue his hobby of biography which had interested him for the previous fifteen years. Having made a thorough study of the biblical biographies of Samuel, David, Joseph and others, he was reading John Newton's biography with profit.[34] About ten days later the *Record* published his article on Newton's life.[35] Later he greatly enjoyed the biography of Charles Albert Blanchard. He was of the opinion that each new generation of Wheaton teachers should read it "to maintain the spirit of the fathers."[36]

The spring of 1938 also brought a partial return to the pastoral ministry. The Gospel Tabernacle which met in the Masonic Hall in Wheaton had been established by Swedish students in 1926.[37] From the time he came to Wheaton, Dr. Edman taught a popular Sunday school class there which attracted "a large student following" because of "his ready wit and sense of humor."[38] When the student pastor John Ballbach graduated in 1938, the congregational choice for a pastor was the popular teacher. He preached until

September, 1941, when Billy Graham, his favorite student, succeeded him in the pastorate.[39] Billy had preached twice that spring. In a rather unorthodox fashion, before he got final approval by the board, Dr. Edman had asked him by letter to assume the pastorate at $5 a week. Graham's fiancée, Ruth Bell, felt at first he should not take it, but after prayer they both felt it was God's will.[40]

When his father died, Dr. Edman was carrying on his summer work at Bethany Camp. One August day as he was heading for the dining hall with his family for the evening meal, he was called to the phone. His brother Elner said, "I have some bad news for you. Dad just died this afternoon very suddenly." This was a shock because his father had been at Winona Lake just the week before and had gone fishing with his grandsons at 4:00 A.M. Dr. Edman went by himself to pray and face the shock. As he put it, "After all, I had only one dad." His regard and respect for his father were deep and abiding and were reflected in his writings and life.[41]

Further responsibility came when Dr. Orrin E. Tiffany, who had been chairman of the department of history and social science since 1929, resigned as chairman on December 13, 1938. Dr. and Mrs. Tiffany recommended to the faculty that Dr. Edman be the new chairman. The faculty accepted the recommendation on January 3, 1939, and the board of trustees approved it in mid-January. He held the position until he became president. The promotion was announced in the *Record* with the news of Dr. Tiffany's retirement.[42] Assuming leadership on September 1, 1939, Dr. Edman was given a raise in salary to $3,000, less 5 percent, and promoted to the rank of professor.[43] Dr. Tiffany expressed his pleasure at the choice of the new chairman as "one with the gracious personality and the evident organizing ability" necessary for the task.[44]

As professor and department chairman, Dr. Edman had

reached the peak of the academic ladder. He humbly planned no radical change but wanted to strengthen and develop what Dr. Tiffany had begun. He had become an increasingly popular speaker with church groups and service clubs and was a favorite speaker in chapel. He worked loyally to bind the faculty together through social and prayer groups. God had indeed set His seal on the move to Wheaton which He had made known to Dr. Edman on that cold January night in 1936.

12.

For Such a Time

Dr. Edman did not function long as chairman of the department. Events were moving swiftly to carry him to the Wheaton presidency — a post he held for a quarter century. When he began his academic work as chairman in the fall of 1939, he knew that there were problems that the incumbent president faced, but he kept out of them except to try to mediate to keep the peace.

J. Oliver Buswell, Jr., had so impressed the faculty, students and trustees when he took a series of meetings at Wheaton that he was asked in 1926, when about thirty years of age, to become president of Wheaton. This offer was made shortly after the death of Charles Albert Blanchard. Dr. Buswell ably filled this office until 1940 when a series of problems led to the decision that brought his college service to an end.

His support of the Independent Board of Foreign Missions, organized by J. Gresham Machen, led to his trial before the Judicial Commissioners of the Presbytery of Chicago. This trial ran in a series of sessions from June 14, 1935, to February 26, 1936. That body admonished him "to desist from his course" of support of the independent board. Appeals to the higher church courts of his denomination were rejected. Because these appeals were not successful, he and others of like mind withdrew from the Presbyterian Church, U.S.A. to found the new Presbyterian

Church of America later in June. Dr. Buswell became the moderator of this new church at its general assembly in late October, 1936. The group later took the name Orthodox Presbyterian Church.

The secular press spread news of the trial from coast to coast. It was widely discussed in religious magazines. Because Dr. Buswell was president of Wheaton College, which enrolled many Presbyterian students, the unfavorable publicity was a matter of concern to him and to the board of trustees. They proposed in their June meeting in 1936 that a letter of explanation be sent to the constituency concerning this matter.[1]

Dr. Buswell possessed strong convictions about his orthodox theological views. His ability as a vigorous debater and his willingness to stand up for his views sometimes created tensions.

He and the trustees were also increasingly concerned by the annual deficits for some years. These deficits came partly because of the growth of the college and partly because of the recession of 1938. They grew larger from year to year until the total reached nearly $200,000 by June, 1939. Through cooperation of the faculty, staff and administration, it had been cut to less than $90,000 by graduation in June of 1941.[2] Economy moves worried the staff and faculty in regard to the security of their jobs.

Friction increased when a professor criticized Dr. Buswell as an evolutionist because he taught the possibility that the days of creation in Genesis 1 might be eras of years rather than twenty-four-hour days.[3]

Friction also developed over an athletic coach. The trustees finally decided that they must take action. The coach had been a player under the famous Alonzo Stagg of the University of Chicago. Dr. Buswell had engaged him to begin in the fall of 1936 the task of coaching what Dr. Buswell hoped might be winning football teams.

The coach was vigorous and forceful. His unbending stand on issues led to disagreement between him and others in the administration and faculty. When the vice-president in academic administration and the registrar had to notify some students in the summer of 1939 that their poor school record made them ineligible for athletic activities in the fall, the coach vigorously protested the decision and appealed to the president to reverse it. The sportsman ordered athletic equipment in such large amounts that the vice-president in business administration, who was trying to weather the 1938 recession, became disturbed. To make matters worse, the coach had deficits in his departmental budget.

Dr. Buswell brought in a former athlete and missionary in the fall of 1939 to teach Bible and head a committee on athletics to relieve some of the tension. But this man and the coach clashed dramatically. On one occasion the coach ordered him off the basketball court.

The coach experienced more difficulty with the dean of students because he ordered buses directly rather than following the accepted policy of chartering them through the dean's office.

The president's spirited defense of this man and an attempt to dismiss the dean of students alienated students, faculty, alumni and many friends of the college. This man became the wedge that finally separated Dr. Buswell from the college.

While all this was going on, V. Raymond Edman, according to many of his colleagues, tried to help by mediating between the parties in the dispute because he had a deep interest in athletics.

He was also in the midst of a kindly discussion with Jeanne Cook in the pages of the *Record* as to whether or not, in view of the war in Europe, the Washington Banquet for 1940 should be canceled. He proposed that instead students give the money they would spend on the banquet for the relief of suffering in war areas, such as Finland and China. The banquet was canceled, and the money was used for Finnish relief.[4] One of Dr. Edman's students, Don Hoke, now president of Tokyo Christian College, thought that this proposal put Dr. Edman in the early vanguard of those evangelicals who wanted the gospel to have a social as well as personal impact.[5]

In the meantime, concerned students individually or in group statements had contacted the trustees concerning the problems of the college, especially as they concerned athletics.[6] Faculty members, administrators and alumni had already made their views known in vigorous terms.

Matters came to a head at the meeting of fourteen of the nineteen trustees on January 22, 1940, when a communication from ten Chicago alumni as well as letters from the faculty were read. Dr. Buswell stated that the trustees had three courses of action: They could dismiss the president, they could give him a vote of confidence, or they could continue the present situation. He proposed that they let the coach go at the end of the year, keep on the dean of students as a teacher or as dean, and give the president a vote of confidence. He then withdrew from the meeting.

When the president returned, a trustee informed him that they were unable to provide the desired vote of confidence. The trustees decided to terminate the president's services at that time but to give him his salary, home, office and secretary in the transitional period. Another motion terminated the services of the coach at the end of the academic year. Harvey Chrouser was later made head football coach.

The problem of Dr. Buswell's replacement remained. The vice-presidents of academic affairs and business and the dean of students could not be appointed because they had been too closely involved in the controversies which led to the departure of President Buswell. The trustees had heard how well Professor Edman got along with students, faculty, staff and administrators, of his desire to keep the peace, of his acceptance with the general public in his speaking engagements, and of his effective teaching and gracious personality.[7]

Dr. Edman was at home playing pingpong with son David when the chairman of the board telephoned, asking him to come to the meeting of the board on that Saturday evening. Not knowing what had gone on in the meeting up to this point, he was surprised to learn they had voted that he become president. He "reluctantly" accepted the position of acting president, and the three top administrators were called in and informed.

A statement issued on Monday, January 2, praised Dr. Buswell's work for the school. During his presidency the student body had more than doubled, the plant had been modernized, and the curriculum expanded. It also admitted there had been "certain difficulties in administrative cooperation" which had necessitated a change. Dr. Edman was announced as the acting president. He thought that this position would be temporary until the trustees found a permanent president.[8]

When students and faculty heard via the usual academic grapevine of the solution and change, the news burst like a bombshell on the campus. The venerable Darien Straw, both a teacher and trustee of the college for years, spoke in chapel on the topic, "Fear not little flock, it is your Father's good pleasure to give you the kingdom." He then formally announced Professor Edman as the acting president. Dr. Edman closed with prayer and called a faculty meeting after chapel to pray for the school and himself. The chairman of the board addressed the faculty meeting concerning the budget problem and the need for cooperation on the part of all.[9]

The *Daily Journal* of Wheaton carried pictures of both men with the trustees' statement as well as statements by and biographical information about both men. Dr. Buswell urged everyone to be loyal to the college and to Dr. Edman "in his difficult position." Dr. Edman expressed "his very highest esteem and affection" for Dr. Buswell and promised that he would attempt to carry on the work his predecessor had done so well in this thirteen years as president.[10] Both were gracious Christian gentlemen in their relations during this difficult period.

Dr. Tiffany had again to resume his duties as head of the history department, although Dr. Edman continued his teaching load for a time. He taught his freshman course in European history until the 1944-45 school year when the author relieved him of that responsibility.

He frequently consulted with the trustees, faculty and students concerning the state of the campus and his duties in order to act wisely. He talked on occasion with Billy Graham, a senior student, about feelings and attitudes of students and of spiritual conditions on campus.[11] Billy was president of the Christian Service Council and knew the spiritual condition of the campus.

Because the board felt that Dr. Edman needed more salary with his increased responsibilities, they voted that his salary be increased to $4,500 a year, less the 5 percent economy reduction, and that he have free use of the president's home.[12] Westgate had just some years before been purchased from the Oury family with the help of faculty gifts to become the home of the president. The college looked after its maintenance.

Dr. Edman's first problem with the students in chapel loomed as April Fool's Day drew near. This traditionally was a time for jokes, such as alarm clocks going off during chapel services, seniors wearing ludicrous costumes, or changing from organ hymn tunes to Mendelssohn's "Wedding March." Because he believed that chapel was a time for family prayers, he announced in chapel on March 31 that there might be jokes at breakfast or in classes but added, "For example, tomorrow I have the large lecture section in survey of European history. History calls for dates and an understanding of the passage of time; and it would be, therefore, quite appropriate to punctuate the class period by the use of alarm clocks. There is always the possibility some students will thereby become fully conscious." He went on to add, "However, we shall have nothing of the kind in chapel. This part of the day that we spend in family worship is dedicated wholly to God, and nothing inappropriate to worship should be here."

Chapel went off undisturbed, but the students took him at his word, and alarm clocks went off in his class until he announced after the second had gone off that there would be a surprise quiz unless the alarm clocks would miraculously cease going off. They did.[13]

He also broke the juniors of the habit each spring of pitching pennies to the seniors who for several Fridays just before commencement always marched into chapel in a body with their gowns and caps. He appealed to the maturity and dignity of the seniors to ignore the juniors' childish conduct and separately quietly "asked" the juniors to "cease and desist" their practice.[14]

David L. Roberts, now director of development at the college, as editor of the *Tower* of 1941, announced on May 28, 1940, that the *Tower* of that year was dedicated to Dr. Edman. He indicated that it was because of his "genuine humility, deep spirituality, profound understanding, godly wisdom, sweet simplicity, appropriate humor, and adept leadership." Prexy was also described as "vitally active in campus life as professor, pastor and friend."[15] This honor spoke of the love he had won.

He was overwhelmed with the responsibility for the $756,000 budget that the board set up for the coming year at their meeting in late June, 1940. He knew it was the result of months of study. As he walked home from the meeting about midnight, he stopped halfway down the double row of maples lining the road to the western limestone gates to the college which were just opposite Westgate where he lived. He looked up through the canopy of leaves and prayed concerning this tremendous sum which seemed so big to one who had so little of this world's goods. Once again, as on many occasions in the past, he sensed the presence of God and His willingness and ability to make this large sum available as needed. He went home in peace to sleep well.[16] Perhaps this is why at every meeting of the board he had devotions involving a Scripture passage with his brief meditation on it and a prayer for God's blessing on the meeting.

The trustees were convinced by the time of their January, 1941, meeting that what Dr. Edman thought would be an interim task should become his permanent responsibility. Alumni, friends, faculty, staff and students seemed to be collectively happy with him. Thus the board knew that it was "evident that Dr. Edman was the Lord's choice for the leadership of the College," and they unanimously elected him as president.[17] At his request they also set May 9, 1941, his birthday, as the date for his inauguration as president. The alumni magazine carried his picture with the caption "He's All Ours Now" and announced the details for the day.[18]

His inauguration and birthday proved to be busy on that lovely day in May. The Anders V. Edman memorial chimes, which his mother had given to the college, were played for the first time from 9:15 until 9:30 a.m. A morning convocation for faculty, students and representatives of Bible colleges and seminaries followed. Edgar F. Dival of the board of trustees presided, and Dr. Edman's friend, Thomas Moseley, president of the Missionary Training Institute at Nyack, gave the invocation. Charles Washburn, also from Nyack, read the Scripture. Dr. Harry Ironside, pastor of Moody Memorial Church and a member of the board, gave the address, "Forgetting and Pressing Forward." Dr. Edman's friend, Ernest M. Wadsworth, director of the Great Commission Prayer League, gave the prayer of dedication to the new president. Dr. Edman's "favorite singer," Professor Mignon B. Mackenzie, sang what was an appropriate song for his administration, "O Jesus, I Have Promised to Serve Thee." Greetings from the faculty, student body, alumni and trustees followed. Then Dr. Edman spoke on the theme, "Brave Sons and Daughters True."

Ground-breaking for the new alumni gymnasium at the corner of Franklin and Adams followed at 11:30 A.M. Dr. Edman used a spade specially gilded for the occasion to break the first sod. He used the trowel at homecoming in the fall to place mortar around the cornerstone of the new gym. The spade and trowel were to symbolize his interests in securing new buildings for the college.

Harvey Chrouser, the dynamic and aggressive football coach, and Dr. Edman had a common love of athletics. Dr. Edman realized that the earlier plans for a gymnasium and swimming pool were too ambitious and in his quiet way suggested to Harvey that he work on a modified plan. After a game at western Maryland, Harvey brought back plans for a gym that would cost $85,000 and fit Wheaton's need. Dr. Edman had him and Coach Coray talk to the board on February 18, 1941. After the presentation, R. E. Nicholas, vice chairman of the board, asked, "Who is going to pay for all this?" Chrouser replied that the alumni would, because he had just come from enthusiastic alumni banquets concerning this and knew that the college already owned steel which could be used for the building.[19]

The board promised to break ground on May 9 if $75,000 was raised by May 1. By that date $82,000 was available, and Dr. Edman broke ground for the new building as part of the inauguration ceremonies. By November, $101,500 of the $155,000 needed for the building had been collected in cash and pledges.[20] Herbert A. Brand was the architect, and the Julian Construction Company erected the building. This was the first of over a dozen buildings that were to be constructed during Dr. Edman's administration. The cornerstone was laid at homecoming, and the building was first used for a long chapel on Friday, May 29, 1942, and dedicated at commencement on June 14, 1942.

A luncheon was served in the Lower Chapel at 12:00 noon after the ground-breaking. The new chimes were then played at 1:15 P.M. for fifteen minutes before an organ recital which preceded the afternoon inaugural service for representatives of the academic world and friends at 2 P.M.

The colorful academic procession moved to Pierce Chapel between two rows of students who served as an honor guard. Herman A. Fischer, the chairman of the board, presided. Dr. Charles Koller, president of Northern Baptist Seminary, gave the invocation, and Evan D. Welsh, then pastor of College Church and later chaplain of the college, read the Scripture after the singing of the hymn, "How Firm a Foundation." Guy E. Snavely, executive director of the Association of American Colleges, spoke on "The Liberal Arts College in an Upset World." After an anthem by the Men's Glee Club, Stephen Paine, president of Houghton College and a graduate of Wheaton, talked about "Service that Lives." Dr. Edman was then inducted into the presidency by Herman Fischer, who gave him a brief charge. Dr. Edman responded with a pledge to uphold Wheaton's standards. Darien A. Straw, teacher and trustee, presented the seal of the college to the president.

Dr. Edman then gave his inaugural address, "For Christ and His Kingdom," indicating that the motto would be the goal of his administration. He spoke of the importance of democracy and its characteristics as practiced in America and related the independent liberal arts college to American education and democracy. Then he pointed out how Wheaton had been founded by men who feared God but upheld freedom for all men in the fear of God.[21] After another anthem by the Men's Glee Club, the benediction was given by Dr. Lewis S. Chafer, president of Dallas Theological Seminary.

The official delegates and their wives were received at an informal reception on Hiatt lawn. The formal banquet came at 6 p.m. in Lower Chapel with David O. Fuller presiding. Speeches of congratulations and good wishes from representatives of Bible institutes, Wheaton churches, the city of Wheaton, the student body, the alumni, the faculty, the trustees and the Illinois Federation of Colleges followed the dinner. Afterward the Womens' Glee Club gave a concert of classical and sacred selections. The new president and his wife then retired, tired but happy, to Westgate.

Earlier in the day, Professor Laurin King had presented Dr. Edman with the key to a fine mahogany desk that, unknown to him, had been put in his office. Gifts of students and faculty paid for this birthday present. Professor Effie Jane Wheeler's article, "In Safe Hands," in the inaugural issue of the college bulletin summed up in that title the sentiment of all concerning the new president. Student opinion was well expressed in the words of a student, Werner Graendorf:

> Wheaton today inaugurates more than a president. It inaugurates a personality. Unassuming and quiet, Dr. V. Raymond Edman embodies a dynamic of character and variance of background that make the fourth presidency of Wheaton replete with the sparkle of a genuinely great figure. . . . Perhaps no more eloquent tribute to his position on the campus could be given than the fact that the fickle student mind in college parlance, ranks him simply and unanimously, "Tops."[22]

Frank E. Herrick, of the class of 1899 and a local judge, wrote a poem for the occasion which ended by thanking God for the new leader in these words:

> Our grateful hearts as one their thousand thanks uprise
> To Him who sent this man to guide and lead and bless.[23]

Dr. Edman in an article in the college student paper wrote of what were to be the two dominant themes of his administration. He believed that it was the duty of the college to state clearly, concisely and enthusiastically "such basic political principles as popular sovereignty with its emphasis on the intrinsic value of the individual, constitutional government 'of laws and not of men,' separation of powers between the major departments of the state so that no one is paramount, and a proper division of authority between the federal and state governments." His second point was that Wheaton was founded in the fear of God by men who upheld the cause of Christ as expressed in the writing on the cornerstone: "For Christ and His Kingdom."[24]

Mrs. Edman had her part in the inauguration too. She was given a lovely basket of calla lilies which must have reminded her of the arch of calla lilies at their wedding at Quito in 1924. Her speech of thanks recounted how she had prayed at a stump for the will of God in her life and how soon thereafter she had met Dr. Edman. William Geidt, a student writer, wrote that "Ellie Bailey . . . went to Dr. Edman's office with the request that the girls be given the afternoon off to search the woods for a stump to pray by."[25] She must have found her stump, for Bill later married her!

Dr. Edman was asked at about this time, "Just what does a president do?" He wrote, "There is plenty of spare time between two and four-thirty in the morning. During the day there are usually just details — a mountain of correspondence, friends of the College to meet, committees to help, chapel talks to give, messages to churches and organi-

zations all over the land on a wide variety of topics, interviews, articles to write, buildings to plan, promotional efforts to organize, money to raise."[26]

He spoke of his lifetime habit of early rising in an article
in *His* magazine. He got up no later than 5:30 A.M., even
earlier in later years, to care for the furnace and have "a
quiet time with the Lord." The family arose at 6:15, and by
7:15 the family was ready for morning prayers which often
involved the memorization of psalms, of which they had
memorized twenty-one by 1942. He went to the office at
8:30 for daily prayer with members of the faculty and staff;
at 9:00 he had a half hour for reading the Bible to "get food
for the inner man and light essential to the way." Then would
follow the routine of the day.[27]

His report to the board in June, 1940, revealed that the
deficit of over $200,000 in June, 1939, had been reduced to
$141,000. In June, 1941, he reported that his proposals of
1940 had already been put into effect and were functioning
well.

He was honored in 1941 by election to the Scholastic
Honors Society of Wheaton College. Houghton College further honored him on June 9 by asking him to give the commencement address and awarding him an honorary degree
of Doctor of Laws. He was asked to head the subcommittee
on education of the Taxpayers Federation of Illinois. The
Conference of Church Related Colleges asked him to serve
on the important committee on resolutions for that organization in the west central area.

College work went on until the shock of the attack on
Pearl Harbor on December 7, 1941, forced Wheaton along
with the rest of the country to face the reality of war. Dr.
Edman said two days after this event, "Our patriotic duty
at the present time is to perform our routine tasks to the best
of our abilities." He urged students to go on with their

studies until called for service, and to make sacrifices "by saving time, energy and necessary materials."[28] When all listened in chapel on the day before to the declaration of war by President Roosevelt, he added that he had prayed many times in chapel "that such a thing might not happen in this generation."

Dr. Edman heartily concurred with the suggestion of Billy Graham that the bell in the tower should be rung each day at 5 P.M. to call everyone to pause and pray for those in service and for peace. This practice began on Thursday, April 22, of 1943 and was continued for the duration of the war. This custom would help the college family to remember, as Dr. Edman put it, "that our highest patriotism is to perform the tasks committed to us by our fathers and to perpetuate the contribution of Wheaton to the spiritual life of America and the world."[29]

The need for more money for the new gym nearing completion became apparent in March, 1942. The faculty proposed to raise $2,000 for classrooms and office space on the second floor, and the alumni under the leadership of Russell Mixter took the responsibility to raise $30,000 for equipment.[30] The building was ready for long chapel on Friday, May 9, and was dedicated on Sunday, June 14, with Dr. Edman as the main speaker at the baccalaureate service held at the time. He had now completed the first building to come into being under his administration.

He was happy when at their June 13, 1942, meeting the trustees elected his beloved "Uncle Joe" Evans to their number. At the same time they accepted his proposal that the president of the college be elected annually to his position. The board also began at his suggestion the granting of an annual award of merit at each commencement for meritorious service by some staff member.

A personal note from Ed Coray, director of physical education, was among Dr. Edman's treasured file of letters of appreciation. He wrote two years after Dr. Edman had become president, "I want to express my appreciation for your human friendly attitude toward faculty and student alike, for your capable leadership, and especially for your humble devotion to do God's will in all things."[31]

The president urged the board at its fall meeting in 1942 to study the matter of appointing an alumni secretary to coordinate the work of the alumni and to keep them in touch with the college. The faculty later received with enthusiasm his announcement that the board at the same meeting had voted to end the 5 percent reduction in salaries and to aid new faculty members with their moving expenses.

The board showed its appreciation of his work by raising his salary to $5,250 at their midwinter meeting in 1943. This added increment to his pay did not loom as large in his thinking as did the revival of 1943 which he happily reported to the board at the same meeting. He also mentioned to them his plan to call a conference of faith mission leaders during that year to plan how best to prepare workers for the mission fields of the world when the war ended.[32]

Harold P. Warren, pastor of the North Baptist Church of Flint, Michigan, had been asked to be the special speaker for the midwinter Bible conference from February 7 to 14. Al Smith, a noted singer, was asked to be the song leader. The day of prayer on Tuesday, February 9, proved to be one of unusual spiritual concern. After the evening meeting President Edman invited all those who wished to become Christians to go to the hall behind the platform. Lee Simcox, now a Presbyterian pastor, told him that he lacked clear assurance that he was a Christian. Dr. Edman invited Lee to ask God to forgive him and save him. He took a piece of chalk and made an "X" on the blackboard, then told the boy, "Now, Leland, the next time the devil tries to tell you that you haven't been saved, you just remind him of this exact time and place. 'X' marks the spot." No longer could Simcox say in the words of Horatius Bonar, "I Was a Wandering Sheep." This hymn in the service had bothered him.[33]

Mr. Warren preached on confession as the basis for forgiveness in the chapel on Thursday morning. After the message the captain of the cross-country team, who had already enlisted in the army, came to the platform and confessed that he had led his men in a race on Sunday without the knowledge of the college authorities.

Dr. Edman responded, "If there are others who have need to confess their wrongdoing, they may do so now."

Students stood all over Pierce Chapel and in quiet order confessed to criticism, pride, cheating, worldliness and other sins. Lunch and dinner were ignored as one after another spoke until the evening service. Many responded to the call after the evening meeting to pray or to become Christians. The same pattern followed the chapel on Friday and went on all day.[34]

Mr. Warren invited Billy Graham and Al Smith to speak at his church in a Saturday night meeting. Ten came forward in that meeting of five hundred. Many others confessed their sins in the Sunday morning service after Pastor Warren described what had happened at Wheaton that week.[35]

A girl student was visited in nearby Elmhurst Hospital by her roommate who told her of the revival, but the patient resented her roommate's testimony. However, she became a Christian later while lying on her hospital bed. The new believer wrote to her home in Washington, D.C., and her mother gave the letter to their pastor. When he read it in the evening service, more than sixty people came forward without any message or invitation.

In February, 1943, Dr. Edman helped to organize the Christian Service Brigade which had been carried on informally for some years by Joseph Coughlin and his student friends. Dr. Edman served as a member of its board until 1948.

His alma mater honored him by asking him to give the Nyack 1943 commencement address late in May. He also participated with others in the Wheaton Bible Conference during intersession of June. The rest of the summer was devoted to speaking in various Bible conferences across the land.

An Army Specialized Training Program Unit No. 3672 was assigned to the college after much negotiation. The military program was scheduled to start on August 19. On July 18, 80 men arrived, to be followed by another 150 the next week. Before the starting date, 250 were present under the leadership of Major Joseph Peot.[36]

The college upheld its standards, at Dr. Edman's insistence, while negotiating the contract for the unit. Major Peot was told that there would be no smoking, swearing or drinking on the campus. The men of the unit observed these restrictions quite well, and many of them became Christians during the fall meeting. Eventually the men of the unit became a part of the campus and rooted loyally for Wheaton teams during games.

It was partly Dr. Edman's advice that led to the adoption of AWOL ("At Wheaton on Leave") as the theme for the 1943 homecoming. Large cardboard figures of Dr. Edman in his World War I uniform and Charles, his son, in the blues of the Seabees were placed on his lawn with the words "Like Father, Like Son."[37]

Earlier on September 28 he discussed with the faculty his plans for the future of the college. He asked them to pray definitely for a student union, a dining center, completion of North Hall, men's dormitories, new library, science and music buildings, an enlarged infirmary, and new academy buildings.[38]

13.

Confidence Crisis

RUMBLINGS AMONG SOME FACULTY and alumni in the late forties involved President Edman's ability to give proper academic leadership and planning for the future. Some pressed for professional leadership among the faculty to overcome "the static nature of our educational thinking." Others noted that the Russell Survey and the North Central Report of the thirties were both outdated. The Harvard Report of 1944 indicated some of the ferment wartime developments had precipitated upon the broad field of education.

Effie Jane Wheeler and Clyde Kilby of the English department and Lamberta Voget met in the hallway at the west end of Blanchard Hall one evening and talked of the necessity for some action. They added Paul Wright of the chemistry department to their number and went to Dr. Edman with the request for a long uninterrupted conference. They were invited to his home for tea where they told Prexy of the unrest and recommended leadership and action on his part. They acknowledged his lack of formal training in educational administration. He had not studied it as Dr. Buswell had at the University of Chicago while he was president.[1]

The faculty's committee on committees after consultation with the president reported to their associates the nomination of special committees to study the future of Wheaton and make recommendations. S. Richey Kamm was named chairman of the academic planning committee, with Clyde Kilby and Paul Martin as his associates. Paul Wright headed a campus planning committee with Effie Jane Wheeler and DeWitt Jayne as his associates. All were relieved of half their teaching load and given secretarial help for the 1944-45 school year.[2] A committee on spiritual life and standards was set up to handle the chapel services, a task which had been formerly performed by the president and his office staff.[3]

Between June 25 and July 22 the campus planning committee and Dr. Kamm visited college and university campuses, such as Wabash, Dartmouth, Harvard, Bryn Mawr, Antioch, Oberlin, Swarthmore and Purdue. They all agreed on their return that the best site for the proposed student center was on the south side of Kenilworth between Adams and Irving.

Dr. Kamm worked on procedures for his committee after his return. Clyde Kilby read widely in academic literature. Paul Martin prepared statistical studies. They adopted as their goals studies of the history of the college, the development in detail of an educational philosophy for Christian higher education in a liberal arts college, faculty selection and compensation, curriculum development, and the selection of students. The campus planning committee was charged with the responsibility for ". . . the presentation of an adequate over-all campus plan, building needs, design and functional arrangement of any new buildings."[4]

Dr. Edman met with representatives of the student council and student publications of the college on August 5 and 6 at Winona Lake where he was speaking and vacationing. They discussed such matters as freshman orientation and chapel.[5]

He had also recommended to the board that spring that they have their annual meeting in October rather than in

June. This would give them a complete fiscal picture for the past year and enable them to plan more intelligently for the fiscal year beginning in the fall when they met at homecoming each year. This change was approved and put into effect that fall.[6]

The fall meeting in October, 1944, brought other decisions of long-range importance. A promotional committee chaired by Robert Walker, publisher of *Christian Life,* and consisting of trustees, alumni and faculty, presented their Wheaton Centenary Plan for buildings. In addition to approving the completion of North Hall, they set 1948, the "Blanchard Anniversary," as the date to complete the Memorial Student Center; 1953 to complete the dormitories, the "Illinois Institute Anniversary" year; and the science, library and music buildings to be finished by the "Wheaton Anniversary" in 1960. The board enthusiastically accepted the plan and authorized the building of "a model of the completed plans for the College campus" which could be used for publicity pictures. Dr. Edman, who had first been personally sold on this plan by Walker, was happy with the results of the presentation which he had arranged.[7] DeWitt Jayne made the model, and Dr. Edman had it placed in his office.[8]

The appointment of Roger Voskuyl in the fall of 1946 as academic dean helped to allay criticism of the president's lack of academic leadership. The report of Dr. Kamm's committee in the fall of 1945 completed the work of the academic planning committee which was replaced by the North Central Committee annually. The comittee on campus planning under Dr. Wright was continued.

Late in 1944 Dr. Edman became interested in the possibility of wartime service. He filled out detailed papers for a naval chaplaincy in December after he learned that he could qualify. He preferred the navy "because of its kind of service." This plan did not go beyond the filling out of papers.[9]

The alumni reorganized their association in the summer of 1944. The organization had begun in 1923, and in 1928 an alumni magazine was launched. An alumni fund to aid the college was begun in 1944 and in that year amounted to more than $34,000. Members of the alumni office staff were deeply concerned over the alleged lack of academic leadership on the part of the administration and often urged Dr. Edman to take more leadership in this area.

The students in the midst of campus ferment did not forget the ever present war. They staged a bond sale in March, 1945, to help the war effort. To stimulate interest they announced that Dr. Edman's beloved 1937 model wide-brimmed "Old Gray Hat" would be auctioned. Bill Stand-ridge, the student actioneer, got the bidding on bonds up to $768.75 before he let the hat go to a student named Axel Anderson.[10]

Dr. Edman left on March 9, 1946, for the first of his many and extensive travels outside the continental United States. This involved a two-week trip to Central America with Mrs. Edman and two friends to survey missionary schools and to visit missionaries and national workers. Dr. Edman spoke five times in Honduras in Spanish after having been away from the field for fifteen years with little use of Spanish. The party was also entertained at the American Embassy for lunch. They went on to visit in Guatemala, Costa Rica, Nicaragua, San Salvador, and Mexico. They were happily received by the missionaries and the national Christians.[11]

Affiliation with West Suburban Hospital Nursing School in Oak Park completed another of Dr. Edman's dreams. He had been asked in 1940 to recommend a head nurse for a missionary hospital in China. Esther Salzman, a nurse at the college infirmary, volunteered to go, and from that time he claimed that he had the dream of a school to train nurses with a liberal arts degree for similar service.[12]

Dr. Oscar Hawkinson, chairman of the training school committee of West Suburban Hospital, thought of affiliating the Nursing School with some college. He contacted several educators in the Chicago area, but only Dr. Edman responded with any enthusiasm. Dr. Edman reported this request to the board at its February meeting in 1946, and the trustees moved "approval" of affiliation with the hospital. The faculty in early March approved recommendation of a nurses' training program to the board. The plan was put into effect in the fall of 1946.

The nurses were to come to Wheaton to complete their bachelor of science degree after three years at the hospital in nurses' training. Dr. Russell Mixter was named coordinator of the program. Some faculty members taught basic college courses at the hospital. The girls had social interchange with the college by attendance at college functions, and a nurses' choir was organized. The hospital since beginning that program has not lacked nursing students, while many hospitals have had difficulty in securing sufficient nursing trainees.

The addition to the North Hall girls' residence in 1946 became the second building constructed during Dr. Edman's administration. Ground had been broken at commencement in 1945, and excavation begun in August. The new unit was ready for occupancy in the fall of 1946. Two large dining halls in the basement, two lounges and a recreation room made the building useful for more than one purpose. This provision for another 160 women made possible the housing of a total of 275 women in this building.

Dormitories for men students also became a reality in 1946. Two units, now called Elliot and Saint halls, after the Wheaton men martyred by the Aucas in January of 1956, were built through the generosity of three friends who together gave $80,000 of the $120,000 which each dormitory cost. This was short of the needed sum, but Dr. Edman's comment was, "Faith in God is a basic proposition with us. I often quote a favorite saying of Hudson Taylor: God's work done in God's way, will never lack God's supply."[13] The two buildings provided room for 180 men and their supervisors in the fall of 1946.

It was in this year that Dr. Edman became more closely associated with the various projects of the LeTourneau family. He was already a member of the LeTourneau Foundation with Mr. and Mrs. LeTourneau.

The students of Wheaton College in the spring of 1946 also brought into being a magazine named *Kodon.* It contained articles and original stories by students. It was to provide "entertainment" in order to "take the tension out of the first days of school."[14] Dr. Edman for some years contributed a half-humorous, half-serious column entitled "To My Way of Thinking." In it he answered student questions and made comments on life at the college.

His starting of Christmas Tie Day in January, 1947, provided a minor but interesting and humorous note on which the year began. He had been given a loudly colored tie as a Christmas gift. He announced, because he hesitated to wear it alone, that each man should on that day wear his loudest and most execrable Christmas tie. This replaced the annual fall loud tie day that had started in 1937.[15]

He and "Uncle Joe" Evans made a trip to Greece in March and April of this year with Paul Yphantis and Stavros Deliyannides, who had been his classmates at Nyack and with whom he was associated in the work of the Greek-American Missionary Association, to help set up a parochial school and a Bible institute for the evangelical churches of Greece. He commented in a letter to Dr. Ironside that "the international conditions made the trip to Greece increasingly significant, as that country now appears to be the last frontier for the Gospel and for the western way of life against Communism."[16] The students wanted to raise money to help the Greek churches when they heard of his trip. They raised over $1,500 for Greek Christian work before he left.

The party left on March 24 to travel to Birmingham, England, where Dr. Edman spoke at a Youth for Christ meeting to help introduce that organization in Britain. They flew on to Stockholm where he spoke in Swedish in two churches on March 27. They then flew on to Geneva to see about "printing conditions" and to Rome from where they went to Athens on April 12. They remained in Athens for ten days where they carried out their main mission. They returned to Wheaton on April 25 by way of Paris and London.[17]

He and Uncle Joe went to Ethiopia in May at the request of Emperor Haile Selassie, through his minister of education, to conduct a missionary school survey. Dr. Edman reported to the emperor after his survey on the need for the establishment of a teacher training school. Dr. Edman had a warm admiration for the emperor, who he felt was a real Christian with a deep interest in the promotion of Christian education in his county. It was this interview with the emperor he was describing in chapel on the day of his death in 1967. He had the pleasure on June 13, 1949, to present to the emperor, through the Ethiopian ambassador, the degree of Doctor of Laws.[18]

These years from 1940 to 1947 brought pleasure to the president as he secured buildings for Wheaton, added new programs, and traveled on behalf of the missionary cause to Central America, Greece and Ethiopia. The next year was to bring new opportunities for service but also was to be the year of greatest crisis in his life.

14.

Trial by Fire

DR. EDMAN EMBARKED upon a new venture during the school year of 1947-48 that was to launch him as an author. He applied for the alumni research grant which, beginning with the previous year, gave a Wheaton faculty member one year off with salary to do research and to write. Although he applied late that year, the committee making the decision decided to give him the grant. He proposed to do research at the Widener Library in order to write a book on missions from apostolic times until the days of William Carey. While he desired that the book be scholarly, he also wanted it to have a spiritual message and to promote the cause of missions which was so dear to his heart. The grant was announced in February, 1947.[1]

The board gave him a leave of absence for 1947-48 and appointed Roger Voskuyl as acting president in his absence. Miss Marianna McGill was to serve as his secretary and to help him with the research and writing. The college would assume the responsibility to pay half her salary.[2]

The Edmans made their headquarters that year in Dr. Evans' home in Boston. Even though he was busy with research on the projected book, Dr. Edman came back to Wheaton on such occasions as the annual meeting of the board and homecoming.

Perhaps the impending crisis that was to develop during the year and to cause him so much concern and grief was foreshadowed in his article for the fall *Bulletin* of the college in which he wrote, "Despite difficulty, delay, distress, desertion by others we are to press forward. . . ."[3]

He reminded the faculty in his address to it in the September, 1947, conference that they were to be "a people of prevailing prayer, of deep persuasion of the truth of the Scriptures and of the task committed to us, and of evangelistic passion to move men God-ward." The college had always held to the three "R's" of revelation — persuading men of the truth of God; redemption — giving passion to teaching; and the return of Christ to give perspective to understand history.[4]

If Dr. Edman could have forecast the difficulties he would face in the summer of 1948, one wonders whether he might have accepted the invitation that came to him by phone and in a letter in early November, 1947, from H. M. Shuman, president of the Alliance. Dr. Shuman requested that Dr. Edman become the president of Simpson Bible Institute for a three-year period.[5] Edman told Mr. Shuman in his reply on November 12 that since the spiritual crisis he had experienced on the ship *Boskoop* in 1928 he was willing to go anywhere if it was in the Lord's will. He had, however, "no liberty in the spirit to accept the invitation" which he so much appreciated.

The firstfruits of his voluminous work as an author came in 1947 with the publication of an earlier address in pamphlet form under the title, *Swords and Plowshares*. It was a scholarly treatment of the problem of world peace.

He began work on his manuscript on missions in October in the stacks of the Widener Library. The librarian who assigned his carrel thought it unusual that a college would release its president to do scholarly research.

Shortly after he started his work, one of the problems that were to plague that school year emerged. A young European who wanted to study Christian education in

America was made a graduate fellow to teach German while he was observing education on the campus. He began also to hold Bible classes and soon had a student following. On Tuesday, October 28, he lectured to the social science organization, Pi Gamma Mu, on a Christian philosophy of education. Students were present in large numbers but no faculty members were there because there was a faculty party that night.

The *Record* published its view of the "inference" of the young fellow's talk that even Wheaton College might be moving toward secularization in the same way that formerly Christian schools in Europe had become secular. This occurred because they mixed humanism with Christianity, made Christian education compulsory, and developed spiritual pride.[6] The visitor tried to clarify his talk by a letter to the editor in which he pointed out that the paper had misunderstood that he was speaking of education and colleges in general rather than about Wheaton in particular.[7] Several letters also set forth student views of his talk.

All would have been well had not the president of a Bible school publicized the *Record* article in his paper as an evidence of the need of prayer for a Wheaton that was, in his view, slipping spiritually. He asked prayer for the college. The young graduate fellow wrote to this man to correct the misquotations of his talk both in the *Record* and in this man's magazine, but to no avail. While Dr. Voskuyl handled this problem as acting president, Dr. Edman had to deal with it several times later in correspondence.

Dr. Edman returned to the campus again in February, 1948, to give the midwinter convocation address entitled "Brave Sons and Daughters True." He reported that his research and writing were going well and that a third of the first rough draft was done. The work would be completed by summer.

Shortly after his return to Boston, when he was ministering with the track team on a Sunday in Worcester, he
had an attack of kidney stones which crippled him with
intense pain. This illness delayed his work on his project
for some weeks.[8]

He did, however, find time to write short articles for an
"If I Were You" column for the *Record* which the new editor of the *Record* asked him to prepare.[9] Royal Peck had
only won the editorship in January after a close vote of
thirteen to twelve. David Howard, the next student council president, played an active role in the favorable decision. Peck had served for some years in submarines and
had more than three years of experience as editor of his
high school paper. He was also a close friend of Dr. Edman's son Charles and greatly respected Dr. Edman. It is
interesting that no article which might have caused trouble
for Dr. Edman in his year of crisis appeared in the *Record*.

Problems and criticism of Dr. Edman's administration began to accumulate in the spring and summer of 1948. A
group of the alumni believed Dr. Edman was not providing
the necessary academic leadership. This objection was supported by members of the faculty and administration. Dr.
Edman's desire not to hurt anyone led some to conclude
that he furnished what were apparently conflicting answers to people who were seeking information on college
matters.

A faculty group met informally and occasionally in the
home of one of the teachers until that person broke with
the group when he realized his friends were interested in
forcing Dr. Edman to resign or to become a glorified public
relations representative. Because Dr. Voskuyl had made a
name for himself in his field by participating in the Man-
hattan atomic bomb project, and had proved to be an able
educational administrator, it was rumored that they hoped
to make him president. Dr. Voskuyl knew nothing of all

this. The group also wanted to limit the enrollment of the college to 1,200 and eliminate the academy and graduate school as soon as possible to release more money for faculty salaries.

Rumors concerning Dr. Edman's lack of judgment concerning members of the opposite sex were added to the charge of lack of academic leadership.[10] His complete innocence was proven increasingly as the author interviewed others and studied the data concerning the matter.

The dean of students and the director of public relations flew to Boston on Dr. Voskuyl's recommendation to discuss the rumors with Dr. Evans and another board member. These men advised the staff members to contact Mr. Fischer and Mr. Nicholas, leading board members. The latter two carefully investigated the matter and assured a group at a meeting in the dean's office of Dr. Edman's integrity.[11] The most that could be said was that Dr. Edman in his position of leadership should have been extra cautious to give no grounds even for rumor.

Mrs. Edman's ill health during the year did not make matters easier for them. Dr. Edman gave much time to her comfort and happiness.

In the spring of 1948 circumstances led to the resignation of a faculty member with much influence among the students. On top of that, the director of the public relations office was dropped on grounds of economy and Dr. Edman's secretary was let go. All this created more tension among certain alumni and faculty and students on the campus for summer school.

The popular faculty member in June of 1945 had signed his copy of "The Platform of Wheaton College," which each member signs annually, but had crossed out the word "premillennial" in Article 7. Dr. Edman wrote a note asking him to come to his office to discuss this matter. The teacher had also been counseling students to go to seminaries which, in the opinion of Wheaton leaders, were liberal in theology. There was discussion of the reservation this man had on premillennialism and the professor assured Dr. Edman that he was not a postmillennialist.

The professor was later asked in December, 1947, to prepare a statement of his views for the board and did so at length. In his letter of January 8, 1948, he said he held to a cataclysmic view of the return of Christ along the lines of the Westminster Confession. He did not, however, mention the millennium in the letter. On April 29, in a second letter, he stated that he saw no discrepancy between premillennialism and covenant theology after further study of books by reformed theologians. Thus he believed that he could accept Article 7.

His criticism of Dr. Edman's lack of academic leadership and the fact that in the mind of the president and some of the trustees he was linked with other critics of the administration led Dr. Edman to suggest in June, with the backing of the board, that he might well consider leaving Wheaton. The board agreed to pay his salary up to a year until he obtained a suitable position. He submitted his resignation on July 13.

All of these rumors and problems cut deep. Royal Peck indicated the extent of Dr. Edman's concern. One evening in the early spring of 1948 he was in the Edman home watching television with his buddy Charles. The boys were surprised when Dr. Edman dropped into the home on his way back East after speaking in Texas. He told them that he had been called home by phone to meet with the board in a special session and that some members of the board felt he should no longer be president. He asked them to pray with him about this matter. The prayer period lasted about half an hour, and Royal remembered Prexy's anguish of heart in prayer. At one point he prayed, "O God! I want only Thy will." He told God he would resign if God made it clear that his work at Wheaton was finished, but so far he did not have that conviction. He also asked God to search his heart and reveal anything "unseemly or sinful" and to give him "strength to stand for what was right in the difficult hours ahead." It was this prayer meeting that kept Royal from breaking all these matters in a news story in the *Record*, even though friends in the faculty, administration, student body and his close friend, Dave Howard, to whom he owed his position as editor, asked him to do so.[12]

Herman Fischer, chairman of the board, wrote a long letter to Dr. Edman early in July. Describing the problems facing the president which were matters of deep concern to many, he advised Dr. Edman to come back to campus as soon as possible and be at home as much as he could during the summer. He recommended a clear-cut delineation of Dr. Voskuyl's duties so that no dissident group could play him against Dr. Edman.[13]

Dr. Edman in his reply assured Mr. Fischer he would do as he had requested. He added at the end of the letter that Psalms 3, 35, 41, and 84 had been "especially helpful" to him and that Kipling's lines, "If you can keep your head when all about you are losing their's and blaming it on you . . ." had helped him to keep balance.[14]

Concerned students were yet to be heard. David Howard, the son of a member of the board, was to be the student council president for 1948-49. He had gone home to Philadelphia until the start of summer school. Upon his return to campus he found the students disturbed about the "dismissal" of their favorite professor. The students wanted Dave as student council president to do something about this.

Dave talked to the faculty member who had resigned, the dean of students, some trustees, the alumni secretary, townspeople, the director of public relations and to faculty members. The dean of students sent Dave home to get his father's advice on how he might deal with the situation. He and other students also had a session with Dr. Edman.

Three members of the class of 1947 later constituted themselves a committee to write a long letter to Dr. Edman concerning the resignation of the professor who had been their class sponsor. Dr. Edman wrote a long reply to their letter on August 3 explaining his actions.[15]

The Board also met in August at the request of some of their members to consider these problems in greater detail. A few felt Dr. Edman should resign, but the majority gave him full support. Robert Van Kampen, a publisher and friend who accidentally heard of this meeting, phoned Dr. Edman and advised him to come back at once to be at the meeting.[16]

Mr. Fischer met with the faculty after this and made it clear that the professor involved had not been dismissed by action of the board and that there were no charges against him although there were "differences of interpretation of the Second Coming of Christ." In October, Dr. Edman wrote a long letter to the executive secretary of the North Central Association of Colleges to explain the circumstances involved in the professor's resignation because the secretary had been asked to investigate the matter.[17]

David Howard remembered that at the fall retreat of student officers at which Dr. Edman was present some students were bitter in their questions about the August meeting of the board. Dave asked Dr. Edman if he wished to speak. Dr. Edman broke down and wept while he talked for an hour through his tears. The student campus leaders present authorized Dave to issue a statement to the students supporting the actions of the board and the administration.[18] The meeting ended with the motion "that the Council recognize the full and honest investigation of the Board of Trustees and prayerfully support the decision. Dr. Ed-

man informed us that the Trustees had commended his
course of action. Therefore, although we realize that no
open decision has been publicly announced, Dr. Edman's
words of 'going on from here' seem to embody the minds
of the Trustees which we have voted to support."[19]

Early in the school year Dr. Edman in chapel said, "If
I have offended anyone this summer, I am deeply sorry."
One of the senior fieldmen told him that he should make a
clearer statement bearing more directly on the issues, and
he did. Dave Howard later arranged for a chapel in which
the students cheered and clapped when Dr. Edman came
in and Dave Madeira welcomed him home. He was given a
Bible, and Mrs. Edman was given some lovely flowers. Dr.
Edman then went on with his chapel message.[20]

The professor who had left wrote a letter to Dr. Edman
about a year later. He still stood by his own theological
position but asked forgiveness for what should have not
been said or done by him or was based upon rumor. He felt
that Dr. Edman had been misinformed about him on some
points. It was a gracious letter and received a gracious
reply. The same man later came back to Wheaton to participate with Dr. Edman's full approval in a conference on
campus.

These experiences marked the deepest crisis of his life.
But throughout he had the same deep sense of the presence of God he had experienced in other crises. In Boston's
Tremont Temple where he had been invited to speak, Dr.
Edman told one of the fieldmen that he felt as if the Lord
Himself had put His hand on his hand and told him to be
quiet because everything would work out right.[21] He also
wrote in a letter to a friend on the board "that in recent
months we have ridden through a terrifying tornado." He
added, "I have had some unspeakably wonderful experiences, especially during the past summer, of my Lord's
presence and power with me. One morning He said to me

as clearly as you ever heard me speak to you, 'I will be *with* him in trouble, I will deliver him and honor him.'" He noted that Psalms 3, 27, 31, 35, and 46 had been helpful.[22] His son Charles expressed amazement at the way in which "through trial, joy and pain his heart remained gentle."[23]

The experiences of the year seemed to deepen his spiritual life, but he never lost his sense of humor. The writer and others remember, however, that before these experiences he was in the habit of almost continual facetious punning, but after the experiences of the year he rarely punned.

15.

Blessings Unlimited

THE DARK CLOUDS of misunderstanding during 1948 were followed by blessing for both the president and the school. The college was given part ownership of the W.K.M. Company of Texas in the fall of 1949 and the longed-for library became a reality through the gift of board member Robert E. Nicholas and his wife.

Spiritual blessing swept Wheaton with revival early in 1950. Finally, Dr. Edman was able to have his research published as a substantial book on missions and to further aid the cause of missions in other ways.

Hours of editing during the tense summer of 1948 prepared his manuscript on missions for printing. The Van Kampen Press published it in the spring of 1949 under the title, *The Light in the Dark Ages*. The author was "thankful that there was opportunity to complete that project, which for a long time had been on the shelf; and we trust that it will prove helpful in the cause of foreign missions."[1] Apart from his Ph.D. dissertation, this was V. Raymond Edman's major scholarly work and the second full-length book he published.

During that same year of crisis in 1948 he brought together chapel messages of previous years and combined them with later spiritual experiences for the book, *The Disciplines of Life*. Many of the "disciplines" became personal triumphs as he endured the problems and rumors at the college which threatened his useful ministry.

His longing for closer relations with the faculty was achieved in some measure when he invited faculty members to bring their bag lunches at noon to his office. After lunch he urged mutual discussions of college matters, which gave him a clearer indication of the feelings of the faculty.[2]

Another project during 1948 concerned the cause of missions. The president could think of no one who had ever sent a book to him and Mrs. Edman while they were on the mission field. He persuaded business friends, especially Robert Van Kampen, a publisher who became a member of the board in October, 1948, to share the expense of blessing missionaries with books. These volumes, sent as a Christmas remembrance, went to Wheaton alumni in missionary work in all parts of the world.[3]

Students shared in this first project for Christmas, 1948. Dr. Edman asked James Elliot, martyred in 1956 in Ecuador by the Aucas, to mobilize the Foreign Missions Fellowship for preparation of the packages for mailing. Robert Van Kampen's generous aid enabled Dr. Edman to send a small library of seven books to every Wheaton missionary family.[4] His files still contain the letters telling of blessings this gift of books each year brought.

The second Inter-Varsity Christian Fellowship — Foreign Missions Fellowship convention at Urbana, Illinois, during the Christmas vacation of 1948 featured Dr. Edman as the main speaker. Wheaton had the largest chapter of FMF with a membership of about 400. David Howard, a student that year at Wheaton, was the national president of FMF.[5]

The Edmans, accompanied by their close friends, Mr. and Mrs. Robert Harris of Detroit, made a trip to Central America between February 28 and March 8, 1949. Dr. Edman sought out Wheaton graduates who were on those mission fields. During the two days at Merida in the Yucatan Peninsula of Mexico he found time after the annual "Washington banquet" of wild boar and venison to visit the ruins of Chichenitza. The party flew on to Guatemala City where they visited missionaries and national Christians. Firsthand information was shared with the faculty and students when he returned to campus.[6]

Dr. Edman and the Wheaton family were saddened when Effie Jane Wheeler, beloved teacher and gracious Christian, became ill with inoperable cancer. She wrote a warm letter before her death in mid-June, 1949, which Dr. Edman read in chapel. It told of her faith in Christ and of her joy in His will for her. She urged the students and faculty to serve Christ more faithfully. Dr. Edman, who conducted her funeral service, described her as "one of the most radiant and inspiring Christians I have ever known — an earnest believer in the Lord Jesus Christ and an effective and energetic teacher."[7]

Wheaton and Chicago newspapers played up the dramatic news in October, 1949, that Wheaton College had become part owner of the $5,000,000 oil well valve and pipeline equipment operations of the W.K.M. Company. Fred McManis, Sr., of Houston, Texas, had organized W.K.M. in 1918. When he needed capital in the fall of 1929, he had gone to Chicago and visited with his wife's cousin, Cary N. Weisiger, Jr. Cary told Mr. McManis as they walked to meet his train that he should remember the Lord and give to Wheaton College whenever he could. He never forgot his cousin's words and over the ensuing years contributed about $5,000 to Wheaton. He had been very pleased with the personal notes which Dr. Edman sent to him acknowledging each gift.[8]

Mr. McManis called Dr. Edman in the fall of 1949 from Chicago and asked him if money was needed at Wheaton. The oilman refused Dr. Edman's offer to send a car and instead took the train to Wheaton to see the campus. Dr. Edman called trustees Herman Fischer and Taylor Ferguson to come to his office. They had earlier discussed in

detail how they might handle such a transaction, little real-
izing they could soon put their plans into effect. Following
the conference, Mr. McManis sold his company to Wheaton
and to Southwestern University in Georgetown, Texas, making each an equal partner. He chose the Texas college
because its president had been pastor for twenty-five years
of the church which he and his family attended. The two
colleges sold the business to the American Car and Foundry
Company in the spring of 1954 and placed the money in
their endowments.

Dr. Edman's correspondence shows that after Fred Mc-
Manis died, his wife looked to Dr. Edman for spiritual,
family, and business counsel. Part of the main women's
residence was renamed McManis Hall in honor of her husband.

The dream of a library became a reality just before
Christmas in 1949. Robert E. Nicholas, a board member
who had a real estate business in nearby Oak Park, told
Dr. Edman he would provide the money for a new library
but that it must be an anonymous gift. Dr. Edman announced in chapel on January 6, 1950, that a gift of
$250,000 had been given for a library which would seat
half the student body and provide shelf space for more
than 100,000 books.

Ground was broken for the library on commencement
day in June. Dr. Edman and Miss Julia Blanchard, who had
been librarian for many years and was the daughter of
Charles Albert Blanchard, laid the cornerstone on December 10. On that Sunday afternoon Dr. Edman said, "As
we lay the cornerstone of the new library we remember
that our Lord and Savior is called in Scripture 'the chief
cornerstone' and we are all 'living stones' in the building.
We trust that Wheaton's brave sons and daughters true
who pass through these doors will go far afield to add other
'living stones' in that spiritual building."[9]

When the building was ready for occupancy, librarian John Kephart and his staff moved 95,000 books on December 5, 1951, from the old library in Blanchard Hall with the help of a human chain of students, faculty and Dr. Edman. The building was formally opened on Friday, January 18, 1952. Miss Julia Blanchard cut the ribbon across the door. Dr. Edman couldn't resist a pun. "She will be the last one to cut up in the library," he said.[10]

The years 1949 and 1950 also brought the problem of controversy over the location of the Memorial Student Center. Faculty, students and alumni were all participating in the raising of money for this memorial to the thirty-nine Wheaton students who had lost their lives in World War II. The building, according to the campus planning committee, was to be located on the north side of the campus to the right of Breyer Hall.

Robert Salisbury drew up the architect's sketch of the center, and the building committee of the board in February, 1949, agreed to let bids for the building as soon as $70,000 was raised. Edward Coray, director of the physical education department, was put in charge of raising the $70,000 of the $120,000 that the board felt was needed to start the building whose final cost was estimated at $262,000.

The students and alumni favored a site on the far north side of the campus. The building committee of the board, like Dr. Edman, preferred to have it in the Blanchard quadrangle between Williston and the bookstore. Porter Butts of the University of Wisconsin, who was a specialist in planning student centers, told the student council, faculty, and alumni who wanted it on the north side of the campus that this location would remove it from the crossroads of the campus and spoil its usefulness. His advice was heeded, and the present location was chosen.[11]

Ground-breaking came at homecoming in October, 1949,

and work on the building began in April of the next year. The cornerstone was laid during the 1950 June commencement season. The finished building was dedicated on June 11, 1951, although it had been in use since just after Easter vacation. During that same year an addition to the heating plant was made to handle the extra heat load demanded by the new buildings.

Tension over the location of the student center did not hinder the outpouring of spiritual blessing in the revival of 1950. There were earlier evidences of unusual spiritual interest on the campus that year. Two hundred seniors in their fall retreat seriously faced their responsibility to the younger students, adopting as their motto for the year, "To know Him and to show Him." The class leadership felt a special urge for prayer during the first semester.

During the week prior to the revival at the college, Torrey Johnson, a graduate whose heart had been touched in the 1943 revival and who had been a leader in the founding of Youth for Christ, was ministering at the Academy's special services. Mothers of the children in the Academy from the town of Wheaton met to pray for the meetings. Their own hearts were touched and convicted as they prayed, and many went to their children to correct home situations by asking forgiveness of their sons and daughters. News of this awakening stirred college students.

Edwin Johnson, a graduate of North Park College and Seminary who was then pastor of the First Mission Covenant Church in Seattle, was the speaker for the midwinter services at the college. George Beverly Shea was the song leader and when he was absent, Bud Schaeffer, an outstanding basketball player and an earnest Christian with musical talent, was his substitute. William Wareham, chairman of music for the Christian Service Council, was the pianist and Wallace Dunn the organist. Services began on Sunday, February 5, and ran to Sunday, February 12.[12]

Edwin Johnson, whose heart had been stirred by a revival in which he had shared in the Seattle area, spoke on Sunday evening from 2 Chronicles 20:12 on the words, "Neither know we what to do: but our eyes are upon thee." Tuesday, February 7, was set aside as a day of prayer with no classes.

The meeting in Pierce Chapel on Wednesday evening, February 8, did not seem to promise any unusual spiritual movement. Bud Schaeffer led in a couple of hymns and the chorus, "Send a Great Revival in My Soul," prefacing each with a Scripture verse related to singing. Two students gave a special cornet number, and a student in the front row led in a short prayer.

That morning a student had asked Dr. Edman if he could have a moment in the evening service to tell the students how God had forgiven his sin and given him victory in his life. The president told this student that at about 7:15 P.M. he could give his word. Afterward, other students also rose and spoke. Two students, dissatisfied with their spiritual experience, requested prayer, and Dr. Edman told the second, Eugene Lye, that there would be prayer for him after he spoke. By the time Lye had finished at 7:30, many others had stood to await their turn. Sixty were standing in a moment, and Dr. Edman did not get to pray. Quietly, one after the other gave their word throughout the night. Dr. Edman stood all through this until nearly midnight when one student thoughtfully suggested that he sit down.

Someone sent a note about 2 A.M. stating that since some students had been standing a long time to testify of God's grace, to ask forgiveness of someone or to confess sin, that Dr. Edman ask them to sit in the choir seats to await their turn at the microphone.

Testimonies continued all day Thursday except for a brief message on Psalm 1 by Pastor Johnson at 9 P.M. Dr. Edman felt constrained at 9 A.M. Friday, February 10, to end the public meeting. He told those who still desired to speak to come into Arrow Hall which was just behind the platform. The meeting went on there until 2 P.M. Friday. Nearly all the students and many faculty members had spoken by this time. Dr. Edman decided to close the main meeting because word of what was going on had drawn many curiosity-seekers.

Each person spoke quietly, earnestly and sincerely. Some told of finding Christ as their Saviour. Others confessed cheating, holding grudges, criticizing the teachers or administration unfairly, or their lack of prayer and unwillingness to do what they knew was the will of God. Nearly everyone who spoke made reference to the portion of Scripture which the Spirit of God had used to bring him to the point of correct relationship with God. Each seemed to experience a sense of the presence of God.

Those who gave testimonies generally followed the principle of making the confession only as wide as the sin. If they had wronged another, they righted the wrong, and then spoke of victory in their life after stating that the matter had been confessed to the one wronged. If several were involved, the confessions were confined to the group. Only when the whole college community was involved, was the sin mentioned. Thus there was no opportunity for sensation seekers to listen to lurid testimonies of wrongdoing. Little wonder that as all sang the favorite hymn "Wonderful Grace of Jesus" that Friday evening it seemed as if the volume of praise would lift the roof of the chapel.

There are several notes in Dr. Edman's files which students had written to him during the service. One requested that the testimonies be kept short so that those in the back would "get a chance" to say a word. Another note told of a phone call from Billy Graham who had heard the news in Atlanta and was having a special prayer meeting for Wheaton that night. A girl wrote of cheating in history class on an examination and that she wanted to confess it. Another girl, now a professor with a Ph.D., wrote, "I've done you an injustice, I must confess tonight. If time runs short, please include me." She was one of the campus leaders who had been particularly critical of him during the crisis in 1948.

News of the long testimony service reached Chicago newspapermen. Reporters were dispatched to cover this unusual story. John H. Thompson, military editor for the Chicago Tribune, wrote that he came to campus to cover the event "with the cynicism of his trade," but he soon came to "marvel at the intensity of emotion and the obvious sincerity of the students." He confessed in his article that he had never before "seen anything like this."[13]

News releases of the revival were on the front pages of papers in Miami, Los Angeles, Seattle, New York, and particularly Chicago, as well as numerous other cities across the nation. *Life* ran a long article with pictures of the chapel scene. The coverage was generally objective but sympathetic. Dr. Edman wrote notes of thanks and testimony to several of the editors for their fair treatment of what might have been sensationalized unfavorably.

The worst sleet storm in years hit the area after the Sunday evening meeting on February 5. Power was cut off from the campus by fallen wires. Emergency generators were put into operation to run the public address system and to light the lobby lights in the Alumni Gymnasium where Dr. Johnson was to give his final sermon Monday evening. More than 2,000 students and townspeople filled the darkened gym and listened to the speaker in the semi-darkness.

News of the revival was carried to other parts by voice as well as by newspaper report. Bud Schaeffer was asked by Edwin Johnson to fly to Seattle after the Saturday night basketball game to tell about the revival to churches in the

Seattle area. He slept only half an hour on the plane that night and spoke eight times on Sunday in different churches and four times on Monday morning. Bud returned to Wheaton on Monday night and had to play another basketball game on Tuesday night. He could still thank "the Lord for strength and did not get tired at all."[14]

A student from the University of Chicago, who was an atheist son of atheistic parents, phoned a newspaperman to beg a ride to Wheaton. He arrived about 3 A.M. Friday and was so convicted that, with the help of some students, he became a Christian and found, as he put it, that the Lord was "the solution to the world's problems."

Asbury College, the London Bible Institute in Ontario, Canada, Seattle Pacific College, Lee College in Tennessee, Simpson Bible Institute in Seattle, Nyack Institute, and North Park College and Northern Baptist Seminary in Chicago all experienced similar movements among their student bodies and faculties at about the same time. Many lives were directed toward God in total Christian dedication for various professions to be entered in later life.

Renewal reached the Wheaton chapel choir in the bus en route home from a midwinter tour in Florida. The debate team also had its period of confession and prayer on the way back to Wheaton between Louisville, Kentucky, and Wheaton. Several churches in Wheaton also experienced revival.

Dr. Edman in his report to the people on the college mailing list described the revival as "days of heaven upon earth."[15] Royal Peck and Dr. Edman's son Charles came to the conclusion that God had by this revival set His seal on Dr. Edman and showed that he had done no wrong in the previous year.[16]

When Dr. Edman was later asked to name the happiest moment of his life, he wrote, "What happiness can surpass that of seeing young hearts conquered by the Savior and then becoming more than conquerors through Him."[17]

He summed up the 1949-50 school year in these words for the *Record*: "The past year has been unusual and outstanding: the gift from Texas, beginning of the Memorial Center, gift of the library, and above all, revival all in one year."[18]

Dr. Edman summarized the developments of the first ten years of his presidency in his report to the board at the annual meeting in October, 1950.[19] He wrote of the work of the ASTP army unit on campus from 1943-44 and of the increase in the size of the student body, the faculty, budget and assets of the college. He reminded them of the acquisition of the Academy property at Prince Crossing, the Memorial Student Center, the library, the heating plant, the completion of the women's dormitory and the two men's dormitories, the Alumni Gymnasium and of the Black Hills Campus for summer science studies. He spoke also of the fine work of the two special committees under the leadership of Dr. Kamm and Dr. Wright and of what had been done with their recommendations. He wrote with particular relish of the revival in February and of his deep concern for Wheaton's spiritual integrity.

Dr. Edman was also asked to speak at the March 25, 1951, 6 a.m. Rose Bowl Easter Sunrise Service which more than 10,000 persons attended. His sermon was based on the text, "I am alive for evermore," in Revelation 1:18. He declared that the resurrection is our guarantee of life in eternity. The service was carried in full or part by over 600 stations on the Mutual Broadcasting network during the day so that he had a national audience. On April 28 he gave the devotions at the International Christian Leadership prayer breakfast in Washington for members of the executive, judicial and legislative branches of the national government.[20]

The fifty acres and buildings at Honey Rock on the east shore of Long Lake in northern Wisconsin were added with Dr. Edman's support to the assets of the college in 1951. The physical education department planned to use it for a summer camp for boys and girls in which students in Christian education and physical education could serve as counselors, gain practical experience, and add academic credit.

The president asked in the winter of 1951 that the college enter the Social Security program.[21] He was always interested in improving salaries and benefits for the employees of the colleges.

Two more books were added to the list of his publications during the year. *Storms and Starlight* was a devotional book, and *Finney Lives On* revealed his interest in revival. In May, 1951, he began writing the "Spiritual Clinic" column in *Christian Life*. He gave this up in 1967 to become editor of the *Alliance Witness*.

The ROTC became a part of campus life with his enthusiastic support during 1952. Since his army days he had been convinced of the value of such service in terms of discipline and manliness. He sincerely believed that the Bible taught that a Christian should bear arms at the request of his country, although he respected those Christians who took the position of biblical pacificism. Later the board at its annual meeting in October, 1950, approved "the policy of attempting to institute an ROTC on campus." The board finally approved the acceptance of the unit to be activated at Wheaton on June 20, 1952.[22]

Dr. Edman believed that this training would help to teach the students "patriotism, discipline, dependability and courtesy." He wrote to the alumni that "military service is a part of today's pattern of being." Christian young men should have opportunity for officer training at a Christian school and, when needed, should serve their country as officers rather than enlisted men. He added, "There is a call today for a Joshua, a Gideon, a David, as well as Elijah and a Paul. ROTC at Wheaton is the answer."[23]

Dr. Edman began his long association with the John H. Rudin Company at about this time. This company published a multivolume edition of the King James Bible with picture and commentary to illumine the Bible for young and old. From about 1951 until his death he contributed an inspirational column to each issue of the company magazine (the *Success Builder* and now the *Life Line*) for their salesmen with the title "As I See It." He became a director of the company in about 1956; in 1957 he was invited to be the chairman of their board.[24]

The library had been opened for student use in 1952. It was a further pleasure for the president to break ground for the new dining hall and to see it rise to completion so that students could eat there after their return from Christmas vacation in 1952. The publication of the devotional booklet, *In Quietness and Confidence*, was the main event in his literary work for the year.

He accompanied R. G. LeTourneau on the first of three trips to Liberia between December 26, 1952, and mid-January of 1953. The party of eleven left from Vicksburg, Mississippi, on December 27, 1952, on the trip that was to total 18,000 miles. They flew in the LeTourneau plane, "Snippy," a converted A-26 bomber piloted by "Barney" Barnwell. They stopped at Miami for the annual dinner of the Christian Businessmen's Committee, then went on to Bermuda, Santa Maria in the Azores, and then made the final flight of over 2,400 miles to Liberia. Dr. Edman wrote that during this trip and others, "We sit for long hours at a table on the plane, saying nothing, R. G. with his slide rule and I with my pencil and copybook."[25]

Visiting missionary radio station ELWA in its early stage of development, he was thrilled with the progress "his" boys were making in this new venture to give Africa the gospel by radio. His earlier counsel to Watkins, Steeley, and Thiessen was beginning to bear fruit.

The party also took a one-day trip of 1,000 miles each way across the Sahara to Casablanca, where Mr. LeTourneau had to go on business. Because Mr. Barnwell had no maps of the area, he navigated with a map of Africa from a copy of the *National Geographic* which Dick Ross, one of the ELWA workers and a Wheaton graduate, brought to the plane when he was invited to go along. When they arrived in Casablanca, the French officer in charge of the airport was astonished that they had flown from Liberia across the desert because French army pilots had orders to avoid flying over the Sahara lest they be downed and lost. While the officer was berating Dr. Edman for their foolishness, Mr. Barnwell was listening in the cockpit with great glee; neither told the officer they had navigated from a magazine instead of elaborate maps. Dr. Edman rode during the night in the nose of the plane, enjoying the sight of the Southern Cross and "a very real sense of the presence of the Lord."[26]

They returned home in January by way of Natal, Brazil, where they had breakfast because they had left Liberia at 3:30 A.M. He reported on this trip to the college constituency by an article in the college *Bulletin* with the title "Bulldozers and Bibles" and the subtitle "Blisters and Blessings."[27]

He again flew with Mr. LeTourneau between March 30 and April 20 to help in the development of the work at Tournavista in Peru. Here the LeTourneau family had a million-acre concession from the Peruvian government in return for building a thirty-one-mile road and developing the area for colonization and the lumber industry.[28] He was able to visit radio station HCJB and the Wheaton alumni who ministered as missionaries in the area.

He and Mrs. Edman then led a party of twenty-seven

from June 27 to August 11, 1953, on a tour to Bible lands for Dr. Joseph Free's Wheaton Tours. He spoke of the trip as "a great spiritual uplift and source of information. The Bible is a new book when one has been in these places."[29] It was on this trip as well as during an earlier meeting in Florida that he made such an impression on one of the participants that he later by will left Wheaton $1,500,000.[30]

Dr. Edman wrote to another friend, "We have had an interesting and eventful summer under the good hand of the Lord, following His footsteps over the hills of Judea, through Samaria, especially around the Sea of Galilee (which we crossed and recrossed by moonlight), and down through the Jordan Valley. All of it was eventful and meaningful to us because of Him. Calvary's hillside and the empty tomb at its base were the most tender places at which no eyes were dry."[31]

During December of 1953 he had an enforced stay at West Suburban Hospital because of an attack of gallstones. The little card which the basketball squad sent to him appealed to his sense of humor. It read, "Congratulations in having rocks in your gall bladder rather than in your head like most people!"[32]

The establishment of the Christian Character Scholarship Award in 1954 pleased him. He thought that good work in part-time employment might be rewarded by a cash bonus based on the rating the supervisor gave to the students working under him. Students had to apply and then had to do good work to get a favorable rating which would make them eligible for the award.[33] He believed that this would help to foster dependability, initiative and honesty.[34]

Williston Hall also received a face-lift during this summer with the removal of the porch and the treatment of the brick so that it would match other buildings. The board, in addition, approved the construction of a main-

tenance building. Much of the work on it was done by
the maintenance staff, and the building was ready for use
by the summer of 1955.

This same year brought publication of *The Delights of
Life,* a companion to his *The Disciplines of Life,* and of
the devotional booklet, *Great Is Thy Faithfulness.* Its companion, *Not Ashamed,* was published in 1955. Much of
this work was done in the early hours of the morning or
on plane trips.

Dr. Edman had been pleasantly surprised at the annual
staff-faculty-trustee dinner on March 14, 1955. After the
dinner for the 325 guests in the new upper dining hall, a
life-size color portrait of Dr. Edman in academic garb by
Orlin Kohli of Wheaton Studios was unveiled. Then Dean
Fadenrecht and Taylor Ferguson of the board gave him a
set of car keys and invited him to look out the window
where a 1955 red Chrysler with white upholstery was
parked. This was a combined gift from staff, faculty, and
members of the board to celebrate his fifteen years as president. He nicknamed it "Paleface" and said it would replace his blue "Pocohontas."[35]

He flew to Quito in April. Then he was taken by car to
Otavalo where he saw some of his Indian friends and converts. All the living members of the first class of the Bible
Institute met with him in Teresa Reed's home in Guayaquil. Afterward he spent two days in Lima, Peru, in the
new home of the Wycliffe Translators. He had a chance
to visit Cornelia Morse of the class of 1950 in Santiago,
Chile. The party then flew across the Chilean Andes
Mountains and the pampas of Argentina to Buenos Aires
where he spoke to a Bible institute student body on Wheaton's year verse, Jeremiah 29:11. From here he went on to
Montevideo to be with old friends, the Reuben Larsons.
Later he went on to Sao Paulo, Brazil, for a Youth for
Christ Congress where he was one of the main speakers.[36]

He was back on campus by Monday, March 25, to report in chapel on his trip and God's work in South America. The trip had been even more pleasant because he had been accompanied by good friends E. Joseph Evans, Wendell Loveless and Robert Van Kampen.[37]

Administrative work, speaking, traveling and adding the two booklets, *Sweeter Than Honey* and *Not Ashamed,* to his list of publications climaxed the fifteen years of his administration in 1955. The years from 1955 to 1965 were to see continued progress in needed buildings, publication of books, increasing the endowment and strengthening the academic program. But along with material progress he deeply desired spiritual advancement.

16.

Wearer of Many Hats

THE *Tower* of 1955 described Dr. Edman's doing, living, smiling, praying and leading, "For Brave Sons: An Example Worth Following."[1] Trips, new buildings, counseling students and others off campus, and academic changes filled every waking hour.

He and "Uncle Joe" Evans were asked by World Vision to go to Korea and Taiwan during the first week of September, 1955, to minister to conferences of pastors. That week more than five hundred pastors came from the plains and the cities and from the aboriginal tribes of the mountains to listen to the two visitors expound the Word and engage in earnest prayer.

Shortly after his return home he engaged at homecoming in October, 1955, in the dedication of still another structure — the Breyer Science Building. Board Chairman Herman Fischer, Jr. had announced at the 1951 homecoming the death in February of that year of Dr. John H. Breyer, a 1905 graduate of the college who left the bulk of his estate to Wheaton College for a science building. When the estate was settled, more than $500,000 was given to the school.[2]

Dr. Edman took a second trip to Liberia in January, 1956, with R. G. LeTourneau to inspect the progress of the work at Tournata and to be present at the inauguration of William S. Tubman as president of Liberia. They arrived by plane via Brazil in time to attend, all resplendent in top hat and tails, the inauguration on January 2.

On the way home they stopped at Tournavista in Peru to see the progress on that project. While there Dr. Edman visited Yarinacocha, the jungle base for Wycliffe Translators in eastern Peru. Here he received word of the martyrdom of the five missionaries to the Aucas, and he and the people at the base prayed for the widows. He wrote to the Philip Howards, whose son-in-law Jim Elliot was one of those slain, that he spoke to the people at the LeTourneau project on the words, "Why this waste of the ointment?" from Mark 14. "What seems a waste to materialistically-minded people like Judas," he said, "is love and devotion to the Lord Jesus. Nothing given to Him is wasted!"[3]

When he arrived home, Kenneth Kennard, professor of philosophy, yielded his place in chapel on January 14 so that Dr. Edman could speak on Revelation 5:9 and announce the death of the five men. He was moved to the point of tears in telling of the tragedy, for he had known and loved Ed McCully, a prize debater; Jim Elliot, a fine wrestler; and Nate Saint, a skilled airman. He wrote to the alumni:

> Hearts have been deeply stirred and saddened here on campus by the martyrdom of three of Wheaton's brave sons, and two other stalwart servants of the Lord, in the jungles of Ecuador . . . and stirred to face the challenge of picking up the torch where they dropped it and carrying the light into Auca darkness. Life's last chapter is written in eternity and not in time, and only when we reach that last chapter shall we fully understand how the seeming tragedy was used by the Lord of the Harvest to bring Aucas and other Indians of the forest to the Savior.[4]

This assessment became a reality. Fifteen men in one week told him that they planned to work with the Aucas. Rachel Saint, sister of Nate, and Betty Howard Elliot, the

widow of Jim, were able some years later to live among the
Aucas and lay the foundations of a church that is still
prospering.

People all over the land wanted to help the widows and
their children in a tangible way. At the suggestion of Clarence Jones and Abe Van Der Puy of HCJB, the "Five Missionary Martyrs Fund" was set up in April, 1956. Dr. Edman, Clyde Taylor, and General Harrison, who was retired
from the Marines, were made trustees by action of the
board of directors of the Evangelical Foreign Missions Association. Dr. Edman was named as chairman. The fund
was continued until 1967 when the widows and children
received final disbursements from it. The fund with interest
amounted to almost $100,000.[5]

Meanwhile at the college more buildings were built. Cement grandstands were erected with the help of interested
friends for the seating of spectators at athletic events on
McCully Field. Ground was broken for the Health Center
at homecoming in 1956 after the old Wayside Inn was razed.
The cornerstone was laid in June and the twenty-five-bed
center was dedicated at homecoming in 1957.

His special interest in the widows of the slain missionaries
led him and Mrs. Edman to visit over Christmas of 1956
in Ecuador. This was Mrs. Edman's first return to that
land since her departure in 1928, and they visited the mission station at Riobamba where they had been stationed
just after their marriage. They also enjoyed a reunion with
ten of the members of the first class of the Bible Institute.
Dr. Edman spoke on a special Christmas Eve broadcast
over the shortwave station of HCJB, now in its twenty-fifth
anniversary year. Most of the time was spent, however,
with the widows and children of the five slain missionaries.
Dr. Edman was taken in a helicopter to see Palm Beach
where the men had been killed and to see the Auca village

from the air. He also met Dayuma, an Auca woman, for the first time.

Publication was not neglected in this year saddened by the martyrdoms. Another devotional book, *Just Why?* was published. An additional booklet entitled *Fear Not* appeared in 1957.

He easily weathered a minor protest early in 1957 over plans to change the tower entrance to Blanchard Hall. Ed Coray reported that the alumni board unanimously opposed the change because it would spoil the appearance of the building and because the funds could be better used elsewhere. An alumnus of the class of 1900 even wrote a poem concerning the proposal:

> To many of us
> The Tower is the
> Face of Wheaton College
> We do not want it "lifted."

He wisely bowed to the wind of alumni opinion and changed the plans. Internal changes greatly improved the appearance of the entrance and provided a small, attractive reception center.

Plans for the centennial year of 1959-60 took an increasing amount of Dr. Edman's time after 1956. He asked the executive committee of the board to appoint a centennial committee of faculty, trustees and administrators to plan for the event.[6] Some time later he told them of the need of a coordinator who could give half his time under the direction of David L. Roberts in public relations to coordinate all the programs of that year.[7] Richard E. Gerig, a graduate of the college, was selected for this work.

Because he found a number who were concerned about Wheaton's position regarding the creation of man, and because he believed that doctrine helped to determine one's theology of man, Dr. Edman asked the members of the science division to prepare a statement on the creation of man. The final statement asserted the fact of the special creation of man and limited change to that within groups of creatures. He submitted the statement to the board in 1957.[8] This statement took its place beside the statement which the Bible department members had prepared earlier on the issue of the inspiration of the Scriptures.

When Ralph Edwards honored Billy Graham on his "This Is Your Life" program, he invited Dr. Edman to be present for the November 13, 1957, telecast. Dr. Edman said of Graham's first meeting with Ruth Bell that he could tell "it was love at first sight even through my bifocals."[9] He also presented a Bible to Edwards.

His third visit to Liberia was made with R. G. LeTourneau from late March to April 5, 1957. Dr. E. Joseph Evans accompanied them but returned home via Lisbon and London. Dr. Edman enjoyed leading the staff of ELWA in a service in which he spoke on Zechariah 4:10, "Who hath despised the day of small things?"

Most of the time was spent at Tournata in helping to reorganize the schools and educational projects. He drew up an elaborate report on this matter. The party left Roberts Field at 4 A.M., had breakfast in Brazil, dinner in Trinidad, and he arrived in Wheaton in time for the evening meal the next day.

Shortly after his return, he and Mrs. Edman entertained Rachel Saint and Dayuma, the little Auca woman who had been won to Christ by Rachel. When Dayuma expressed a desire to be baptized, Miss Saint suggested that Dr. Edman might baptize her. The service was held in the Evangelical Free Church in Wheaton with Dr. Edman baptizing her by immersion on the evening of Tuesday, April 15, 1958. Dr. Carl Armerding gave the English message which Miss Saint interpreted into Auca for Dayuma. Evan Welsh, the college chaplain, baptized Dayuma's eight-year-old son, Ignacio, in the same service.

Plans for buildings to be completed in the centennial year were discussed at the board's 1958 spring meeting. The new gymnasium was to be built as soon as $400,000 was available, and Mr. Nicholas reported that $300,000 had been accumulated at that date. The board adopted this building as its special project. Ground-breaking for the gym came on November 2, 1958, and it was dedicated on September 27, 1959, just before the opening service of the Billy Graham centennial crusade.

Ground would be broken for the new chapel when the alumni effort reached three-fourths of the amount which was their responsibility.[10] The faculty in October adopted as its centennial project the provision of $20,000 for bleacher seats on the chapel platform and $14,000 to add to the research fund. Each member was to give 1 percent of his income to these projects.[11]

Dr. Edman again served the cause of missions during the intersession when he taught a missionary leadership course to seventeen. Many expressed gratitude for the help given them in the course. Students also went out to help for the summer on various missionary fields in the first summer missionary project. Money for the project was raised by the students, faculty and staff.

Dr. Edman was pleased to give the sermon, "Freedom's Holy Light," on August 3, 1958, at the Rockingham Meeting House in Vermont where Dr. Jonathan Blanchard, the first president of Wheaton, had attended church. The church had not functioned since 1907 but was opened each year for this one service. He was glad as Wheaton's current president to speak in the church where the first president had worshiped.[12]

Dr. Edman was busy in January, 1959, with participation in the Anniversary Year Preaching Mission of Park Street

Church in Boston. His subject for the week was "The Person and Work of the Holy Spirit." On January 27 he took part in the inauguration of Robert Loveless, a graduate of the college, as president of Honolulu Christian College. He used his favorite theme, "The Hinge of History," for the address.

He then flew to another island where Billy Graham was resting with his wife and the Grady Wilsons. Graham had had a serious infection in his left eye, and he hoped it would clear up in time for the Australian and New Zealand crusades. Dr. Edman enjoyed his period of prayer and Christian fellowship with them and was a blessing to Graham.[13]

He, Dr. Evans, and Robert Van Kampen and his wife left on March 19 for Tokyo to be present at the first graduation of the Tokyo Christian College, which was founded by Don Hoke, a 1941 Wheaton graduate. Dr. Edman gave the commencement address. Just before closing with prayer, he said, "I have a surprise and would like to talk to you people for one minute. We came from the United States two days ago. . . . I and the Board love your President and felt we would like to give him an honorary degree of Doctor of Divinity." He then called Don and his wife, Martha, to the podium, gave him the diploma, and placed the hood on his shoulders. The Japanese do not like to show emotion, but Mr. Van Kampen said they were wiping their eyes with their fingers because they had no handkerchiefs in their graduation gowns. That evening Dr. Edman spoke at a Wheaton banquet.

From Tokyo they traveled to Hong Kong and up to the Chinese border. He commented to Mr. Van Kampen as they looked over into Red China with its need of Christ, "Now I know how Moses felt looking into the land of Canaan." They stayed in Manila over Good Friday and stopped briefly in New Guinea en route to Australia.

They spent eight days in Australia, four of which were with Billy Graham and his team in a Queensland coastal resort.[14] He and Uncle Joe met with the team members daily after an early breakfast to read Scripture — each one reading a verse in turn, extensive study on the passage, and a period of prayer, often with "tears and burdens" for the coming meetings. These seemed to weigh heavily upon Billy. They studied 1 Thessalonians 3 and 4 as well as Job 22:21 and Joel 2:21 extensively. Billy left to take care of his correspondence at about 10:00 A.M. until the group met for lunch at an outdoor table overlooking the Coral Sea. Golf or swimming was the order for Billy early in the afternoon, on his doctor's advice. Dr. Edman spent as much time as possible while on the plane and in Australia completing the manuscript for his next devotional book, *He Leadeth Me*. Dinner at 7 P.M. was followed by personal devotions and bed at about 9 P.M.

They all had a special sense of God's presence on the last morning of their rest. Dr. Evans remarked, "For this we came to Australia. Now our mission is completed."

Dr. Evans and Dr. Edman flew with Billy to Sydney and from there to Auckland, New Zealand, where they were able to participate in the first meeting of that crusade. Immediately after the meeting he and Uncle Joe left for Honolulu and home.[15]

Perhaps these experiences were a factor in leading him to address the faculty at the fall workshop in September, 1958, on "The Perspective of Premillennialism." He reminded them that everything was to be undertaken in the light of Christ's return. It alone gave meaning to history, eternal values, holiness of life, and the hope of final triumph at the consummation of time. The coming centennial was not to glorify Wheaton but God for what He had done through Wheaton in the past.

Centennial planning took up increasing time during the

school year. Richard E. Gerig, the coordinator, sometimes wondered whether there was much interest in the centennial, but Dr. Edman encouraged him to go on and was always optimistic and positive concerning his proposals. Gerig was amazed at Dr. Edman's flexibility and adaptability during the centennial year. He had "enthusiasm and vision" for what the year could do and sought "to scripturalize and spiritualize" all the parts of the celebration. In this connection he made Psalm 100 the centennial psalm and spoke frequently from it. He also wanted the Graham Crusade to be the first event of the centennial year in order to indicate the importance of evangelism in Wheaton's program.

An Abundant Century Festival in the spring of 1960 was to feature Wheaton graduates in service for Christ against the odds of pagan forces. The two forces were symbolized by Elijah and Baal in a production which ended with emphasis on the need of dedication for the next century of Wheaton's history. Dave L. Roberts, now director of development at Wheaton, brought these ideas of service and dedication together with the phrase, "Dedication in Education." Dr. Edman looked upon the centennial year as a plateau for reflection on the past before going on and upward.[16]

The Billy Graham crusade from September 27 to October 4 was to be the first major centennial event. It was to be followed by a laymen's conference over the weekend of October 2 to 4, with Graham speaking at a banquet for about 1,000 men. Academic symposia by the various divisions were to occur throughout the year, and a special celebration on January 9 and 10, 1960, was to honor Charter Day. The Abundant Century production on May 27 and 28, 1960, was the last major event scheduled for the year.[17]

Plans for the centennial chapel building matured slowly, for no one was satisfied with the designs submitted for consideration. There was, as Dr. Edman put it, "a discipline of delay" until another firm was called to submit its plans. Dr. Edman said of these: "This is it! That was the unanimous exclamation of the trustees including myself, when we saw the design of the new chapel. . . . And there will be a place for all of us! Our hearts were glad." Enough money came in so that ground-breaking could be at the June, 1959, commencement. The main chapel was to measure 193 by 130 feet and have a 125-foot tower. The east wing was to be 108 feet by 56 feet and was to contain the small New England-style Wurdack Chapel. The large chapel was planned to hold 2,500 people.[18]

The building was to cost $1,250,000, of which it was hoped the alumni would provide $500,000. Dr. Edman wrote to Stanley S. Kresge, whose foundation donated money for the Kresge Assembly room in the east wing, about his idea for the chapel: "When we began discussing the project with Mr. A. Harold Anderson who designed and constructed the chapel, I made just two requests: 1. It is to be of Georgian Colonial, because then it will never grow old. 2. It should be broad and deep. Harold inquired 'Why?' I answered, 'because 95% of the use will be the daily chapel service, and I want the students as close to me as possible.' "[19] Harold Anderson's firm did get the contract, and he helped to provide the lovely $100,000 Schantz organ for the chapel.[20]

The cornerstone was laid on October 18, 1959, and the first chapel service was held on May 18, 1960. The Abundant Century Festival was also given in it, but the formal dedication was not until homecoming in October, 1960. Dr. Edman spoke on the theme, "What Mean These Stones?" at this service.

The president was surprised and pleased when the board named the building Edman Chapel. He said he was "completely overwhelmed when Brother Nicholas made a mo-

tion that the other part of the chapel [the main building]
to the left be known as *The Edman Chapel*. Heart is
greatly humbled."[21] It became known as Edman Memorial
Chapel after his death in 1967.

A major break with the past leadership of the college
came when Miss Julia Blanchard, the daughter of the second president of the college, died on May 6, 1959. The
librarian for many years, she had given Dr. Edman much
help concerning the ideals for Wheaton which her father
and grandfather had held. At the funeral service in College Church, he again affirmed that Wheaton would be
true to the Book, the Saviour, and the platform of faith of
the college and the vision of education which his predeces-
sors had held.[22]

The new Centennial Gymnasium was dedicated just before the first Sunday afternoon meeting of the Billy Graham
crusade on September 27. The keys of the building were
formally turned over to Dr. Edman and to Harold Faulkner,
the business manager, by the architect and the builder.
Billy Graham gave the dedicatory prayer. About 18,000
were present for the first meeting of the crusade which
came immediately after the dedication. Because of rain, the
chapel service on Monday and the evening crusade meeting were held in the new gymnasium.

Although Billy Graham confessed that he came to Wheaton with fear and trembling because of the difficulty that
most evangelists had experienced in making an impact in
that city, God did remarkably bless his work. Because of
doctor's orders he did not speak in the morning chapels
but delegated that work to Leighton Ford and Grady Wilson. Dr. Edman later delighted again and again in letters
telling of the results of the meetings. Total attendance in
the evenings was over 100,000 and in the morning chapel
services about 15,000. More than 2,800 people responded
to the invitation after the sermons. Of these, 62 percent

were making first-time decisions to become Christians. Both the Monday and final Sunday meeting on October 4 were forced indoors by rain. Over 16,500 were accommodated in four college buildings and in two local churches where Grady Wilson and Leighton Ford preached. The budget of $30,000 was met so that the final Sunday offering of $6,000 could be designated for the "Hour of Decision" broadcast expenses.

Follow-up Bible classes and a Christian "buddy" system were established to help the new converts. Dr. Edman himself held a two-month Bible class in Blanchard Hall on "the basics of Christianity" for many of the converts.[23]

Even though the crusade had been a busy time, Dr. Edman traveled to Toccoa Falls Bible College to give a message concerning Betty Elliott's first Thanksgiving among the Aucas. During this service Russell Kadle, a student who thought God was calling him to the field of Christian education, was led to study the Bible carefully and to pray concerning whether he should not become a missionary. This experience led him later to become a missionary in Ecuador.[24]

The Secretary of State for Illinois honored the centennials of Wheaton and Augustana colleges by making the Illinois automobile license plates orange and blue for 1960. Dr. Edman was assigned plate number 1860 000.

Early in the fall he began to plan for a December 27 to January 1 conference in Lima, Peru, with missionaries when he and Uncle Joe would be the main speakers. He suggested that the format include an early morning prayer session, good fellowship at meals, and sessions for prayer and Bible study.[25] He talked frequently over shortwave radio that fall with the promoter of the conference about the meetings. Dr. Edman wanted the conference to be a "Peruvian Keswick" with a stress upon a victorious Christian life.

His Bible studies during the conference were on the person and work of the Holy Spirit. He told a friend, "There were times of tenderness and tears with renewal of fellowship and courage on the part of the Lord's people there!"[26] About eighty missionaries attended. He was also able through the planning of his friend Reuben Larson to speak to the English-speaking group in Guayaquil on a Sunday morning. Again he met some of the graduates of the Bible Institute of his missionary years.

The production of the Abundant Century Festival and the commencement of 1960 brought centennial-year activities to an end. Mark Hatfield, governor of Oregon, was the speaker. Dr. Edman summed up the centennial-year activities in this manner:

> By the Lord's good hand Centennial year has been a plateau of achievement providing a time to remember the Lord's help and provision in the past. From Billy Graham in the early autumn to Commencement with Baccalaureate in the new Chapel and Governor Hatfield's message to the graduates of 1960, it has been a good year. Now let us start climbing again. There are new heights to be reached in academic excellence, spiritual effectiveness, and additional facilities, beginning with new residence halls.[27]

The last desire was partly realized with the ground-breaking for the new women's dormitory at the 1960 homecoming and its dedication a year later. It was named Smith Hall in honor of Corinne Smith, for many years the popular dean of women.

Centennial year also led to a summer engagement. Dr. Edman was asked to speak at a Wheaton Week at the Mount Hermon Bible Conference in the Santa Cruz Mountains near Monterrey, California. Carter, a member of the development office, and Cecilia Cody went with him to provide the music, and Mrs. Edman to speak to the women.

Dr. Edman spoke on the person and work of the Holy Spirit from John 14:15-26.

The centennial year also saw publication of two more books. *They Found the Secret* had such a good reception that the publisher later asked for a sequel. *Wiser Than They Thought* came out at Christmastime.

17.

Valley of Shadows

THE CELEBRATION of centennial events and frequent travels were complicated by severe trouble with Dr. Edman's eyes which was diagnosed in June, 1959. He suffered a detached retina in the right eye which Dr. Faye Whitsell, a specialist, repaired on June 27. While his vision was limited for a time after the operation, he enjoyed the Scriptures through the recordings of the New Testament and part of the Old Testament which Billy Graham had given to him when he heard of his affliction. He was still able to comment wryly to the *Record*, "Although my eyes are and have been deeply affected, I'm still able to see through the students."[1]

Cataracts in both eyes advanced during the fall until the doctors felt they could be safely removed. Dr. Whitsell removed the one on the right eye on February 16, 1960, and the one on the left eye two days later.[2]

Healing was proceeding satisfactorily when "dread shadows" indicated the presence of a detachment of the upper retina in the left eye on March 14. He had to return to the hospital for repair of this detachment on March 16. The lower part of the retina in the left eye became detached on April 9. Dr. P. Kenneth Gieser and others who were consulted urged him to go immediately to the Massachusetts Eye and Ear Infirmary in Boston where Dr. Charles L. Schepens had developed a new type of surgery to "weld" retina detachments so that they would hold successfully. He went to Boston with his son Roland, and the operation on April 14 was successful. He then recuperated at Dr. Evans' home for a time.

He endured a further operation early in January, 1962, in Boston for the removal of a plastic tube that had been placed in the left eye in the first operation in Boston. This was done by local surgery, and Dr. Schepens was amused when Dr. Edman told him the correct number of stitches he had put in. Dr. Edman had been busy counting them during the operation.[3] This was the last of six painful rounds of eye surgery over a period of two and a half years.

Letters to friends tell of his feelings during this difficult period. He found it tedious after the first operation to lie still without moving his head and to be in total darkness. He wrote to Rachel Saint that this darkness for him helped him to think of "the real and awful darkness that you face there in the jungle in your efforts to reach these people who know the terror of darkness." His own days of "material darkness" had given him additional time to "look upward for you all there."[4]

After his first illness in 1959, Dr. Edman spent eight weeks of darkness and quiet in the hospital and at home. He was then allowed to go to his cabin at Honey Rock with orders not to stoop, to turn his head suddenly, or to exert himself. This rest, although his eyesight remained poor because of the ripening cataracts, enabled him to participate in the fall centennial activities and the missionary conference in Lima at the end of the year. He was able to follow the news over the radio; Mrs. Edman read to him; and the secretaries read his office correspondence to him during the various illnesses.[5]

When the detachment of the upper left retina came in the early spring of 1960, he wrote to many of the phrase

"treasures of darkness" in Isaiah 45:3. He said that these
treasures for him included more time to pray for friends
and the work of the college, tenderness of others who were
caring for him, trustfulness in their good intentions toward
him, patience while healing took place so slowly and, above
all, the assurance of God's presence even in the darkness.[6]

He outlined for another friend the lessons that the Lord
taught him through this suffering. God did not always at
once give the reason for the testing, but He always gave
the assurance of His unfailing presence and help. God
would make His grace sufficient and impart His strength in
human weakness. He always gave an "extra" word of comfort to the one in need, and He would in His time make
His purpose in these afflictions plain.[7] Still another friend
was reminded that "God tests us and comforts us so that
we can be better comforters of others, as Paul put it in II
Corinthians 1:4-5."[8]

He wrote after the first detachment of the retina, "I have
been learning my lesson, too, on delay and patience. . . .
Lying in complete darkness and immobile for two weeks
in the hospital was extremely tedious and there was tempta-
tion at times to discouragement and fretfulness of spirit.
But I learned that God's promises shine even more brightly
in the dark as do the stars."[9] His courage in suffering was
revealed in his letter to Alan Redpath, former pastor of
Moody Memorial Church, in which he wrote, "By the good
hand of the Lord upon the doctors, the eye surgery for
cataracts was completely successful. Eyes will be tearful
and tender for some time to come, but with the Lord's help
will be stronger each day. For the children of light there
are 'treasures of darkness.' The Lord is good. Nahum 1:7
is a good promise."[10] When the detachment in the upper
left retina occurred, he wrote, "Thus I shall have the 'Discipline of Darkness' for another eight or ten weeks. . . ."[11]

The greatest test came when the final detachment occurred in the lower left retina in April, 1960. He remarked in his letter to Grady Wilson that he had "dread of another round of that delicate surgery" but was encouraged by Wilson's reading of Psalm 20 over the "Hour of Decision."[12] He became conscious one afternoon of inward "terrifying flashes of light." Next morning when Mrs. Edman brought his coffee and turned on his Bible records of Isaiah, he began to walk back and forth in the room, thinking of the possibility of blindness. He had revealed his fear of blindness to Dean Fadenrecht.[13] He went on in the manuscript, "Again, Face Your Fears," to write, "It was just then that there came to me the most wonderful sense of the Lord's presence. He assured me, 'I will never leave thee nor forsake thee. I am with thee.'"

Dr. Edman also found Isaiah 41:10 inexpressibly wonderful and personal. In another letter to a former student, Ross Rhoads, he wrote, "There was a real meeting with the Lord, and assurance that everything was committed to Him. . . . There was a gracious sense of His presence and hope."[14] He was afraid, but with the psalmist in Psalm 65:3 he would trust in the Lord.

He never revealed the full depth of his feelings in complaint but did confide to friends, "This has been a deep and long valley, to be sure; but the Lord who is the light of life had always been with us."[15] He wrote again, "For me this has been a dreadful winter."[16] He summed up his experience some years later for a friend:

> All that we are and have belongs to the Savior. The lesson was deeply impressed upon me when the eye surgeons came to the persuasion that they just could not make the retina stick to the eyes, despite repeated rounds of surgery. I assured them that the eyes belonged to the Lord and that His will was the best for them. In His gracious providence He restored sight in both eyes as indicated in that testimony.[17]

His manuscript, *But God*, came out of this period of testing.

His physician, Dr. Faye Whitsell, wrote that he too had learned spiritual lessons in caring for Dr. Edman: "I wish to give you some little word of my deep appreciation for what you mean to me. I have learned some deep spiritual lessons while being privileged to take care of you."[18]

Others during all this illness, apart from his dark glasses and his need of an arm to guide him, did not realize just what deep waters he was going through while he participated in the activities of the centennial year. He well deserved the Centennial Award given to him on Founder's Day on January 9, 1960, which read, "In recognition of distinguished service and achievement which have contributed to the spiritual and cultural welfare of the College."

He used the centennial Psalm 100 in his Sunday, January 10, chapel message on the theme "The Lord Is Good." He said man belongs to God by virtue of his creation and by his redemption in Christ.

His mother passed away also in this period of illness. She had a heart attack and was taken to the hospital where she remained four weeks until another coronary took her life at the age of eighty-three.

Founder's Day was marked by a convocation in the new gymnasium. Dr. Harold Ockenga, pastor of Park Street Church, brought an interesting and learned address without manuscript entitled "For Christ and His Kingdom." More than nine hundred people came to the evening dinner which specially recognized the hundredth anniversary of the college. Dr. Edman announced the renaming of the graduate school building as Buswell Hall in honor of Wheaton's third president who was present at the dinner.[19]

Just before Christmas of 1960 Dr. Edman received a note from Richard M. Nixon, then Vice-President, thanking him for a copy of *He Leadeth Me*. Mr. Nixon wrote, "You may be sure that Pat and I will value it particularly because of your inspiring inscription and autograph." He went on to state, "In these trying and complex days, we must gain strength and the capacity for understanding the problems in our own world from our faith in God."[20]

The invitation to speak at the televised Chicago Sunday Evening Club service on January 15, 1961, was a further opportunity to present his political and economic views which he believed were biblical. He took the subject, "The True Liberal," pointing out that contemporary liberals had completely reversed the meaning of the word by denying economic freedom to the individual and were in danger of exchanging democracy for some form of dictatorship. Numerous letters of approval were sent to the college.

The problem of human origins which involved Wheaton's position on the origin of man took up much of his time from early in 1961. The science division held a symposium on "Origins and Christian Thought" on February 17 and 18. Topics such as "Origin of Life," "Origin of Species," "Origin of Man" and "Origins and Christian Thought Today" were discussed.

The *Record* stated that the meeting led to the conclusion that natural science will agree with special revelation when both are properly interpreted. Disagreement came in discussion over the order in which things were created.[21]

A Wheaton pastor who was present at the meeting took notes and spread the information that Wheaton was teaching evolution because of some statements at the conference by some of the speakers. Indignant letters soon came to the president's office protesting this "apostasy" or requesting the truth about the meeting. Two very conservative religious magazines publicized the matter. Dr. Edman replied to all that Wheaton did not teach "theistic evolution."

Copies of the platform of the college, Dr. Edman's own writings on the subject, and the paper, "Christianity and

Science at Wheaton," which Dr. Mixter and his colleagues had prepared earlier, were sent to all those who wrote. Dr. Edman wrote to one friendly inquirer that Wheaton had no scientist on its faculty who held to organic or theistic evolution but that all held that God created man by a distinct act and that Adam and Eve were the first human beings. He also pointed out that the views of the guest speakers who seemed to hold to theistic evolution were not approved by the college nor their views necessarily accepted. Many of the statements about the symposium were misrepresentations or perversions of the facts or were removed from their proper context.[22] He told several that the controversy had a beneficial effect in helping all to see the problem in clearer perspective and to sharpen their presentation of scientific and biblical truth concerning creation.[23]

Members of the science division signed a letter to Dr. Edman in which they asserted that all of them were believers in special creation of man. A long statement prepared by the Bible and science faculties, supporting and explaining special creation, appeared in the May, 1961, issue of the college *Bulletin*.

Despite all these efforts to clarify the position of the college, Dr. Edman continued to receive letters of complaint for several years on this matter. Minutes of the executive committee of the board and of the board itself have much material concerning this issue between 1961 and 1965. In all of this difficulty Dr. Edman in many letters loyally stood by the science faculty when he was sure of the position of the men. He himself took a strong stand in favor of special creation as biblical.

He appointed a committee of the Bible department and the science division to work out a statement on the creation of man as an amplification of the article concerning creation of man in the college's doctrinal statement of the college. After much discussion in the executive committee of the board, the board on October 13, 1961, adopted this motion:

> Realizing our great need of safeguarding Wheaton Col-
> lege from the inroads of error and apostasy, I move that this
> statement — "They are convinced creationists who believe
> in an historical Adam and an historical Eve the parents of
> the human race who were created by God and not biologi-
> cally descended from lower forms of life . . ." be incorpo-
> rated in our statement of faith which every trustee, faculty
> member and full-time staff member signs in good faith
> every year.[24]

These ideas were formed into an addendum to the article
on creation in the college doctrinal platform.

Because the first Laymen's Conference had been so successful in the centennial year, a second Laymen's Wheaton
Retreat was held in October with the theme, "living epistles
known and read of all men" from 2 Corinthians 3:2. Dr.
Edman in his characteristic way headed a column in the
program with the words "The Bible Is Shoe-Leather."

From November 12 to 19, 1961, he was in the Hawaiian
Islands with Dr. E. Joseph Evans for a Bible conference at a
Chinese church for which he gave a series of messages from
the book of Habakkuk. A visit with the parents of David
Iha, who had been the cocaptain of the football team in
1960-61, was an added pleasure. This family with great effort, though of moderate income, had sent their children to
college.

His penchant for hanging onto a hat long after it had
outlived its usefulness was humorously revealed when a
friend from Texas sent him a new broad-brimmed hat. He
wrote his thanks:

> When a fellow really wants to use his head, he should have
> a Texas hat! This has long been my persuasion, and over
> the years I have worn a modest sombrero from your fair
> part of the world. It has become quite dilapidated and ev-

ery spring Friend Wife says she is going to put it in the
trash can. However, I have rescued it each time and after
having it cleaned I have put it away until the autumn.
It has now reached a point of almost "no return." And
then comes this new one; much bigger and better, and just
. the right size![25]

The Nyack Missionary College Alumni Association meeting of four hundred alumni in Miami named him alumnus
of the year, and the class of 1922 gave him an engraved
desk pen set. This was an unexpected but gratifying honor
because of his affection for that institution and his desire to
help it in any way possible.

Planning for McAllister Conservatory took up much of
his time in 1962 and 1963. His assistant, Wyeth Willard, had
in March of 1949 contacted Charles B. Phillips, an elderly,
wealthy man in Aurora, Illinois. Mr. Phillips expressed a
wish on one visit that someone bring him a gift instead of
asking for one. When Mr. Willard returned to visit him in
November, 1950, he brought Mr. Phillips a sack of bananas.
He told Mr. Willard that that was the first thing anyone
had given him since John D. Rockefeller had given him ten
cents years before. He added, "Don't be surprised if I do
something for Wheaton College." He did give to obtain a
large annuity which later provided nearly $100,000 for the
new music building. When he came to campus, the first
thing he said to Dr. Edman was, "Thank you again for those
bananas."[26] The much larger amount of the needed funds
came from the McAllister estate, and so the building was
named in honor of William H. McAllister.

Ground-breaking came in April of 1962, and the building
was dedicated after the baccalaureate service in June of
1963. Dr. Edman, according to Director Edward Cording,
was pleased because the work of the conservatory had always been important to him.

Dr. Edman also participated in plans for the spring, 1962, Chicago crusade of Billy Graham. He delighted in letters to several friends to point out that more than 30,000 attended the crusade each night and that 116,000 were present in the Soldier Field meeting on the last Sunday.

He and Uncle Joe went to Aruba in the Netherlands Antilles from August 4 to 15 to minister to missionaries of The Evangelical Alliance Mission. Dr. Evans talked on prayer and told of the Welsh revival in which he had been converted as a boy. Dr. Edman gave messages from Haggai and Zechariah. Many letters from missionaries at the conference were summed up by the comment of one that it was "not only one of the best conferences but the best yet."

Another book, *But God,* appeared in 1962. He had recorded it on the Dictaphone, and the secretaries in the office typed and edited it. Many commendatory letters told of the help it gave to people in need.

He and Mrs. Edman spent Christmas of 1962 in the Holy Land with one of Dr. Joseph P. Free's Wheaton Tours which he led from December 21 to January 6, 1963. His seasoned advice as a traveler to one asking for help in how to lead a tour revealed his traveling ability. He urged that each member of the tour have all his papers in order; have large tags with distinctive color to identify his luggage easily, be sure to count the number of bags each time, drink no unpurified water, eat no raw vegetables or fruits without a skin, drink no milk nor use dairy products that might be contaminated and, finally, not buy a lot of useless "souvenirs." He advised that they visit mainly the biblical sites.[27]

His group of sixteen traveled to Palestine by way of Copenhagen, Beirut, Damascus and Cairo. They were in Bethlehem for Christmas Eve and spent nearly a week in and around Jerusalem. Then they had two days in Athens on the way home. While meditating on Mount Carmel, he adopted Deuteronomy 31:8 as the college year verse for

1963-64. He described the trip as "the most satisfactory we have ever had" to biblical lands because "we saw more in the seventeen days of this trip than in the eight or nine weeks of a previous trip."[28]

Dr. Edman announced the appointment early in 1963 of Hudson T. Armerding, who had come to the college as a history teacher in 1961, as provost to take over part of his administrative load. Dr. Armerding said that his duty was "to relieve the president of details so that he can concentrate on public relations contacts, and to streamline administrative channels."[29]

The visit of some to campus early in 1963 to promote charismatic gifts and tongues caused concern. Dr. Edman decided to give several messages in chapel on the person and work of the Holy Spirit. The author remembers the charitable spirit and adherence to biblical principles of these chapel talks. They later found their way into print as articles in religious periodicals.

A troublesome hernia had to be dealt with by surgery in April. Once again Dr. Edman sampled the hospitality of West Suburban Hospital and the work of his nursing "lassies." Healing was slow and painful and he was out of his office for some weeks.

These problems were no doubt forgotten in the pleasurable trip with the seniors on their "sneak" to Colorado. The triumphant juniors who had obtained possession of the "senior bench" exhibited the bench to the seniors in a truck when the train stopped in Mendota, Illinois. The seniors swarmed off the train, seized their bench, and triumphantly took it on the train with them to their sneak. Dr. Edman with delight explained the situation to the startled passengers. One of the windows in a pullman car was broken when one junior in his excitement at losing the bench threw a stone, but the cost of replacing it was met by the class treasury.

A bequest of $1,000 from the estate of his friend and a member of the board came to him in October of 1963. Hugo Wurdack was an industrialist from St. Louis for whom the small chapel in Edman Chapel was named. Dr. Edman wrote to Mr. Wurdack's widow that a bequest like this was a new experience for him, and he wanted to express his gratitude for such thoughtfulness.[30]

He picked up a phrase in David L. Roberts' report to the board which indicated the philosophy he followed in promotion of the college: "Friend-raising must precede Fund-raising."[31] For this reason, as the united witness of the college field representatives testified, he preferred to be friendly and helpful to people, trusting that God would move them to help Wheaton. If not, at least Wheaton had been of service to them. Service to people with estate problems grew out of this philosophy. His letters to donors, whether of large or small gift, were models of friendliness and helpfulness.

He had always been interested in plans for retirement income for the faculty. Thus it was a matter of gratification to him to announce on November 5, 1963, in the faculty meeting that the college's retirement plan was to be transferred to the TIAA-CREF plan for college teachers financed initially by the Carnegie Foundation. The college and the teacher paid in equal amounts to be invested by the organization for retirement benefits.

The Christian Medical Society, meeting at the college late in December, awarded him its first honorary membership, even though he was a medical layman. The citation indicated it was because of his "valuable counsel and faithful guidance" of the society from the days when it was started by Dr. P. Kenneth Gieser and because of the role of Wheaton College in the advance of medicine at home and on the mission fields of the world. The society enlisted 3,500 doctors in its ranks of whom 700 were medical missionaries. It also encouraged short-term medical missionary service by doctors in mission stations around the world.

Dr. Edman was more than happy to announce to the faculty earlier in October that the board had elected Billy Graham to become a board member and that he had accepted the position.[32] He and Billy had talked and written about the matter for some time, but until now Graham had hesitated because of his responsibilities. He wrote to Dr. Edman that one of the reasons he agreed to serve was "my own personal loyalty and friendship to you. Only eternity will reveal what your life has meant to me through the years."[33]

18.

Finding His Elisha

DR. EDMAN RECOGNIZED in 1964 the need for relief from the load of the presidency. He knew at last that he must consider the matter of a replacement.

January, 1965, would mark the completion of twenty-five years as a leader at Wheaton. That, he reasoned, would be an appropriate time for change. In a letter to Billy Graham, he said he thought he would ask the personnel committee of the board at its next meeting "in anticipation of my retirement or assuming the duties of chancellorship" to make a study of the qualifications of a president for Wheaton.[1]

He took up the matter of surrendering his position with the executive committee of the board in a meeting on July 9, 1964, and at that time the board voted to recommend that he become chancellor of the college in June, 1965.[2] The committee moved "to concur in the request of Dr. Edman that he be relieved of administrative responsibilities in order to serve more effectively in a larger field, his title to be Chancellor of Wheaton College, such request to be subject to action by the Board of Trustees."[3]

The personnel committee of the board, until the board as a whole acted on the matter, gave consideration to the qualifications of a future president and discussed possible candidates. Some time earlier when Dr. Edman had been in Boston for Dr. Evans' birthday, "Uncle Joe" had advised Dr. Edman to think of his coming retirement and the train-

171

ing of a man who could take his place. Evans added that he had in mind the man who should take Dr. Edman's place. He mentioned the name of Hudson T. Armerding whose work at Gordon College he had watched carefully through the years Dr. Evans had been a trustee of that institution.[4]

When the committee reported to the board on September 10, 1964, it recommended that Dr. Edman be appointed chancellor and outlined his duties "to be the official representative of the college in interpreting the spiritual, academic and educational philosophy to its constituency, represent the college officially at special functions, alumni groups, conferences and other gatherings for the purpose of developing contacts and expanding public knowledge of the college, to develop relationships with foundations, trusts, large donors and other groups where his official position can make a significant contribution to results" in cooperation with the director of public relations. He was also "to be a consultant to the Board of Trustees in matters of educational policy, standards and policies."

They also unanimously recommended that Hudson T. Armerding be named president. He had experience as a teacher, dean at Gordon College, and provost at Wheaton which fitted him for the position. Dr. Armerding was invited into the meeting of the board and was told that he was elected as president. He accepted the honor and both he and Dr. Edman made brief statements.[5] News of the change came through the *Record,* but unofficial word had leaked out before that issue appeared.[6]

Dr. Edman immediately wrote to his "Dear Fellows" (sons) telling them of the way in which the board "unanimously and enthusiastically" elected him as chancellor. A double installation of him as chancellor and Dr. Armerding as president was scheduled for January 8, 1965, the birthday of the college and the twenty-fifth anniversary of his elevation to the presidency of the college.[7]

Two days after the action of the board, Dr. Armerding wrote a moving letter to Dr. Edman in which he reminisced on the older man's counsel and classes when he was an undergraduate and of their association when he was provost. In all of this, Dr. Edman's "life has been an inspiration and blessing," and he said that in the days ahead he would "count heavily upon your advice and counsel and your prayer support."[8] Dr. Edman did pray and give counsel when asked but acted as a true statesman in giving up duties to another without interferring with his successor's decisions.

A letter to a friend expressed Dr. Edman's confidence in his young successor:

> I look forward with anticipation to the new responsibilities of the Chancellorship and have great confidence in Dr. Armerding as he comes to the presidency. Wheaton will continue to be centered around the person of Christ and guided by the Book under his administration. As you know, he was one of my students in earlier days and I have had opportunity to observe his academic and administrative leadership over a long period of years.[9]

Many letters of congratulation on his new position came to Dr. Edman from many sources. His pastor in the Bible Church, Malcolm Cronk, wrote:

> Your godly life and testimony, your faithfulness to duty, your unswerving loyalty to the cause of Christ have been, are and shall continue to be a source of deepest inspiration and encouragement to me, and multitudes like me. Your writings are such a blessing, and wherever you have opportunity to minister the Word, it is always freighted with the blessing of the Holy Spirit.[10]

Two former students, Chaplain James Hutchens, Wheaton graduate and Vietnam veteran, and his wife, Patty, spoke for many graduates when they wrote to him after they received the news of his new position. They spoke of his influence in their lives in this manner:

> We wanted to write and tell you that we are thankful to our Lord for your faithful witness to us and to many thousands more — you have been greatly used of the Lord and I don't think anyone can really measure the extent of influence into the hidden crannies throughout the years. I have appreciated your positive attitude and so often that has been a stay for me when I have wanted to complain and be dissatisfied. I have read your books with great pleasure and appreciated them so much the more because I knew for a fact that your life backed the words up. It was a joy to know you during our years at Wheaton and at Honey Rock and our young eyes were on you and your life — you proved a real example and that means so much to us in these days when there is so little to look up to. We have always felt that you were our friend, just as much as any great persons you have known, and Jim and I have counted that fellowship dear. Prexy — you've just been a real example of a Christ-follower — so that we didn't have only Biblical examples to go by, but a 20th century example.[11]

The college *Bulletin* that announced the change of administration summed up the gains during Dr. Edman's administration. There were now 1,800 students instead of 1,100; 125 faculty members; assets were now about $8,000,000 instead of $2,800,000; endowment was $7,500,000 instead of $660,000; and the budget was $4,500,000 instead of $730,000. He had traveled over 500,000 miles by air on college business and spoken on six continents. He had also written more than twenty books and numerous articles.[12]

His election on November 6, 1964, at the annual meeting of the Billy Graham Evangelistic Association as senior vice-president of the association loomed nearly as large in mind as the chancellorship. He wrote Mrs. Mina Hill of the college publicity office, "This position will give me large responsibility in the world-wide work of the Association. However these duties will not in any way conflict with those of the Chancellorship, rather they will complement each other."[13] He had been a member of that board since 1957 and, since 1959, chairman of the team committee. He handled delicate situations well and took much of the load from Graham in handling personnel problems. He had also served on the executive and finance committees for years.

Governor Kerner honored him by extending to him an invitation to become a member of the board of trustees of the Lincoln Academy of Illinois. This organization had been set up in 1964 "to recognize, honor, and encourage the outstanding achievements of Illinois citizens."[14] It gave Lincoln Medal awards for such service. Dr. Edman was a trustee of the organization until his death.

His sons added to the pleasure of the occasion when, in honor of their father's new position, they gave $5,000 to build a delivery room in the obstetrics division of the Presbyterian hospital in Taegu, Korea, where Dr. Howard Moffett is a missionary doctor. Dr. Moffett, who had been one of Dr. Edman's political science majors, had also experienced the president's "guiding hand and wise counsel" in the days when he was a student.[15]

Dean John H. Fadenrecht at the January 5, 1965, meeting of the faculty, Dr. Edman's last as president, presented him a plaque from the faculty with a citation on it under the college colors. The citation spoke of his contribution to the college, his work in enlarging its facilities, his representation of the college and Christ in public relations, his humor and his example in life for all. Dr. Edman thanked the faculty for its members' "loyal support over the years" and commented that he had noticed that "Wheaton's principal impact is its spiritual impact" and added that "uppermost is the need for our awareness of the spiritual, for this is what the students remember more than anything."[16]

The inauguration climaxed his twenty-five years of service as Wheaton's fourth president. He looked forward eagerly to the duties of chancellor in his pleasant quarters in the McAllister Building. He did miss the students coming in for counsel but busied himself with travel and writing.

19.

Into the King's Presence

THE DOUBLE INAUGURATION of Dr. Edman as chancellor and of Dr. Armerding as president on January 8, 1965, ended Dr. Edman's twenty-five years as president of the college. It also marked beginning of two and a half years of service as chancellor. Nearly 4,000 inaugural invitations, of which 1,800 went to students, were sent out; 14,000 announcements of the event were mailed later to friends of the college. More than 100 colleges and universities and 14 academic societies sent representatives for the occasion.

The ceremony at 10:30 A.M. was brief, in keeping with the wishes of the two men, but in it the spiritual heritage of the college was emphasized. Dr. J. Oliver Buswell, Jr., president from 1926 to 1940, gave the invocation. After an anthem based on Psalm 100 was sung by the concert choir, Evan Welsh read Psalm 100. Then the congregation sang "O God Our Help in Ages Past."

Clyde Vroman, president of the North Central Association which accredits the college, brought greetings from that organization. Norris R. Aldeen, speaking for the board, commented that it would be difficult to speak no longer of Dr. Edman as "Prexy" but said that he would make an ideal "Good Will Ambassador-at-large" as well as a good chancellor. Aldeen felt that he summed up the feelings of Wheatonites in the words, "Prexy, we love you and thank God for you." Dean Fadenrecht brought greetings from the faculty to the two men and spoke of them as "strong and firm in vision of purpose and wisdom of action." He expressed the "genuine appreciation" and "sincere admiration" of the faculty for Dr. Edman's leadership by preaching and example in encouraging the faculty and students in searching for "scholarly excellence" and "moral and spiritual values." Ted Ryan, student council president, spoke for the students.

Herman A. Fischer, chairman of the board, then installed Dr. Edman in the office of chancellor and Dr. Armerding in the office of president. The father of the latter then led in a prayer of sincere commitment of the two men to their respective tasks. Dr. Edman gave the charge to the new president, after which Dr. Armerding gave the main address with the title "Entrusted with a Vision." Dr. Edman's "Uncle Joe" pronounced the benediction.

A luncheon for nearly 650 guests was given in the Centennial Gymnasium. Greetings from the city by the mayor, from the association of ministers, from the town churches, alumni, the Federation of Illinois Colleges, Christian colleges and the faculty were brought by their various representatives.

The Wheaton College Women's Club were hostesses at an afternoon reception in the Heritage Room of Edman Chapel for the two new officials and their wives. Here many congratulated Dr. Edman on his new position and thanked him for his past leadership. Many of the students were able to participate because classes had been dismissed for the day.

The Alumni Association presented him with a desk plaque on Founder's Day on January 9. His gift for friendship was emphasized by the words "A Personal Friend of Students and Alumni" which had been engraved upon it. A long scroll with the signatures of all the students under the simple heading, "Thank You 'Prexy' for . . . Everything," eloquently expressed their opinion of him, even though some might not have agreed with all his ideas.

Dr. Edman described his new status in a letter to a friend in this way: "The recommendation for a change of responsibilities was my idea. . . . As President Armerding put it we shall have an 'outside president' and an 'inside president.' "[1] He commented to another friend that "the duties will be somewhat like that of the 'Chairman of the Board' in industry."[2]

H. S. Sutherland, president of Biola College, congratulated him on his "years of outstanding service" to Wheaton and to the Christian public while he was president in these words: "Your name has become synonymous with the cause of Jesus Christ, both as an able expositor of the Word of God and as a most effective administrator of what is doubtless the outstanding Christian institution of higher learning in the whole world."[3]

Dr. Edman wrote to his eye doctor, Charles Schepens, "The chancellorship is a sort of retirement with a hyphen. I spell the word 're-tire,' which means putting on a new set of tires and then to get going again. The best years are ahead!"[4] Dave Howard well expressed Dr. Edman's past contribution and future work in a letter in these words: "We have always felt that the Lord has given you unusual gifts of meeting people individually and of a platform ministry."[5]

He and his secretary, Rowena Carr, took over his well-furnished offices in 212 McAlister Building. This he called his "Island" where he and his "Friday" could carry on his writing and correspondence apart from the bustle of the campus. He did not confine himself to his office but in his January, 1965, schedule traveled to points in Texas and the Northwest and in February to the East and Florida on behalf of the college.

Rather than detain President Armerding, who had sold

his house, from moving into the president's home at West-gate, Dr. and Mrs. Edman temporarily moved to another college-owned home until the college could ready the chancellor's home at 818 Scott Street for them. With Mrs. Edman's ability to make a lovely home, they soon had a delightful place of their own. They lived here or at his cabin at Honey Rock until his death.

On May 6 he went to Europe to be with Billy Graham for the week of a crusade in Copenhagen. Here his prayer and counsel were helpful to Graham who encountered un-usual opposition in the meetings, even though they were an eventual blessing to many people.

Later he spent several days in West Berlin with a Ger-man friend, Peter Schneider, whom he had met in Wheaton. Peter took him to visit East Berlin where Dr. Edman was deeply disturbed by what he saw along the "Wall of Shame," the shadow of which fell heavily on his spirit until he re-called Psalm 74:12. He often referred to the wall and what it symbolized in Germany in later editorials in the *Alliance Witness*. This period of grief for Germany gave way to the joyous visit with alumni at the Bible Institute of the Greater Europe Mission at Seeheim near Heidelberg. He ended the trip with a meeting of alumni and friends in Paris.

Upon his return to Wheaton he found that in his absence the council of the Alliance had elected him as editor of their official paper, the *Alliance Witness*. Psalm 90:16-17 was a help in deciding whether to accept this new position along with his other responsibilities. He wrote to his friend Gerald Wellbourn, "On arrival home I was surprised, chal-lenged and humbled by the word from General Council about election to the editorship of the *Alliance Witness* for the next three years."[6] His editorial labors as well as the writing of articles for the paper forced him to give up his question-and-answer column in *Christian Life*.

Miss Anita Bailey, the managing editor of the *Alliance*

Witness, spoke of his work as editor in these terms: "I believe he was the most prepared man I have ever known, and so practical." She also mentioned his gift of appreciation of all who helped him. His copy was always "clean" and ready for the printer with a minimum of work needed to put it in final form.[7]

Jack Shepherd, an Alliance minister, wrote to him of his "breadth and openness of spirit" and "the depth of your understanding of God's truth. In addition, you have a very winsome competence with the pen and a discerning appreciation of the Alliance fellowship."[8]

Dr. Edman in his report as editor for the year 1965 expressed his loyalty to the full inspiration and authority of the Bible, and the preeminence of Christ. His objective as editor was to exalt "the Savior and the Scriptures." Beyond that, he wanted to keep the Alliance fellowship informed of events at home and abroad in their fellowship by picture, news item, and story. An examination of his work as editor reveals that he fulfilled these objectives well.

In addition to his work as chancellor and editor, he was chairman of the board of John Rudin and Company and senior vice-president of the Billy Graham Evangelistic Association.

He and Mrs. Edman and Trustee and Mrs. George M. Traber left on October 29 for a trip to South America, stopping for one evening with Billy Graham in the Houston crusade in the Astrodome. The party arrived on Saturday, October 30, in Quito, Ecuador. They were guests at HCJB, where he spoke over the radio and appeared on television. The next day he spoke in chapel at the Bible Institute and at noon had dinner with many of his former students. He also took the Wednesday service.[9] On Monday, November 1, he and Mrs. Edman had the joy of visiting Otavalo where he had been first stationed as a missionary in 1923. He ministered to the Aucas in their first Bible conference from Wednesday, November 3, until Friday. The Edmans had some time in Guayaquil on their return trip to the United States.

The ministry to the Aucas had first place in Dr. Edman's later speaking, correspondence and writing. Using seeds and different types of ground to teach the spiritual truths of the parable of the sower in Mark 4, he had also instructed the Aucas concerning their part in the Great Commission of Christ and of their need for baptism. The chancellor had the thrill of baptizing eleven of these Aucas in the river on the last morning of the conference. Two of the elders who had helped to kill the missionaries in 1956, Kimi and Dyuwi, assisted him in baptizing the others.

Another joy was helping the Aucas to hold their first celebration of the Lord's Supper in their little bamboo church. He used Mark 14 and 1 Corinthians 11 in explaining the meaning of the supper before dispensing to them boiled yucca for the "bread" and a banana drink from a gourd for the "wine." They commissioned Dyuwi and Tonia after the Lord's Supper by reading from Acts 13 and laying hands upon them as missionaries to the Aucas farther up the river.[10] The pictures he took on the occasion were used in meetings all over the United States to show the power of the gospel. He also wrote articles on the conference for several religious papers.

Dr. Armerding at a dinner for the faculty, staff and board members in January, 1966, took special note of the fact that Dr. Edman had served thirty years at the college to that date. In his letter accompanying the thirty-year service pin he remarked that Dr. Edman had left "a substantial and indelible contribution to the work of the Lord here" and that he would continue to add to it in his present ministry as chancellor.[11]

Although he had completed thirty years of work at Wheaton, his pace of work changed rather than slackened. His report of March 28, 1966, to the president told of counseling duties on campus, working with the fieldmen, speaking at twelve Bible conferences, holding many church services, speaking at alumni meetings, and many visits to friends of the college in their homes or offices. He also maintained a heavy correspondence with friends of the college whom he had come to know over the years.

From May 19 to June 9 he was tour leader of a trip to Bible lands under the sponsorship of the Billy Graham organization. Billy Graham's mother, the Robert Van Kampens, and Mr. and Mrs. Glenn McMahon of the college field service went along on the trip. Dr. Edman and Roy Gustafson, who was in charge of the Graham trips to Bible lands, prepared a Bible study guide to relate the Scriptures to the places which they would visit in the Middle East.

Mr. Van Kampen, who sensed that Dr. Edman was doing more than he should with the changes of climate, time, and a two-day trip to Egypt, urged him not to go to an alumni meeting in Beirut. But Dr. Edman would not cancel his appointment even though he was exhausted.[12] When he had severe pains in arms and shoulders during the night, he realized that he was suffering from a heart attack that might kill him. In later letters and articles he emphasized his sense of the presence and peace of God because he knew that he had a right relationship with Christ, that he had served Him as well as he could, and that his estate had been properly cared for in his will. Romans 8:11 became real to him. He knew this was an encounter with death similar to one he had experienced in 1924 when he had been ill with typhus fever.[13]

When Lavand Syverson, a Wheaton graduate of 1954 and the associate director of the American University Hospital, visited the tour group the next morning, Dr. Edman told him of his chest pains. Dr. Edman was taken to the hospital where he was given the best of care for four days. Then he became a welcome guest in the Syverson home where he remained for several days until he was able to return home in easy stages by air. His doctor at West Suburban Hospital made several tests and ordered him to cancel his numerous engagements until after Labor Day and to spend the summer resting. He was assured that there was no permanent damage to his heart.

He enjoyed this rest during the summer at his cabin on the shore of Long Lake near his beloved Honey Rock Camp. Looking out to the east in the morning, he could see the sun rise over the pine and hemlock forest behind the cabin; and from his picture window in the evening he could see the setting sun and the lake through the trees. Here he rested, relaxed and recuperated during the summer. His sons, their wives and children helped to make the summer happier when they visited him.

He was concerned when one of the graduates of Wheaton who had a deep fear of communism published a book during the summer of 1966 in which he accused many Wheaton professors and its administration of steps toward socialism and doctrinal declension which, in his opinion, amounted to apostasy. Fortunately Dr. Edman did not let it become a major problem to himself, but he agreed with others that the wisest course was not to "dignify the matter by any official report or action."[14] He did reassure those who wrote to him of the doctrinal integrity of the college. He was more interested in the final work on his new book *Windows of Heaven.*

In the fall he reported to the board that his health was much improved and that he would resume work again. Plans were made to be with Billy Graham for the West Berlin Crusade and to attend the following Congress on Evangelism where he was to read his paper on "The Conflict of Spirits."

What turned out to be his last crusade with Billy was a

joy to Dr. Edman as he sat beside Billy on the platform, prayed with him, and usually rode to their hotel with him. He stayed on for the Congress on Evangelism. Dr. Edman specially appreciated the testimony of Aucas' Kumi and Dyuwi whom Rachel Saint brought to the conference. He was heartened by the stress on the authority of the Bible, Christ's lordship, and His second coming. He sensed the warm Christian fellowship of the meetings, prayer sessions and meal hours together.

In mid-November upon his return home he participated in the annual home convention of the Oak Lawn Alliance church by speaking several nights during the week and twice on Sunday, November 13. While resting in the afternoon, he complained of pressure in his chest. Mrs. Edman urged him not to take the evening service, but he felt it was his duty. On Monday he had more pain in the office, and on Tuesday he had to go home before chapel. Dr. Wyngarden moved him to the hospital that day and ordered that all his engagements be canceled. He remained in the hospital until the week before Christmas when he was sent home to rest and to follow a strict diet. He expressed his attitude to the doctor's orders in this way: "Since I believe that one of God's merciful provisions for us is the care of competent physicians, I feel it is only right that I follow their advice."[15]

He suffered a more severe attack on December 21. Mrs. Edman remembered that even in the midst of his intense pain, he commanded her and Rowena Carr to sing "Revive Us Again" which he himself started while they were waiting for the doctor. This attack kept him in the hospital from December 23 until January 14, when he was able again to come home. The doctors ordered him to have six months of rest, and the board freed him from all college responsibilities for the six months. The public relations office took over the responsibility of handling his correspondence.

He likened his experience to that of a train in the mountains. After the sunshine of the Berlin Crusade and the Congress of Evangelism, he had been plunged into a series of tunnels with his heart attacks. He was now on the siding to await the green light to proceed once more with his work.[16]

Both he and Mrs. Edman deeply appreciated the six months' leave granted by the board. As soon as he was able, they went up to the red cabin at Honey Rock. Psalms 61 and 63 and Jeremiah 17:17-18 provided encouragement to him as he recuperated. He likened his time there to that of Elijah who was told to hide himself by the brook Cherith for a time. He wrote Rachel Saint that these heart attacks added new depth to Isaiah 50:10 and his own saying, "Never doubt in the dark what God told you in the Light." The new lesson was, "Do not forget in the light what I told you in the dark."[17]

Billy Graham wrote to him after the heart attack on November 15, assuring him of his thoughts and prayers. He also told him, "Words could never adequately express how much I owe to you" for encouragement, inspiration, support in criticism from others, prayers for and with him, counsel, devotional books and messages. Now that he was experiencing "God's hush," he could rest assured that he and the team were remembering him regularly in prayer.[18]

Grady and Wilma Wilson wrote cheery notes assuring him of their love and prayers for his recovery and of their gratitude for his contribution to their lives. They wrote, "For years we have felt that we were closer to our Lord and better equipped to serve Him faithfully, obediently and well because of your life and the inspiration you have been to us. Eternity alone can reveal what you have meant to us over the years. Thank you again for everything, and especially for your life and intercessory prayer on our behalf."[19]

Daniel S. C. Liu, chief of police in Honolulu, wrote to

thank him for the article on "Trains, Tunnels and Sidings," which told of his spiritual experiences during the period of his heart attacks, and to thank him for his part in "the early morning meetings and breakfast fellowship with you" at the Berlin Congress in these words: "It was a blessed experience to be sitting at your feet and acquiring the 'nuggets of gold' you interpreted from the Bible and recounted from your dedicated life of ministry for God."[20] Paul Rees wrote that Dr. Edman's "*tunnel* has become my *tonic*" after reading his article, and he used Dr. Edman's oft-repeated words to his friends, "As you have often said 'Chin up and knees down.'"[21] One well-wisher who had never met him wrote that others had told him Dr. Edman was "a warm loving man of God but still a scholar and leader."[22]

Although he was uncertain of his future life expectancy and was on a very limited schedule to spare his heart, his thought was of others. Many brief handwritten notes were sent by him to friends in need as he slowly regained strength at home during the cold, snowy winter of 1967.

The author's wife was dying of cancer in Delnor Hospital where Dr. Edman had been a patient earlier. He wrote this note to her just after she was taken to the hospital early in February in which he said, "We are looking up earnestly to the Faithful One for you and for Earle and Bruce. The Lord is good! If you are on the second floor you will meet many nurses I came to know during my many weeks there. Hi to them. Friend Wife adds love. Prexy."

He wrote to the author on February 12, "Often during the day and in the waking hours of the night we look to our faithful Lord for Helen and you all. I have held before the Lord the promise in John 11:4 and 41, He has brought you and constantly there is emphasized — 'for the glory of God that the Son of God be glorified' He will do it! Prexy."

After her death on April 1, he sent this note on April 3: "There has been so much prayer for you, during the day

and in the waking hours, of night — and always with the
assurance of the grace that is sufficient. Be sure, Earle,
that we keep trusting the Faithful Comforter to be the unfailing helper for Bruce and you all." Such was one small
sample of his thoughtfulness of others when he himself was
so ill.

Many times he thought of the family life in Ecuador
with its bright and difficult times, of depression days in
Worcester with the church and in graduate school, of the
lovely hill at Nyack, and the years at Westgate in Wheaton.
Mrs. Edman found the following note dated April 27, 1967,
nearly a year after his death when she was cleaning out
his desk: "Lover, You have always been good to me and
to them [his boys], and with them I thank the Lord for
you. Lover."

A letter of April 4 to his sons started out, "A note to you
four boys" and went on to say that it was not intended to
be maudlin or morbid, even though he was uncertain how
much longer he might have. While able to do so, he wanted
to write "this little word of very sincere thanksgiving to the
Lord for you all." He spoke of the different places they
had lived and the hard as well as the good times they had
had, but he seemed particularly to remember "the jolly
times at breakfast followed by our devotions of Bible reading and memorization and of prayers together before you
all went to the Academy, Junior Academy or Holmes school;
the quiet and reverent three-hour services we used to have
as a family on Good Friday together to read the Word about
our Lord's suffering and death. . . ." He closed with the
thought there might be "much sand in life's hour-glass with
resultant opportunity for whatever limited service the Lord
may have for us. However, in any event, I just wanted each
one of you . . . [naming each of his four sons] to know
that you have been good to me." It never occurred to him

to think of how good he had been to them, how much he had prayed for and loved each of them.

He expressed his concern in a note on April 29, 1967, to his "Friday," Rowena Carr, who was working in Texas, that he was doing so little for the *Alliance Witness* although they were still continuing his remuneration. Also he was deeply concerned that the college was still paying his salary and humorously wrote, "Get paid for praying on the siding?" In a later note on May 31 he commented to her, "There are occasional 'twinges' of pain to remind me I am just one heartbeat from heaven all the time." He spoke in a July 19 note of his need for help with his two new manuscripts and wrote almost plaintively, "There is no Friday with efficiency and patience to be right hand for me."

Just before his sixty-seventh birthday the executive committee of the board in a resolution on May 4 noted that his contribution to the college, the cause of Christ and the world was "substantial and noteworthy" and extended their congratulations and best wishes with prayer for the rich and abundant blessing of the Lord upon his life in the days to come. The whole college family was cheered when he appeared in public for the first time since his heart attack in November, 1966, to be on the platform for the commencement exercises.

Mrs. Edman and he left for Honey Rock and the red cabin as soon after commencement as the weather permitted. His sons David and Norman and their families were with them for two weeks during the summer, and he faithfully reported the sayings and doings of the grandchildren to "Friday." He was able to do tapes on two forthcoming books, *A Personal Inventory* and "hills" of the Bible as well as revising *God's Plan of Redemption* which he thought was the "clearest presentation of the whole scope of salvation" that he had ever seen. Mrs. Edman busied herself with the preparation of meals and housekeeping. She also made some of the little improvements on the grounds that he would have liked to do but could not in his condition.

Dolores Lassen later transcribed his tapes of *A Personal Inventory* in which he mentioned completing "a fairly rough but fairly complete draft" which would need revision. When he completed it on June 27, he added, "But then the snow may fall before we finish the revision of this manuscript." He did not finish the revision and when the snow first fell that winter it fell on his grave.

He planned to carry on his work as chancellor and wrote to Harold Faulkner on September 14 that the doctors were permitting him to resume "part-time responsibilities of his office" again and that the six months' leave granted by the board at its January meeting could terminate as of September 15. Writing and correspondence would form the main part of his work as the doctors would not give him permission to travel or to speak in meetings.

The day which was to be his last on earth began and ended with devotional activities. He awakened at 3:00 A.M. and began to pray for the college — its staff, faculty, students, friends and alumni missionaries. He systematically repeated requests for various persons, groups and areas. When Nathan Bailey, president of the Alliance, visited Mrs. Edman after his death, she told him how Dr. Edman had named the district conferences of the Alliance and had a special burden of prayer for Mr. Bailey.[23] Dr. Edman had breakfast with Mrs. Edman about 6:30 and left to conduct the morning watch service on behalf of the coming special fall services. He had resumed leadership of this daily 7:00 A.M. prayer group in W105 on the first floor of Blanchard Hall with the opening of school. Before leaving to go to this prayer group he had twice said good-bye to Mrs. Edman that morning. He wore the blazer which the class of 1968 had given him.

Seniors Stanley Shank and Paul Rowell, who used to

carry him up the stairs in the Conservatory Building to his office, were both present. Shank thought that he was very alert and buoyant on that Friday, September 22, as he told them several of his jokes. He used Luke 18:1-18 for the devotions and then asked that they sing "Every Day with Jesus Is Sweeter Than the Day Before." After the prayer period they carried him, sitting on a chair, up the stairs to the second floor and saw him go to his office.[24]

He worked until chapel time, making phone calls to Harvey Chrouser, his brother Elner, and to Mrs. Edman. He signed his last letter before leaving for chapel. It was to Mrs. K. M. Frey of the John Rudin Company of which he had been board chairman for several years. The letter contained his manuscript for the column "As I See It" in the company paper. He was cheery when he left the office to go to chapel.

He walked in by the door under the tower just after 10:15 and was met by Richard Beesley of the department of education and Chaplain Welsh. Dr. Armerding and student Scott Monaghan, who was to make an announcement in chapel, came in about 10:23. Dr. Armerding noticed that Dr. Edman seemed a little nervous and preoccupied. Dr. Edman asked Beesley, "How's my favorite author?" to which Beesley replied, "Just fine, how's my favorite author?" Dr. Armerding reached down to pull up his socks and Dr. Edman commented, "I guess we're greatly blessed to have socks at all." He then took a nitroglycerin pill. When Ed Cording, director of the conservatory of music, passed, Dr. Armerding turned half in fun to Dr. Edman and said that he should order Mr. Cording to join them. Dr. Edman said, "Ed, you come here."

They filed into chapel with Monaghan leading and then Beesley, Dr. Armerding, Dr. Edman and Mr. Cording. The audience sang "Like a River Glorious" after the chapel chimes. Dr. Armerding prayed, made announcements, and had Monaghan make his announcement. Beesley prayed after the audience sang "Beneath the Cross of Jesus."

Dr. Edman began to speak at 10:40 on the topic "In the Presence of the King," using his audience with Emperor Haile Selassie in 1947 to illustrate his theme. He told of how he had been briefed on what to wear, when to bow, and what steps to take. He applied this preparation for the audience with the emperor to the need of those who come to chapel to prepare themselves to come into the presence of the King of kings. He spoke of the need for reverence, silence, prayer and worship when one came in and then the need for hearty participation in the service. He began to close his talk about 10:53.

Suddenly he stopped speaking and collapsed after a slow half turn. Dr. Armerding and Mr. Cording bent over him, and hymnbooks were put under his head. Dr. Armerding quietly went to the pulpit, closed the chapel with prayer for God's help, and asked the students to leave.

Mrs. Edman, who had been listening to the service over the radio, guessed what had happened when he stopped speaking, and she dressed to be ready to go to the chapel. A student who was a nurse came to the platform, massaged his heart, and began mouth-to-mouth resuscitation. Others loosened his tie and belt. Dr. Edman was breathing heavily all this time.

Mrs. Norman Johnson, who was in charge at the Health Center, called an ambulance and a doctor and then went over to help. The ambulance soon came, and the attendants gave him oxygen and massaged his chest. But it was to no avail, for he had already entered into the presence of the King of kings. His body was taken on a stretcher to the ambulance.

Dr. C. B. Wyngarden came, having been notified of the situation in the chapel by one of his patients who had met him on the street. He examined Dr. Edman and pronounced him dead. He was heard to comment, "This is the closest thing to translation that I have ever seen." Just then Chaplain and Mrs. Welsh arrived with Mrs. Edman. Dr. Wyngarden took Mrs. Edman to his car and told her that her husband was dead.

When Dr. Armerding went back to the office, his secretary reminded him that Dr. Edman had written him a letter with detailed plans for his funeral in the event of his death.[25] He had written that this letter should be in his file for future use as "the sands may be low in the hour glass," and he wanted these ideas to be known "in case of the Lord's call" to him. Directions were given concerning the mortician, the type of casket, that there was to be no "viewing of the remains," and a private burial service for the family.

He went on to say that there might be a lying in state in the vestibule of Edman Chapel a couple of hours before the service. Then he named the Scripture passages to be read and hymns to be sung, especially his favorite, "Beneath the Cross of Jesus." Any tributes were to be brief and to exalt the Lord rather than himself. He desired Dr. Armerding and the pastor of one of the local churches to take the graveside service after which a volley might be fired and taps sounded. He closed, "And then you all back to the Lord's glad service!"

Dr. Armerding and his council met to plan the memorial service after consultation with Mrs. Edman and his brother Elner Edman. Billy Graham was asked to give the message and agreed to do so.

The flag-draped casket was brought into the chapel foyer at noon on Sunday, September 24, the ROTC honor guard mounted, and two books for visitors to sign were put in place. When the service began at 3:00 P.M., the casket was brought to the front of the chapel.

His beloved "Uncle Joe" led in prayer after Dr. Tenney

read Psalm 24. Dr. Graham used Ecclesiastes 3:1-8 as the basis for his message on the time of Dr. Edman's birth, his manner of life, his speaking ability, his ability to be silent in counseling, his suffering, his sense of humor, his ability to sympathize in time of trouble, and the unforgettable manner in which he died. The 250-voice choir of the college musical organizations sang the "Hallelujah Chorus" from the *Messiah*. Brief tributes from Honey Rock Camp, ROTC, student body, faculty and the administration were brought by Harvey Chrouser, Colonel Meadows, Dan Reigle, Paul Wright, and Dr. Armerding, respectively. Others spoke for the Academy, the Alliance, the West Suburban Hospital and the alumni. His life text, Nahum 1:7, was printed in his own handwriting on the back of the memorial service program. Edman and Wurdack chapels were full and the overflow crowd listened in Pierce Chapel.

Perhaps Dr. Armerding put it best in the mimeographed announcement of Dr. Edman's death to the college family when he wrote, "One of God's very special gifts to us went Home to be with his Savior this morning." The board also expressed its esteem for him by renaming Edman Chapel the Edman Memorial Chapel.

A small private service was held in the funeral home on Monday at 11:00 A.M. for the members of the family and a few friends. Dr. Armerding and Evan Welsh participated in the private service at the cemetery. His favorite hymns, "Beneath the Cross of Jesus" and "Trust and Obey," were sung. The Conguer Rifles squad of the ROTC fired three volleys, and then taps was played. The casket was opened at no time in all these services. Mrs. Edman's last view of him was when he twice said good-bye to her on the Friday morning of his death.

News of his death spread far and wide quickly. Phone calls were made to inform close friends of his passing. Richard Gerig notified WMBI, which broadcast the news of his death. The UPI, the AP and other wire services carried the news across the country. The four Chicago papers had extensive stories of the event. The *Wheaton Daily Journal* had four front-page articles on successive days with a special editorial. *Christianity Today, Christian Times,* and other religious periodicals had either extensive notices of his death or stories.

Both Wheaton College and the Graham organization issued special pamphlets. The college *Bulletin* for November was illustrated with pictures of important moments in his career, had a summary of his favorite sayings, and told of the buildings that had come to Wheaton in his administration and the books he had written. One tribute from a student on the back of the *Bulletin* summed up the feeling of many: "May we not demand from God, even as Elisha did from Elijah, a double portion of his spirit; and looking unto Jesus, remembering this man, go onward through life 'Not Somehow But Triumphantly.' "[26] The Graham pamphlet had a color picture of Dr. Edman at his desk with his Bible open before him, a summary of his life, his chapel talk on the day of his death, and Mr. Graham's message at the memorial service in Edman Chapel.

Dozens of tributes poured into the office and to Mrs. Edman from his friends and correspondents all over the world. One spoke of the impact of his message in a leper colony in the Far East. A nurse in India who had been helped by his book, *They Found the Secret,* told of how the book led her closer to Christ. When she heard of his death in a letter from his secretary, she wrote back of her sense of personal loss although she had not met him personally.[27] The secretary sent cards telling of his death and asking removal of his name from the files of 369 religious periodicals, business concerns, and mission organizations.

His last book came out after his death. It was entitled *Look Unto the Hills.*

His many illnesses and his triumphs in service were now at an end. His influence lingers on in the college in the memories of his many friends, in the many buildings which he helped the college to secure, the West Suburban School of Nursing and the ROTC which he had been largely responsible for bringing to the campus. His spiritual leadership is perhaps his greatest contribution, for he had a real sense of the presence of God and provided a living example of a victorious Christian life. Christ was glorified both in his life and in his death.

20.

The Fruit of His Pen

Dr. Edman's voluminous literary effort was achieved only by getting the maximum from each minute. The outline of an article or book was sometimes jotted down on the back of a plane ticket, an envelope or card. On his return to the office he would put the material on the Dictaphone. Mrs. Rowena Carr became quite proficient in editing these materials for the publishers. A chapel talk, sermon, address or baccalaureate message often became an article for publication, while several of them with connected themes appeared later in books.

His dissertation for the Ph.D. degree bears all the marks of scholarship. The final work of over 400 double-spaced pages of typescript is marked by painstaking care, a vast primary and secondary bibliography, and fine pen and ink maps of the area in Ecuador and Peru.

His first published booklet was the scholarly pamphlet of thirty-one pages published in 1947 by the Van Kampen Press under the title of *Swords and Plowshares*. Using the Scriptures, he demonstrated that the world organization to be set up by Christ at His coming could alone bring final peace and order to the world in the millennium. Both his biblical knowledge and thorough insight into political theory are apparent in the booklet.

The Light in the Dark Ages was published by Van Kampen Press in 1949. A history of missions from apostolic times until the end of the eighteenth century, the book has three divisions: "The Light That Shined," "The Light That Failed," and "The Light That Shined Again." Numerous footnotes, careful writing, and extensive bibliography of primary and secondary sources witness to the careful scholarly study.

The bulk of Dr. Edman's writing, however, was devotional. If sales are a criterion of usefulness, his books had a deep impact upon the religious public. His own sense of the importance of the mystical in relating one to God in prayer and Bible-reading, his reading of devotional literature, and his experience of personal suffering over the years were sources for these devotional works.

The Disciplines of Life, his first devotional work, was issued in 1948 by Van Kampen Press. The book "came out of heart experience and study of the Scriptures — or — some might say the reality of the Word in one's life. One learns these lessons as he walks steadily onward with the Lord despite the circumstances of the moment, or stands still to see the salvation of the Lord when there is every reason for running away."[1] Materials for the book "were gathered over a period of twenty years, but the articles were written at various times, on the train, in a plane, in Ethiopia, or California. Actual writing took place over a period of about five years."[2] These experiences were first used in a series of chapel talks from 1945.

Each chapter was a discussion of a discipline, such as darkness, delay, disappointment, doubt and duty. One man commented, "We all find its lines speaking directly to our hearts, and thus we know that they came straight out of yours, the ripe fruit of your experience. On this account the book is a great comfort and inspiration to us. There is the ring of validity that cannot be imitated."[3]

Dr. Edman's interest in revival after the college revival of 1950 bore fruit in his manuscript, "Finney Lives On," published by Fleming H. Revell in London and Scripture

Press in America in 1951. Dedicated to "Wheaton's Brave Sons and Daughters True," the book included a biographical sketch of Finney's life, a discussion of his evangelistic methods, and a digest of his views on revival's pattern, price and perils from his own writings. Billy Graham described it as "a prized addition to my library."[4]

Storms and Starlight was published in 1951 by Scripture Press, with Mrs. K. B. Tiffany, a longtime friend and admirer of Dr. Edman, doing much of the editorial work on the manuscript.[5] The book was dedicated to "Uncle Joe" Evans "who early taught us prayerfully to read the sacred Word, unreservedly to love the Lord Jesus, and wholly to believe the promises." It consisted of lessons from the life of Christ in the gospel of Mark which Dr. Edman had given in chapel. Each was alliterated with the letter *s*.[6] Dr. Edman expressed gratitude to God "that the Word will get out to many hearts and homes who as yet know little of Wheaton. Most of all we trust that it will speak for Him, the Altogether Lovely One."[7]

The Van Kampen Press in 1953 published a small spiral-bound book of devotions entitled *In Quietness and Confidence*, intended for devotional use by the student nurses.

The companion volume, *Great Is Thy Faithfulness*, was released in December, 1954, by the Van Kampen Press. He wrote of God's faithfulness to man on the left-hand page and cited related devotional thoughts, poems and relevant Scripture verses on the right-hand page.

The Delights of Life, a companion volume to *The Disciplines of Life*, was also published by Van Kampen Press in 1954. In 1953 he wrote that "we have two projects simmering on the back of the stove, one on revival in American history covering the span of American evangelists from Jonathan Edwards to Billy Graham; and a companion volume to *The Disciplines of Life*, to be known as *The Delights of Life*."[8] These twenty-eight chapters, compiled in a period of illness, centered on the theme that "true happiness comes from within because of the indwelling Savior and not from outward circumstances."[9]

Another little spiral-bound devotional book, *Not Ashamed*, appeared under the Scripture Press imprint in 1955.

Just Why? was released by Scripture Press in 1956. Dr. Edman spoke of the book as "an attempt to help bewildered folk see that there is a divine pattern and purpose" in life.[10] Madame Chiang Kai-Shek's note of thanks when she received a copy of *Just Why?* indicated that "if it is as stimulating as your previous work, it will be most worthwhile."[11]

Such letters encouraged him to complete *Sweeter Than Honey* for Scripture Press in 1956. Poems from John Oxenham's *Bees in Amber* were linked with ideas that came to him as he read the poems of this English author.

Fear Not appeared in April, 1957, under the auspices of Scripture Press. Dedicated to his brother Elner and his sister-in-law, this devotional booklet was the product of counseling sessions and chapel talks.

The small book *He Leadeth Me* by Scripture Press was dedicated to Billy Graham and Grady Wilson and their wives. Copies were presented to them at a chapel in Centennial Gymnasium on September 24, 1959, when the book was published.

If one can judge by the scores of letters of comment on it which came to Dr. Edman and by its translation into other languages, *They Found the Secret* ranks with *The Disciplines of Life* as the book from his pen that had the most appeal to his public. Robert Walker, editor of *Christian Life* magazine, had requested articles concerning the spiritual crises of well-known Christians that made them such fine Christians.[12] Dr. Edman gathered materials for twenty articles which later became chapters in the book which Zondervan published in 1960. The transforming work of the "indwelling life of Christ" was the focal point in each life. The book was described by one correspondent from England as "a wonderful gallery of modern saints who knew their Lord."[13]

An article under the title "I, Too Saw an Angel" in the Christmas *Bulletin* of the college in 1959 brought numerous letters of approval and testimonials of the help it had been in developing the idea of supernatural aid to Christians in crisis as stated in Hebrews 1:14. Dr. Edman suggested to Laurin Zorn, a Scripture Press official, that this and other Christmas stories from previous Christmas bulletins might be combined as a volume of Christmas stories. Published just before Christmas in 1960, the book, *Wiser Than They Thought,* was dedicated to the "little folks," his grandchildren.[14] His experience of what he felt was a heavenly visitant in 1924 was the nucleus of this book.

Out of My Life came out of "the long months of darkness and painfulness when there was time to think and pray" during the time of convalescence from eye surgery.[15] Autobiographical incidents were put on the Dictaphone in his home and later transcribed and edited by Mrs. Carr.[16] Zondervan released the book in the spring of 1961. Dr. Frank Gaebelein commented that the reader is impressed "with the warmth of Dr. Edman's writing" and that this book was "a superior piece of literature."

But God was also edited by Rowena Carr and dedicated to the eye doctors who had been so helpful to him in his long bout with cataract surgery and detached retinas in 1959 and 1960. Finally released by Zondervan in 1962, the book was based on the recurrence at least sixty times in the Bible of the phrase "but God."

The phrase "then and there" in the Bible next caught his attention. *Then and There* was the result of this study, released by Zondervan in 1964.

A favorite phrase, "not somehow — but triumphantly," became the title of another Zondervan publication in 1965

which contained the essence of chapel talks from 1940 to
1965.

Moody Press in 1965 published the devotional work *In
Step with God.* It was followed by their release in 1967 of
Windows in Heaven, a series of meditations on Scripture
passages, each accompanied by a religious poem. After his
death, Moody Press brought out *Look Unto the Hills* in
1968. Rowena Carr, who knew his style so well, edited this
series of meditations upon the hills of the Bible, such as
Sinai, Calvary and Carmel.

Dr. Edman collaborated with others by writing a chapter for a symposium. He carefully related ethics to the Bible in a chapter on Christian ethics in the centennial book,
The Word for This Century, by Wheaton teachers.

The indexed list of his articles amounts to about two
hundred articles. In a tenth of them he expressed his regard for the values of the American democratic system.
Others were on Christian liberal arts education, the Aucas,
revival, prophecy, and the second coming of Christ. His
war experiences were the basis for several talks and subsequent articles. His writings appeared in *Moody Monthly,
Sunday School Times, War Cry, Decision, Christian Life,
Christianity Today, The Gideon, The King's Business* as
well as the college publications. This writing gave him
contact with practically every segment of the evangelical
public of this and other countries.

Baccalaureate messages each year, talks to the faculty
in the fall, addresses to groups across the country, and
sermons or chapel talks were often reprinted in tracts or
in the college *Bulletin.* His baccalaureate address to the
class of 1949 became the pamphlet *Karl Marx . . . or Jesus
Christ* in which he contrasted the personalities, philosophies
and programs of Marx and Christ. Over half a million copies
were distributed.[17] It was translated into Chinese to help
Christians in Communist China, and translations were

made into Japanese, Spanish, Greek, German, Turkish and other languages. Part of it was put into Braille.

The Question, put out by the American Tract Society in 1952, is a good illustration of his ability to write arresting tracts. Following the format of the television programs of the day, he asked increasingly important questions about friends, vocation, job, savings, wife and home and concluded with the question as to what plans one had for eternity.

He also found time to write Sunday school literature. A series on 1 Thessalonians was prepared for Scripture Press in 1959, as was a series of topical lessons for the Union Gospel Press of Cleveland.

Many of his meditations also were printed. Those for July 13 to 19, 1964, in *The Quiet Hour,* put out by David C. Cook, were based on Exodus 5 through 14. He wrote several front-page meditations for the *Sunday School Times* in 1964.

The opportunity to try his hand at editorial work was given him after his election as editor of the *Alliance Witness* in May, 1965. His first editorial appeared in the June 23, 1965, issue, and the last occurrence of his name as editor was in the issue of October 25, 1967. His first editorial was entitled "All men are created equal. . . ."[18] This equality was by the act of creation by God which made all men equal before God and before the laws of the land. In another editorial he urged careful study of the broad outline of the premillennial return of Christ.[19] His argument against a welfare or socialist state in the editorial "No Saga for Sagadahoc" was based on a talk which had been published earlier.[20]

Dr. Edman also had years of experience with a question-and-answer column. His column in *Kodon,* the college students' literary magazine at Wheaton, was called "To My Way of Thinking" and consisted of questions from students concerning college affairs and his personal life. In answer to one question on whether he helped with the dishes, he replied, "I have several diplomas in dishwashing, and think it's lots of fun to do things together."[21] When asked whether he kept a diary, the reply characteristic of his humility was "I have never thought that anything that I did was worth the effort of a daily record."[22]

He handled the "Spiritual Clinic" of *Christian Life* from May, 1951, when he took the place of Dr. Harry Ironside of Moody Memorial Church, until April, 1966, when David Burnham, a Wheaton graduate who is now a pastor in Akron, Ohio, took his place. The column was renamed "Personal Problems Clinic" in May, 1955, and "Personal Problems" in March, 1959. His answers were always based upon Scripture. He took unpopular stands on matters but he admitted limited knowledge in some areas and was willing to adopt Christian expediency where no scriptural principle was involved. His loyalty to American political ideals and free enterprise were reflected in several columns. Asked whether communism was inherent in the sharing of Acts 2, he stated that "the Scriptures teach capitalism [private ownership and free enterprise] and not Communism."[23] The right of an innocent party to remarry after divorce was stated thus: "It seems clear to me that the breaking of the marriage vow and the subsequent divorce leaves the innocent party free to marry."[24]

During the years that he was associated with the John Rudin Company of Chicago he wrote a brief inspirational column under the title of "As I See It" for their company paper, *The Success Builder*, from December 26, 1957, until his death in 1967.[25] These were Bible meditations, reports on his travels, illnesses or his experiences to inspire and stimulate the salesmen in their work of selling an edition of the Bible and to help them develop their own Christian lives.

Numerous book reviews appeared over his name in *Christian Life, Christianity Today,* and other periodicals. His ability to give the gist of the book, incisively criticize its weaknesses and assert its strengths made readers want to read those he recommended.

Such was the fruit of his pen. His greatest area of literary service to Christians was the cultivation of their devotional lives, to which numerous letters testify of his success. He often used the fruits of labor by other men but always gave credit for what he used. Though he has gone, this ministry continues in the new editions of many of his works.

21.

Bearing Other's Burdens

THE TREMENDOUS VOLUME of correspondence carried on by great leaders of the church, such as the Reformers, continues to amaze the student of church history. Dr. Edman's files contain correspondence with people all over the world from many walks of life. These letters from others and carbons of his answers to them witness to his effectiveness as a counselor to people of both sexes, all ranks in life, and different occupations.

His students, colleagues, friends of the school, and those who came to know him through his books found him a sympathetic listener able to counsel from Scripture and his wide experience of life as well as to pray with them. His question-and-answer columns in *Christian Life* and the *Alliance Witness* brought additional opportunities to counsel. Often, after chapel services or Bible conferences, he would spend time with those who came to him for help. His approachability and availability contributed much to this demand for his counsel, which was of the nondirective type in which he mainly listened and by questions led the person to his own solution to the problem.

Numerous students sought his advice while he was a teacher and even after he achieved the college presidency, for they thought of him as a friend to whom they could go. One man wrote of him, "To me, Prexy was an intimate friend, as intimate as a college president can get with his students." As a freshman and later as a graduate student he had found that Dr. Edman had given "unhurried discussion of the problem and prayer about it."[1]

Students wanted counsel "for needs that vary from advice about a girl friend who was losing interest to life investment for service."[2] Kenneth Taylor of Tyndale House told of seeking Dr. Edman's counsel in the spring of 1938 concerning his romance with the girl who became his wife. He was impressed with the manner in which Dr. Edman developed principles from the Scriptures which were helpful to him in his particular situation.[3]

One student, now a minister, wrote to him after twenty years about a situation in the 1939-40 school year in his English class. He felt convicted because he had used the notes of a friend from another college to do a term paper for his class in Wheaton. Dr. Edman, as official head of Wheaton, assured him of forgiveness. Then he counseled him to thank God "for his faithfulness in dealing with us so that there be nothing between one's soul and the Savior." Finally he pointed the man to 1 John 1:9.[4]

Philip Lasse of the Africa Inland Mission wrote that a letter from Dr. Edman was as an "encouragement" in a trying time when he and his wife "were in despair" and anxious about the future. His "quiet advice" and the copy of *Great Is Thy Faithfulness* he sent met their need for counsel and was "welcomed beyond measure."[5]

David Burnham, a three-time All-American football player at Wheaton, wrote to him after Dave's father died. Thanking Dr. Edman for all the contacts they had had, he said that "in some of the darkest crises in my life you have helped to bring a spiritual light." He never forgot one occasion in Dr. Edman's office when Dr. Edman told him, "God is preparing you today for what you will be tomorrow." On one rainy night in a game against Millikin, when it looked as if they might be defeated, Dr. Edman had told them, "It's always too soon to quit." He concluded his letter by pledging, "By God's grace we will never quit."[6]

A former woman student wrote to him expressing her appreciation of an unasked-for counseling contact he had made for her that had been very helpful at the right moment. Noticing her "unhappy and troubled countenance," he had put a note in her mailbox, giving her an appointment for "help and prayer." She was impressed that he had concern for her, an average student. By note, prayer, and his advice to her to go to Mrs. Edman for further help, he had assisted her through a crisis in her life. This was "the greatest morale builder and spiritual help" she had known up to that time.[7]

A former Wheaton student was finishing his work for the A.B. degree at a nearby college. He felt a call to the ministry and wondered whether he should start without further training. Dr. Edman advised him to complete his master's degree because "an incomplete sentence always marks down a theme in writing class." Time in graduate school would make it clear whether he should enter the ministry or teach, he advised.[8] Later correspondence revealed that this letter had been a stabilizing influence in the young man's life.

Robert A. Cook, after he had become president of King's College, talked with Dr. Edman concerning his new and difficult responsibilities in this position for which he had had little training. Dr. Edman later wrote him a long letter summarizing the main points of an article concerning the duties of a president that had appeared in *College and University Business* and giving him the bibliographic data so he could look it up for himself. He ended the letter with his idiom, "Keep chin up and knees down!" and signed it with his frequently used signature, "Cheerily."[9]

Robert Evans, founder of the Greater Europe Mission, told the author of how in 1948 he was led to found a bilingual Bible institute in Paris to train young Europeans in the Scriptures so that they could evangelize their own people. When he created an American committee in this country, he got word of misunderstanding and even opposition from European Evangelicals who feared they might lose their students or teachers to this new institution. Greatly discouraged, he began to wonder whether this was God's call to him. He went to Wheaton to see Dr. Edman, who heard him through and then said, "Let's pray about it." His main counsel after prayer was summed up in the question, "What has the Lord told you to do?" If that was clear, no opinion, even of godly men, should change it. Before parting, they had further prayer to tell the Lord that Evans understood and accepted God's call to this work. Dr. Evans' mission now has several Bible schools and nearly 150 missionaries at work in Europe. The once-troubled leaders in Europe now regard this work highly.[10] Dr. Evans was of the opinion that Dr. Edman took special delight in counseling students called to missionary service.

Joe Coughlin had come to Wheaton as a transfer student in the fall of 1937. He and another student, Boyd Hunt, worked with a boys' group in a Glen Ellyn church, and many of the boys had become Christians. After the two were advised by an administrator that they should not have contact with this modernistic church, they met with Dr. Edman in his Blanchard Hall office to ask his advice. He encouraged them to continue their work in love despite the opposition of the administrator and that in the church.

When Joe first organized a larger group of students to do boys' work, Dr. Edman prayed with and counseled the group. When cars were needed to take the students to these meetings, he loaned them his car. He did it on condition that they regularly wash his car because he would not let them pay him for its use. Also, he suggested that the "shares" the boys gave at the meetings be used for Latin America Mission youth camps in Costa Rica. Joe and

his friends set up the Christian Service Brigade officially
in 1940. Dr. Edman was their unofficial adviser from 1937
until 1940, and he was a member of the board of the organization from 1942 until 1948.

Joe told of how on one occasion he was washing dishes
in the kitchen of the College Church after a wedding when
Dr. Edman, who was a guest at the wedding, sensed that
he was discouraged. He told Joe, "I'll tell friend wife that
I'll be helping you." He came back and they talked while
they did the dishes. Joe got over his discouragement as a
result of this time together and went on with his work with
the brigade.[11]

Another counseling session in the spring of 1950 with
Merle Steely, Bill Watkins and Abe Thiessen, three young
married World War II veterans, gave him a part in the
founding of ELWA, the Christian radio station located in
Liberia. The three men wanted his advice concerning their
cherished dream of a radio station in West Africa to broadcast the gospel. Dr. Edman brought such Scripture verses
as Joel 2:2 to their attention and prayed with them before
they went back to their work. He prayed for some time
after they left the office that their faith would make their
dreams a reality.

He had them form a committee of faculty and other
interested friends and contacted a graduate, Norma Bloom-
quist, who had the ear of President Tubman of Liberia because of her educational missionary work. A cable from
Liberia on December 21, 1950, stated that they should send
someone to West Africa to present the idea to the authorities there. The needed $980 for the air fare was scraped
up, and on January 15, 1951, Bill Watkins left for Liberia.[12]
There were delays before he could see the proper official,
until one day he went to the man's home and was able
to point out an error in a survey the man was studying. The

official then heard his story and granted them the necessary contract.

Watkins later went out to clear the area for the station, and in 1952 the group was linked with the Sudan Interior Mission. When Dr. Edman visited Liberia in 1953, he found them building a road and making cement blocks for the buildings. Here again his counsel and vision had been of help in bringing a new important missionary venture into being. ELWA has been a blessing to many Africans through its broadcasts.[13]

He considered his most significant counseling in terms of multiplying his service to be involved with Billy Graham and members of his team. Leighton Ford, Billy's brother-in-law and associate, expressed his view of Dr. Edman's help in these terms: "May I thank you personally for what your ministry had meant to Jeannie and myself. We appreciate with new awareness the ministry of 'another Comforter' in our lives."[14]

Leighton Ford commented that Dr. Edman's role in his life "was that of a respected and trusted father-advisor and counsellor in the faith." He was impressed that Dr. Edman was "not afraid to cry." Both he and his wife agreed "that Dr. Edman's impression on our lives was not so much that of great scholarship or theological insight as that of the reality of the Living Christ who was sufficient in every crisis in his life."

Dr. Edman's historical sense caused him to urge them at meetings of the association to collect carefully and preserve all records on Billy Graham's life and ministry for future historical research.[15]

Dr. Edman's first association with Billy Graham came through his mother, Mrs. Anders Edman, and his brother, Elner Edman. Mrs. Edman, Elner and his family, and Paul B. Fischer were vacationing in Clearwater, Florida, in February, 1940. There they met Billy Graham who was a student at the Florida Bible Institute. Impressed with his preaching, Mrs. Edman urged him to come to Wheaton. When he replied that he could not get in because he was not a top student, she told him she would speak to her son, the president of Wheaton, about him. Mr. Fischer and Elner Edman said that they would aid him financially.[16]

When Mrs. Edman told her son on her return to Wheaton of Billy's ability to preach, Dr. Edman recalled that she asked, "He will get in the College, will he not?" He assured her that Billy would after he had checked his credentials with the proper office.

Billy felt lonely when he first arrived on campus and was impressed with a greeting from Dr. Edman of "Hi, Bill, how are things going?" They also met at Westgate when Billy was trimming the shrubbery around the home. When Billy went to a prayer meeting at the Bostrom home, he sat next to Dr. Edman, who took a real interest in him. He was also a student in Dr. Edman's freshman history class. Billy became pastor at the Gospel Tabernacle in Wheaton when Dr. Edman resigned from that position. Dr. Graham recalled that he sought Dr. Edman's advice "on every major decision of his life."

When some were criticizing him in 1952 for having people who were not Evangelicals participating in his crusades, Dr. Edman's advice to him was to read Galatians 5. He reminded Billy, "They can't fight with somebody who won't fight back." He spoke of Nehemiah, who was too busy building the wall of Jerusalem to come down to talk to his critics.

Dr. Edman had a helpful role as a member of the board of the Billy Graham Association in leadership in the early morning prayer meetings, by keeping business moving, by telling a good joke at the right time to relieve tension in the meeting, by wise advice, and by his membership on the team committee to serve as an insulator for Dr. Graham in personnel problems. While Dr. Edman was chairman of this committee for some years, Dr. Graham felt that his "wise and humane judgment" was useful in personnel problems. He wanted committee or board meetings to move quickly in dispatching business, and at night he urged that they adjourn early for a good night's rest.[17]

Dr. Edman entered into Dr. Graham's problems fully. When he was being harshly criticized in 1952 for some of his supposed "cooperation with modernists" in his crusades, Dr. Edman wrote to Nelson Bell, Graham's father-in-law, that he shared Dr. Bell's "ache of heart and burden of prayer for Billy, and also the great joy in seeing the continued hand of God" on him and his ministry. Wherever he went, he stood "without hesitation or qualification for Billy." He prayed for him in chapel and kept the students informed of his work by notices on the bulletin board.[18]

He and Graham also conferred at length about Dr. Graham's ideas for a Christian university. Dr. Edman was sent a copy of the first issue of the *Decision* magazine for "frank criticism and comments" and replied that the first issue set "an excellent standard in content, format, quality of printing, illustrations." He was specially pleased to see that Graham's ministry had been set in "the perspective of Whitefield and Moody."[19]

When he became chairman of the team committee of the association, he tried to keep acceptance by Dr. Graham to be a member of various boards at a minimum in order to protect his time and energy. Dr. Edman outlined the policy of Dr. Graham, referring such invitations to his committee. Then he would write a gracious letter of thanks for the invitation and appreciation of the work of the organization, state the policy of the association on this matter, and tactfully decline the invitation. The association, partly because of Dr. Edman's advice, adopted the policy that Dr. Graham would not be on boards unless he had "very close control and oversight," and even then his outside associations would have to be limited because of the many demands on "his time and strength."[20]

This committee was also responsible for personnel problems, and it was to check periodically on the ministry of those associated with Dr. Graham. Letters in his files show that he did this work circumspectly and dealt with persons with problems in a kind and tactful manner that would strengthen the ministry of the person and yet not compromise the principles for which the association stood.

Dr. Edman strongly supported the desire of Dr. Graham and his associates to have a pavilion at the World's Fair in New York rather than to have merely a booth in the Protestant Center. God blessed this endeavor at a time when the financial load of the association was particularly heavy.

When Dr. Graham's daughter became engaged to a young man from Switzerland, Dr. Graham and his wife wrote a long letter to Dr. Edman so that he would be the first to know of this happy event. Dr. Edman defended them strongly from mistaken rumors that Graham's daughter had danced at the wedding reception. Reporters who had been at two weddings had confused the reception with another held about the same time in the same Swiss town.[21]

He was gratified when Billy Graham in 1952 expressed an initial willingness to serve on the board of trustees at Wheaton and stated that he would try to be faithful in attendance at the meetings and in making what contribution he could to the work at the college.[22] He was deeply pleased when Dr. Graham did finally become a trustee in 1963.

His main contribution to Dr. Graham's work was well expressed by Dr. Edman in these words: "My ministry is primarily one of prayer and counsel" to him.[23] Thus he flew with "Uncle Joe" Evans to Australia and New Zealand to be with the team for prayer and counsel in 1959.

Often he would lead in prayer at a crusade before the team went on the platform. Sitting by Dr. Graham on the platform, he would occasionally squeeze his hand or pass him a note with a relevant verse of Scripture on it. Dr. Graham told how at the end of one message in the Berlin Crusade, Dr. Edman wrote on a scrap of paper, "The Lord has been glorified here tonight." They would often ride back together to the hotel.[24]

When Dr. Graham was uncertain whether to extend the meetings at a crusade in Minneapolis as some of his associates desired, Dr. Edman said, "You preach and I'll pray, and we'll get the answer." When he finished the sermon, Dr. Graham felt clearly he should close the crusade that night.[25]

Dr. Edman was thrilled when in the late fall of 1964 he became the senior vice-president of the association. Dr. Graham told him that if anything happened to him, Dr. Edman as senior vice-president would "immediately assume command temporarily" until a permanent president was chosen.[26]

Dr. Edman often found Dr. Graham's counsel helpful. He wrote in the summer of 1964 to Graham concerning his feeling that he should perhaps give up the presidency for some other position around the college. Dr. Graham assured him of his prayers and said, "Blessed is the man that decides at the right time" to turn over his work to a younger man rather than to wait until the work and his good name might be harmed. He added that so far as the qualifications of the next president were concerned, "he should be the spitting image of you!"[27]

Few would question the important place Dr. Edman had in Dr. Graham's life and work. Stanley Kresge told Dr. Edman that he appreciated "the great things you have done for Billy Graham over many years. He has told me more than once that you have been the greatest influence in his life of any mortal."[28] Dr. Graham told Dr. Edman in a letter that his "little notes" were among "the most encouraging things that I receive," and "your comradeship in the Gospel through these years has meant more to me than words can ever express." Later in that same year he commented, "Your contribution to my life and ministry cannot be properly evaluated until we stand before Christ at the Judgment Seat. I am forever in your debt and always look forward to your coming to our crusades and the times of prayer that we have together."[29]

Dr. Edman's admiration for Billy Graham was revealed in a letter to a student at Carleton College who wanted information for a paper on the hero in America. He characterized Graham as "a very human person . . . , an enthusiastic and unassuming student while here at Wheaton, and he is just the same today as always."[30]

Dr. Edman was also a helpful counselor and friend to many students who now hold important positions in Wheaton College. Robert Noles, now one of the college field representatives, related how in February of his senior year he had to drop out because of an overload of work and an unexpected appendectomy. Dr. Edman earlier in the month had said to Bob, "The Lord gave me a message for you, Psalm 23:1." When Bob became ill, he arranged for him to enter a hospital to get a chance to rest and took him to it. He then wired Bob's uncle to tell him of his nephew's illness and received word that he would be welcome to go to his home to recuperate. At the end of three weeks, during which he visited Bob frequently, Dr. Edman took him from the hospital to his train for Palm Springs.[31]

David L. Roberts, now head of Wheaton's development department, remembered how his future wife's sister, a student at Wheaton, urged him in the spring of 1937 to visit Wheaton. She arranged for Dr. Edman to meet him. He greeted Roberts warmly and made him feel at home. When Dave told him that he loved working in the business world but desired most to do the will of God for his life, Dr. Edman discussed Scripture passages concerning the will of God and ended by saying, "Dave, let's commit this to the Lord. He'll give a clear answer." They knelt and prayed together. Dave later decided to attend Wheaton and when he came up to the entrance to Blanchard Hall, Dr. Edman happened to come out and said, "Hi, Dave, I knew you were coming. I have been praying for you."

When he became president in 1940, he asked Dave and his roommate Julius Voget to permit him after lunch to use their room on the fourth floor of Blanchard Hall for a quick shower and a short nap each day. The boys got a key for him and became his "Roomies." When he urged the students during special services in Dave's senior year to have prayer with their roommates, he had prayer with his two "Roomies" that day.

Because Dave was president of his senior class, he was kidnapped by the juniors, but he got away. When the juniors said they were going to use pictures of Dave tied up in ropes for their *Tower,* the college annual, Dave asked the seniors and their dates to boycott a concert which the *Tower* staff sponsored to help finance the cost of the *Tower.* But Dr. Edman called a meeting of the *Tower* staff, the class presidents, and Peter Stam to discuss the matter. He read Scripture verses which allocated vengeance to the Lord only. The negatives were turned over to Dave without any duplicates being made, and the seniors and their dates went to the concert.[32]

Marion Wade, a friend and supporter of the college, founder and board chairman of a leading company in franchise and contract cleaning, wrote of his appreciation for

Dr. Edman in these words: "How much you have meant to me, and helped me in the building of my life and my business which is my life and my mission field too."[33]

A Texas businessman ended his connection with his company when the company which had acquired it ordered him to transfer to New York. He shared his problem of how to get another position with Dr. Edman, who wrote to him that the Lord faithfully opens a new door when He closes one, mentioned biblical passages concerning guidance, such as Psalm 37:3-5, and sent him a copy of his book *He Leadeth Me*.[34]

Dr. Edman also had comfort and counsel for those who faced bereavement. A student had just lost her talented and relatively young father after a severe illness. He told her of the help her father had been to him but reminded her to remember that he was with Christ and to remember what he had been to her. He spoke of "the heritage of faith and faithfulness" she had which would help her in her loss.[35] He wrote to a seminary professor who had just lost his wife, quoting Ezekiel 24:18, where the prophet who lost his wife by death in the evening did God's command the following morning.[36] Numerous letters to bereaved persons in his files show his thoughtfulness and sound counsel in the presence of death.

He often received letters from women whose family or other problems left them nervous and distraught. When one asked for an appointment, he wisely and tactfully helped by letter but told her to get an appointment with her pastor. One teacher who suddenly found life uninteresting after years of nervous tension wrote to him. He suggested she might consider working with a Christian organization and referred her to such Scripture passages as Psalm 27:1 and Hebrews 13:5 to allay her fears. He told her that God would not let her be tested beyond her ability to bear it.[37]

The science editor of a prominent Eastern publishing firm wrote to him about Dr. Edman's article, "Facing Death Unafraid," that he had read in the November, 1966, college *Bulletin*. The editor spoke of how he had been terrified to die when he was lost in a private plane in the Ecuadorian Andes. In his reply, Dr. Edman told him of his similar experience over the Peruvian Andes when their plane began to ice up and how Isaiah 41:10 had been helpful in calming his fears. "While there is always initial fear, the one who trusts in God can be quiet and confident," he wrote.[38]

He particularly delighted to help those who were missionaries or were thinking of a missionary career. He advised a thirty-nine-year-old nurse, who was interested in missionary nursing, to contact the offices of EFMA and IFMA to find out what boards might need her services.[39]

When the Baroness Von Trapp gave a concert with her family at the college in 1946, she told Dr. Edman of her interest in missions of her own denomination and of her desire to do such work for a time. He asked her where she might like to serve, and she pointed to New Guinea on a missions map in the room. He said he would like to see her go there. When she and her group returned to Wheaton in 1968 for a concert, she asked for Dr. Edman. Edwin Hollatz, chairman of the speech department, told her of his death. She told him of the talk with Dr. Edman in 1946 and said that as a result she had worked for a year in a missionary outpost in New Guinea and had organized Cor Unum Incorporated to raise money for a mission station of her denomination in the Fiji Islands.[40]

Many people wrote to him about different kinds of personal problems. One woman, an only child, wrote to ask him whether it would be right to institutionalize her mother who had a bad case of arthritis. The mother was making her daughter miserable by constantly coming between her and her husband and interfering with the discipline of the children. He wrote that in his opinion she would be fair to her mother if she placed her in a good home.[41]

Those who asked counsel about their education received helpful response. Miss Lydia Mattar, daughter of the keeper of the Garden Tomb in Jerusalem, wrote for his help in getting into a good medical school. He referred her to a friend who knew of the best medical schools and wrote a letter asking him to help her as much as he could. Also, he quoted to her the Rotherham translation of Jeremiah 29:1 which speaks of God's plans as being for one's good and giving hope for the future.[42]

Dr. Edman was involved in the founding of LeTourneau College in 1946 and was one of its trustees from that time. He was considered by all the LeTourneaus as "a loyal friend, advisor and intercessor through the years."[43] Richard H. LeTourneau, now the president, said his most "reliable counsel" came from Dr. Edman.[44] When Dr. Edman was sent material for board meetings at which he could not be present, he reviewed it and sent a letter telling his views on the matters concerned. He also gave counsel to the family as a member and director of the LeTourneau Foundation which was organized in 1936. His advice about educational and mission work in the Tournata project in Africa and the Tournavista project in Peru was always practical and helpful.

When he was on the board of one Christian organization, he insisted that only the board should make policy, and on one occasion said he would have to withdraw if this policy were not followed by the employees. The tone of his letter was humble but adamant as to principle.[45]

Robert Walker spoke of how helpful Dr. Edman had been in 1956 when Walker set up Christian Life Missions to present the challenge of missions to Evangelicals through modern communications techniques. Dr. Edman as one of the directors never missed a meeting of the board, and his knowledge of the world and especially Latin America made his suggestions helpful.[46]

Many written requests for prayer came to him, and while they did not involve direct counseling, he always assured the writer that he would remember the request in private and college prayer periods. The author can testify that Dr. Edman kept these promises during the early morning prayer services with the staff. Stephen Olford of Calvary Baptist Church of New York expressed appreciation for Dr. Edman's "friendship, prayers, and interest."[47] Dr. Edman was frequently asked to write prayers that might be included in books of prayers for ministers and laymen.

These and the thousands of letters in his correspondence give the fixed impression that he was both approachable and available as a counselor. People were confident that he was interested and would quietly listen to their problems. He listened or read carefully before citing pertinent passages of Scripture which applied to a problem. Then he would pray in oral interviews or write promises in letters that he would be praying. He would send one of his own books that might be helpful. Often he drew upon his own experience to help others work out their problems. The spiritual and the rational were combined in an ethical practical solution to the problem. His counsel was always fresh, original, and nondirected in helping the person to work out the solution to his own problem in a way that would lead to a closer relationship to the Lord.

22.

In Retrospect

LETTERS AND INTERVIEWS agree concerning Dr. Edman's strengths and weaknesses, suggesting stability of character. It appears as if God had marked V. Raymond Edman for His service in a special way from childhood.

His strong belief in the reality of the spiritual produced a marked devotional outlook on life which some thought bordered on the mystical. Christ's "saviorhood as mediator of grace" rather than "His Lordship as King of Truth" was predominant in his thought and life. A writer in *Christianity Today* said this of his emphasis: "The goal of Christian education is an evangelical mission in the world" in order that Christ's saving grace might be fervently proffered to all men.[1] Dr. Edman phrased this idea in a letter to a friend in this way: "The College has always stood for the separated life, not only outwardly from certain worldly practices, but an inward separation of the heart from the world, wrought in the hearts of God's people by the indwelling of His Holy Spirit. There is a deep heart-cry on my part, as well as by many others, that true holiness may mark the life and service of the students of Wheaton."[2]

While he did not neglect doctrine or the practice of Christianity, he did emphasize and practice a devotional life which made him acutely conscious of the presence of God. President Armerding said of him during the memorial service two days after his death, "First and foremost, we

found him one who loved the Lord with a fervent passion. . . . "[3]

This love for the Lord and sense of His presence led him
to spend much time in prayer and in the study of Scripture.
He was conscious of spiritual forces for good or evil, but
there was no question in his life of the presence of the Lord
as a victorious reality in the spiritual life, whatever the
struggle. Love to Christ was a compelling force toward
communion with God in prayer.

This led him to practice early hours for going to bed and
rising. Carter Cody, his assistant, was awakened on one
occasion at about 3:30 A.M. by Dr. Edman, who told him
that Carter's wife, Celia, had phoned and wanted him home.
This was his way of getting Carter up early for devotions
and an early start on their return to Wheaton.[4]

If he were out in the evening at a function for the college,
he would leave for home as soon as politeness permitted.
When he awakened in the night, he would pray until he
fell asleep again. He never rose later than 5 A.M. and
more often at 3:30 or 4 A.M. After a time for reading the
Bible and prayer and breakfast, he would go to his office,
often as early as 5 A.M., to have dictation ready for his
secretary before the 7 A.M. prayer meeting with the faculty,
staff, and students.[5]

He urged the students that "seven-thirty classes should
be preceded by breakfast because physical nourishment is
an aid to intellectual nurture, and breakfast should be preceded by unhurried devotions."[6] He believed in devotions
"at the outset of each day and during the day" for the one
who had "a seeking soul, a sensitive ear, a believing and
obedient heart, and a thankful spirit." He and Mrs. Edman
had early "determined to set aside the first hours of the
day for our devotions. . . . We think the early morning is
the best time for meeting the Lord in His Word and
prayer. Heart and mind are fresh and alert at that time,

and not weary. Neither is there any interruption by the telephone or doorbell since we arise at 4:30 or a little later to have at least an hour and a half or two for the Lord."[7]

This disciplined life of Bible study and prayer each day enabled him to face problems with composure and confidence as he waited on God for guidance as to the right word in each situation. His popularity as a preacher cannot alone be explained by years of formal biblical training, for he had only one year of formal Bible training at Nyack. His successor put it well in these words: "His was a life dedicated in loving obedience to the Word of God and its application to life."[8]

His prayer life led people to think of him as one who lived in the presence of God. Evan Welsh commented that he had an "authentic note of one living and practicing the presence of God."[9] His secretary for over fifteen years said that he was always "listening for what the Lord was saying" in a natural way that had no hypocrisy in it.[10] Dr. Carl Armerding, the father of Wheaton's present president, remembers having a room next to Dr. Edman in the Biltmore Hotel in Florida where he and Dr. Edman were conducting daily chapel services. Though Dr. Armerding himself got up early to pray, Dr. Edman was already up, and he could hear him praying.[11] No matter what issue came up, he would say, "Let's pray about it."

Dr. Edman relished the 7 A.M. prayer meeting with faculty, staff and students during the last ten years of his presidency. He called it the "morning watch" and led it himself when he was home. After reading from Scripture or *Daily Light* for the day, he would often comment on the portion and give an illustration. This was followed by discussion of the matters for prayer and a period of prayer. A song, such as "Trust and Obey," often was used to end the period at about 7:30. He always remembered in prayer the office workers, faculty members, alumni, and regularly the Aucas that they might be won. Other Christian schools were not forgotten. Attendance would vary from six to twelve.[12] Often he would remark after the meeting, "I'm going up to my salt mine," or he would eat a breakfast of cream of wheat and coffee at the Stupe with Clarence Hyde, a staff member who regularly attended the morning watch.[13]

Even when Dr. Edman might have been permitted a touch of human pride in the Wheaton centennial year, Richard Gerig, the centennial coordinator, recollected that he sought "to scripturalize and spiritualize the Centennial." This was why he wanted the Graham crusade to be the first event of the year.[14]

His friend, Robert Van Kampen, who traveled with him in the Middle East, the Far East, and South America remembers that Dr. Edman traveled light but never neglected to have his Bible and a pad of paper on which he wrote the lessons that the Lord taught him from the Word. He would often use the backs of envelopes or correspondence, ticket stubs, or whatever came to hand to record his thoughts.

He also had very strong convictions that a proper observance of Sunday would help to strengthen the spiritual life. He had experienced this in his own home where he had to prepare for Sunday on Saturday by cleaning his shoes and seeing that his best suit was ready. Thus Sunday was free for worship. Simple meals were enough for the day. He avoided traveling as much as possible on Sundays. When he was at the University of Illinois, he decided never to study on Sunday and kept this resolve all through a busy academic career.[15]

His son David spoke of their regular family worship with Bible-reading, memorizing of Scripture, and prayer. They always had their own Good Friday three-hour service at home. Like many boys, they at times thought a good thing could be overdone.[16]

This devotional quality of life did not make him austere and unfriendly; on the contrary, he early became a friendly, kindly, and genial "Mr. Wheaton" both on the campus and among the college constituency. With the gift of genuinely caring for others, he made people feel that they were "an integral part of a fellowship" because he was "a lover of people."[17] He carried a college yearbook with him and prayed for students by name in his private devotions after looking at their picture.[18] His natural ability to associate names and faces after years of separation was strengthened by his frequent remembrance in prayer of alumni, friends and Christian leaders. On meeting a person for the first time, he would be sure to get the name right and then link the name and face with some characteristic of the person. He believed that "everybody is an individual who should be important to us; with the result that I concentrate on who he is, from whence he comes, what he does, and what are his interests."[19]

Once at a Bible conference in California he met a lady whom he had not seen for twenty years and called her by name. She was so impressed with this that her regular large annual gift to the college was much larger that year.[20]

Carter Cody, who was his special assistant and frequently sang and led singing for him, recalled that Dr. Edman made people "feel comfortable" whether they were the humble Arizona cowboy Pecos Higgins, the former army nurse Billie Bigham, or Emperor Haile Selassie of Ethiopia. This quality enabled him to be sensitive to the need of an audience so that he could communicate without strain. He had "an amazing ability to communicate with any level of groups or persons."[21]

David Salstrom, the master of ceremonies for an alumni

banquet in Columbia, South Carolina, started to introduce people to Dr. Edman before the dinner but soon found that he needed no help in remembering the names of alumni or friends. One unsaved young man at the dinner needed counseling, and in a friendly natural way Dr. Edman talked and prayed with him so that he felt no sense of inferiority to this college president but was led to Christ. Dr. Edman seemed to exude "a warm spirit of friendly helpfulness."[22]

For several years he carried on an extensive correspondence with Pecos Higgins of Arizona. Higgins had not gone beyond the second grade but had a gift for writing poetry. Dr. Edman had Pecos come to the Graham crusade and laymen's conference in the fall of 1959 and treated him as a personal friend. Pecos commented on this trip that "the most Education I ever had . . . was at Wheaton College."[23]

Nancy Litteral, a quadriplegic who paints with a brush taped to one arm and types by holding a stick between her teeth to punch the keys, sent the author a long letter about her friendship with Dr. Edman. Nancy did an oil painting of the tower of Blanchard Hall for Dr. Edman, and he sent her some of his books and wrote to her frequently. She wrote, "He is the most giving man I know, I mean of himself. It has always amazed me that such a busy and well-known man would take time out to drop me a few lines and to always remember me at Christmas with a gift of his latest book. He truly was Christlike in his interest and compassion for others."[24]

He also wrote frequently and sent books to Billie Bigham, a retired army nurse who had much illness and suffering. He first heard of her through Maurice C. Smith, one of the trustees. She prayed earnestly for him in the period when he was having much difficulty with his eyes, and in their extensive correspondence they shared their understanding of the Scriptures concerning suffering.

A neighbor in Wheaton sent a Christmas card in 1964 which expressed regard for the Edmans after an initial period of aloofness. He wrote, "You have meant more to us than you have any idea. The way you both live your faith and make it live for others whose lives you touch is more than you can know. Thank you for being you and giving us your friendship."

A graduate student from South America wrote of Dr. Edman's friendliness to him when he came to the college. Dr. Edman called him *compatriota* (fellow citizen) and chatted with him in Spanish. He was invited to the home for meals and was asked to participate in the baptism of Dayuma by giving the prayer in Spanish which Dr. Edman translated into English.[25]

Dr. Edman seemed to combine the best qualities of the mystic with the friendliness of a man of affairs. He was always practical in his outlook and activities. Billy Graham was impressed with the combination of mysticism and practicality in him.[26]

Because of this practical bent he had a sense of the value of time and sought to make the most of his moments. He would jot down outlines of a book, sermon, or some plan for the college, or read his Bible on the many planes he rode in his duties. Much work was accomplished on the Le-Tourneau plane during his numerous travels with R. G. Le-Tourneau. He always attempted to keep the faculty on the subject and to take action as soon as he sensed a consensus had been reached in faculty meetings. He tried to speed up work in the meetings of the Graham organization by moving resolutions at the proper time.

Dr. Edman was also oblivious to rank or luxury. The field representatives tell of being assigned with him on occasion to luxurious surroundings and his humble reaction that he could not conceive of himself being worthy of this luxury. In a natural way he made friends with the workers on the campus and imparted to them a sense that they were important in the operation of the campus. He was not ashamed to pick up scraps of paper to help keep the campus clean.

His keen sense of humor and ability at witty repartee was a factor in drawing people to him. On one occasion he spoke to freshmen at their orientation and solemnly said, "We don't encourage boy-girl relations on campus" and, after a pause in which faces fell, "We don't have to." He wrote to his friend R. G. Harris in Detroit, "Dear You [his friend had addressed him as "Dear Me"] I hardly got a look at that glorious $400 check before it was whisked from under my nose this morning. Seems the girls in my office here have an idea that when an undertaker [his friend's occupation] gives up instead of puts under it's time for fast action and no questions asked— so they run to the nearest bank."[27] He wrote of one of his sons that "during the summer he has been working for a butcher in town, and has become quite experienced in cutting up."[28] A letter of sympathy to Marjorie Glover, who was recovering from surgery went: "This being in stitches is not nearly as funny as alleged in the books. . . . I am sorry that you have been going through the ordeal of cutting up."[29] This ability to pun was pronounced throughout his life.

When it was time for a morning or afternoon coffee break, he would ostentatiously check his pulse and say to someone nearby, "How is your caffein count?" and head for the nearest source of coffee. He humorously blamed this weakness on his Swedish ancestry.

To a frustrated editor of a college publication who wanted to know who had taught him his almost illegible handwriting, he replied, "I was really cut out to write right, but I got sewed up wrong."[30] When asked if baseball would replace dating on campus, he answered, "It is my very pronounced opinion that baseball will never replace dating on Wheaton's campus, because a baseball diamond cannot be easily picked up and carried around."[31]

He described Mrs. Edman's fall on the ice in these words: "Edith fell on the ice and sat down real hard. The doctor says that no bones were broken and the concrete sidewalk seems to be intact."[32] He thanked a friend who had sent him a salt and pepper set thus: "If you are shaky, you can get the necessary salt! Then too, if you just keep grinding away, the necessary pepper will appear!"[33] He wrote to a friend who was concerned with the criticism that he was facing: "I am still able to get bullet proof vests from certain contacts in Cicero, so do not be apprehensive of my welfare."[34]

Numerous letters in his files reveal his thoughtfulness for others. He sent a standard form letter to parents with a new baby, stating that this baby had chosen the loveliest of parents and telling the baby he had enclosed a bib with a Wheaton emblem on it for the use of the young master or mistress. He wrote the president of an insurance company with which he had been insured for thirty years that he appreciated the protection and service that the agent and company had given to him.[35] When his professor and friend at Clark, Dwight Lee, was made the dean of the graduate school at the university, he wrote a warm letter of appreciation and congratulations to him.[36] Dozens of gracious notes thank donors in a humble and considerate way for their help to the school or to the students. Sensitive notes of sympathy were sent to those who were bereaved. If a faculty member had a book published, he could expect to receive a note of congratulations for this achievement.

Karyl Louwenaar of the music faculty one day was asked in a note to drop into his office because he had "an extra to show our appreciation and affection" (for her winning a contest that gave her an opportunity to play in Orchestra Hall). When she came in, he gave her a brown paper bag with congratulations. In it was a small llama rug from Peru with the figure of a musician, a piper, on it.[37] Ray Adkins, a staff member who regularly participated in the morning watch for the last five years before Dr. Edman died, quite often drove him to and from the airport. He would want on his return to be briefed on events at the college. Dr. Edman always brought a small gift for Ray or his family, such as a small brass plate from Egypt, a Hummel figurine from Germany, or a small llama rug from Ecuador.[38]

Eileen Lum, a student from Hawaii, went to his house one winter morning with her coat not fully buttoned. He took her into the entranceway of his home and buttoned up her coat, telling her that she was not in Hawaii and must protect herself from the cold. On another occasion she was flying with him and Dr. Evans to another of the islands of Hawaii when the plane hit some air turbulence. She was fearful and became tense, but Dr. Edman put his hand over hers and smiled until her tension was relieved.[39] This sensitivity to others grew out of the fact that he was himself a sensitive man.

His experiences at Worcester during the great depression made him frugal with his means because he did not want to be a burden on his sons in his old age and because he had a keen awareness from those days of what went into the making of a dollar. He was ever interested in ways of cutting expenses without cutting quality to release more money for faculty and staff salaries. This carefulness with money and his simple way of life made possible the building up of a good-sized estate even though he was a generous giver.

Though he was frugal with his own money and careful in the use of the funds sent to the college, which he recognized as the result of sacrificial stewardship of Christians, he personally was generous in giving to the church or to those in need. He believed that tithing was scriptural, and the tithe was to be based on net income rather than gross income as a minimum of stewardship.[40] He was surprised in 1961 when making up his income tax to find that he had given in that year more than 30 percent of his income to religious or philanthropic work.[41] When the Nazarene Olivet College at Kankakee, Illinois, suffered severe loss from a tornado in 1963, he quietly sent his own check of $100 to the president to help them in their time of need. He gave $400 for two successive years to the work of child evangelism.[42] He contributed a weekly amount regularly to missions through the treasurer of the Wheaton Bible Church.

He wrote to a friend who inquired about principles of Christian stewardship that he believed that "the New Testament teaches definite, systematic giving of one's material substance to the Lord" on each "first day of the week." This money should not be held but should be used immediately in the Lord's work.[43]

His secretaries could expect that when he would return from a trip or at Christmas, he would have some gift with a note of appreciation for their service. He would say as he left at the end of the day, "Thank you for today." One said, "I tried to do my best for him because he was always thoughtful."[44]

When a faculty member would leave the employment of the college, he would send a letter thanking the person for his service and his loyalty to him. Invariably when one received his doctorate, Dr. Edman would write a note of congratulations. He wrote notes each year to thank the director for the wonderful renditions of the *Messiah* that he and his choir gave. When a member of the physics department made an important discovery, Dr. Edman saw to it that the whole faculty was involved in appreciation of this man's achievement. When one individual circulated unkind tales about him even though he had been unusually kind to that person, the most he ever said to the author on one occasion was "That man needs help. We should pray for him." When one needed counsel for error or wrongdoing, he did not hesitate to give firm but loving criticism, even though he disliked confrontations.

His preference to wait, hoping problems might naturally work themselves out, and the sensitivity which made him dislike confrontations that might cause grief to himself and others impressed many as indecisiveness. However, he did have definite doctrinal and ethical convictions which he did not hesitate to express and enforce when necessary, even though others might not agree with him. When a popular magazine began to accept liquor advertising in 1958, he canceled his thirty-five-year subscription and told the editor that he knew of the evil consequences of liquor in life. On another occasion he resigned from a board of a missionary organization whose leader had obtained goods and had not paid for them.

When an occasional faculty member disagreed with the college's doctrinal stand, he would write commending his strong points and then strongly state his own convictions concerning the plenary verbal inspiration of the Bible, or the premillennial coming of Christ. Increasingly after 1948 the indecisiveness which many noticed earlier in handling problems, gave way to a more crisp approach in which he did not hestitate to give a yes or no on the matter, depending upon his convictions.

Those who knew him best spoke of him as a sensitive man who was very much in need of love and understanding and who was deeply hurt by criticism, especially when it was unfair or unjustified. However, he never made outward expression of his hurt, asked for sympathy, or struck back at critics. David Howard was impressed that although he had been student council president when the students had raised questions about Dr. Edman's administration in 1948, Dr. Edman held no grudge but treated him kindly and even had him as speaker in the missionary emphasis week several years later.[45] Dr. Edman also urged others not to answer critics. Billy Graham found this advice helpful on more than one occasion.[46]

The writer was impressed when he saw Dr. Edman promoting or advancing the interests of one who had not been loyal to him or had hurt him deeply. He followed the example of Christ and would not fight back because he believed that the Lord would vindicate him if he were in the right.

This humility did not prevent him from being a virile man with an appeal to athletes. He always had a streak of the adventuresome in him which had surfaced at different periods in his life. Even in 1965 he was willing to live in primitive conditions in order to be with the Aucas for their first Bible conference.

The love of sports as well as an understanding of their value to the student led him to have his regular place on the players' bench at all Wheaton games.[47] Edward Coray, who was for many years director of the college's athletic program, said Dr. Edman supported a vigorous physical education program because he believed that it helped not only to promote good public relations but also offered opportunities for Christian testimony and witness. Sports would also help to promote a positive school spirit and develop physical and moral strength. Games helped to create alertness, cooperation, discipline, courage, loyalty and fitness.[48]

A weakness which was frequently mentioned in interviews was the alleged lack of academic leadership as president of the college. It should be kept in mind that he never had any formal training in administration before he became president and thus had to grow in the position. Preferring to leave attendance at academic meetings of college presidents to the dean, he was cautious lest the academic overshadow and dim the spiritual element at Wheaton. This meant that much of the academic leadership had to come from the faculty until the appointment of a dean. However, he did support worthwhile innovation in the academic program, though he rarely led it. He also wanted to develop individuals who could carry on for themselves and to whom he could delegate authority.[49] Dean Fadenrecht, who held the position of dean for several years, felt that Dr. Edman always gave him academic responsibility and never interfered with him as he tried to carry it out, nor overrode his decisions. Perhaps he did not outline as clearly as he might have the duties of the dean.[50]

Indecisiveness in leadership was often mentioned as an area of concern to many during his administration. This was not because he had no plan in mind but it apparently grew out of his basic optimism and trust in the Lord as well as, at times, an unfounded trust in his associates. He "would wait a problem out" in the hope that time would bring a solution without the need for a confrontation. Since he disliked confrontations or showdowns or having to tell someone that the college could no longer use his services, he often left these disagreeable tasks to his subordinates in administration. His optimism led him to put the best face on a situation or fail to give a complete picture of the situation. Because of this, what might have been minor problems, easily corrected at the beginning, would at times become major crises.

Occasionally his desire to redeem the time led him to ignore proper channels for action. When he gave up his pastorate at the Tabernacle in Wheaton in 1941 because of the press of presidential duties at the college, he wrote to Billy Graham to offer him the pastorate before he consulted the official board. The board was glad to have Billy as pastor, but many felt they should have been consulted first.

His optimism and desire to think the best of people and to grant trust and loyalty to those to whom he gave his confidence led at times to weaknesses of judgment. Some were unworthy of it, betrayed it, or turned it to their own advantage. Some who were brought in during the twenty-five years of his administration with high hopes for their leadership failed to measure up and caused him embarrassment. Occasionally his loyalty to them, even after they left Wheaton, led him to write a too optimistic interpretation of their abilities in letters of recommendation.

His busy schedule and his strict ideas of family discipline and life gave him concern about his relations with his sons. Like many religious leaders who serve the Christian public, he did not have as much time as he would like to have had with his family. Perhaps he too much idealized his strict Victorian father and unconsciously patterned himself along these lines in a day when a more relaxed atmosphere would have helped in raising four sons.

One son commented on the problem of lack of communication with him at times, even though he did try to play games with them, arranged family picnics, and enjoyed family rapport with them on trips and vacations. He never seemed to have time to discuss their possible vocations. Discipline might be arbitrary when he really became concerned, and the Edman boys were often unsure whether any given action or conduct would create bad results. They became unhappy, as letters in his files show, when they were not able to measure up to his high expectations for them in certain situations.

He was, though, very proud of his "four horsemen," and spoke of their doings with fatherly pride in his correspondence with friends. He sought to be with them on special occasions, such as the time of David's commission as an officer in the army or his ordination in New York to the Episcopal ministry. He was quite pleased about his oldest son's giving short-term service in missionary hospitals in Korea, Ethiopia, and other places.

He very much loved his grandchildren and seemed to have a more relaxed approach and excellent rapport with them. He sent them gifts frequently and enjoyed their amusing letters which he often shared with friends. On one occasion his grandson Jeff wrote to thank him for books and stamps he had sent and asked for more. He added concerning Dr. Edman's almost illegible handwriting, "Please print" [in the next letter].[51] He was thrilled when little Carol wrote, "I want to write and tell you that I love you. So do Nancy and Susan. You are the best grandpa in the whole world."[52] His historian's sense must have been gratified when Jeff wrote, "Would you ask the professor of Archaeology some good books to read about Archaeology, for I am quite interested about the study of the past. List them and send the list to me."[53]

He loved to have them visit at Honey Rock where his ideal vacation was "a lovely lake, tall trees, some good books, a gentle breeze, quiet of spirit and contact with heaven."[54] A letter to Carol Ann from Honey Rock is worthy of full quotation:

> Here we are, Carol Ann, in the northwoods of Wisconsin. So sorry to hear that you had the measles, but now you are all better and maybe Nancy has them. When Uncle Charles was a little boy in Worcester, Mass., he had measles. Uncle David was a boy then. One day we could not find David until we looked in Uncle Charles' room and there was David in bed with him, fast asleep. He still didn't catch measles, but your daddy did some time after.
>
> Yesterday, Saturday, was Sarah Grace's birthday in N.Y., and guess who came first thing to see us? a year old deer, same age as S.G. The deer came near our little house to the salt lick, and then began to eat clover in our lawn. She would eat a bit, and then look at us in the window.

After a long visit she wandered N.[orth] into the woods. She will come again.

We have not seen the bears yet because they are far back in the forest. Others here have seen them on the path to our house. They are wild, and not like the three bears who ate the porridge and broke the chair and fell asleep — or was it you!

LOVE TO ALL,
GRANDFATHER.[55]

Little wonder his daughter-in-law wrote that "He was an A+++" as a grandfather and father-in-law.[56]

He also had a deep love for Mrs. Edman, whom he fondly called *Cita*, a Spanish term of endearment, or "Lover," or more often in public when referring to her, "Friend Wife." He believed that married people should be close friends as well as lovers and not take one another for granted. Even during the difficult days of 1948 when his problems at the college and her temporary poor health loomed large, there was a close relationship fostered by common Bible study and prayer each morning. Always proud of her efficiency as a housekeeper and her ability to make a lovely home even in the days when they had so little, he saw to it that he always had an up-to-date will to provide for her if anything happened to him.

When he spent a week at the end of January, 1959, with the Grahams and Wilsons at Hana, Mauai, In Hawaii, he and Ruth Graham were talking on the beach one afternoon about the Graham children. She asked him, "Prexy, now that your four boys are grown and married and moved away, what would you do over again, and what would you do differently if they were little fellows again?" He replied that he would make more effort at companionship in small pleasure, such as picnics and short trips, insist on the cooperation of the children in helping with the home chores, express more confidence in them that they would fulfill their responsibility, would seek to be consistent in his own life and walk before them, and would not hesitate to correct them when there was need of discipline.[57]

This was the manner of man who served as missionary, pastor, teacher and administrator so devotedly and sincerely. He had weaknesses, as do all men, but they were overshadowed by the presence of God in his life. This clear consciousness of His presence was especially experienced just before his long march when he was ill in Germany in 1918, on the streetcar in Boston in 1922 when he needed guidance as to his future, when apparently dying of typhus in Ecuador in the summer of 1925, on the way home on the *Boskoop* in 1928, just before going to Worcester in the depression year of 1929, when Roland was so ill in 1930, on the electric train nearing Wheaton in 1936, after facing his first astronomical budget in 1940, during the major crisis of his life in 1948, and in the periods of trouble with his eyes and heart. This consciousness of God's presence gave him guidance or enabled him to face each crisis with confidence. *Coram Deo* (in the presence of God) provides a fitting motto.

Although his final confidence was in God, he was in the providence of God provided with a friend who was all his life a valued prayer helper and counselor. It was "Uncle Joe" Evans who led him in 1922 to "abandon himself to God," who exerted influence at the Alliance headquarters in 1924 so that Dr. Edman could get married sooner than regulations permitted, who had him teach a year in his Bible School in 1926 and 1927 when Dr. Edman was recovering his health, who helped him to get the church at Worcester in 1929 when he had to leave Ecuador, who advised him to go to Wheaton in 1936, and who finally helped him to think of a suitable successor when he felt he should step down from the presidency. E. Joseph Evans was, under God, one who had more influence for good in his life than any other human being. He was certainly Dr. Edman's Elijah.

Chancellor Edman left a large contribution to the cause of Christ in many ways. He always had a deep interest in missions and missionaries. Not only did he counsel students and inspire them to consider the mission field, but he traveled to mission fields whenever possible to visit and encourage missionaries. He was deeply involved emotionally in the martyrdoms by the Aucas and in the later effort to evangelize them. Perhaps his service to missions was greater after 1928 than it was before or could have been had he been able to stay on the field as he so much desired to do.

Through his voluminous production of devotional literature, his quiet biblical exposition in churches and Bible conferences, his visits and his correspondence, he was able to help people all over the world. Because of him, these people also became friends of the college and assisted it by prayer and gifts.

The gilded spade for breaking ground and the trowel for laying cornerstones became symbols of his work in helping to secure more than a dozen buildings on the campus, thus greatly facilitating the college's educational work. His interest in athletics helped to produce winning teams and stimulate manliness on the campus. His friendliness and his sense of the presence of God helped him to provide leadership that welded students and faculty into a team seeking the excellence in higher education that he also desired.

The secret of his life was well summed up by a doctor in Brooklyn: "The message of your life conforms to the message you preach."[58] Doctrine and practice were uniquely combined by a spiritual devotion to Christ that enabled him to live constantly in the presence of the King.

Bibliographical Essay

THE FOOTNOTES in this volume indicate the many firsthand sources from which the author drew his material. Because each footnote describes the source fully, it seemed that a bibliographical essay would be more useful than a detailed bibliography.

Interviews with Dr. Edman's boyhood friends or relatives, the high school and university yearbooks which he edited or helped to edit, and information in his writings helped in the establishment of the facts of his early years. Letters to the girl who became his brother Elner's wife, written from France and Germany during 1918 and 1919, and his scrapbook of his military experiences were invaluable sources for his military service. His autobiographical book, *Out of My Life,* gave information about his life which was checked against other unpublished sources.

Interviews with Mrs. Edman and dozens of letters from missionaries and Ecuadorians gave authentic information concerning his missionary career from 1923 to 1928. His sermon notebook for 1924 to 1929 contained many outlines of the books and texts of the Bible that he had worked out for teaching and preaching.

The period from 1929 to 1935 at Worcester as pastor, radio preacher and graduate student was fleshed out by interviews with members of his congregation, newspaper files, his file at Clark University which the authorities there graciously permitted the author to xerox, and his sermon

241

notes to the Worcester congregation as well as manuscripts for his broadcasts over WORC.

Interviews in New York with leaders of the Alliance, as well as examination of what records were available in the office there, gave understanding of his pastorate at the New York Gospel Tabernacle in 1935 and 1936. Papers in the files of the registrar and the catalogs of Nyack Bible Institute were useful sources for his work as a teacher at that institution.

The long period from 1936, when he came to Wheaton as a teacher, until his death in 1967 was documented by more than 60 interviews with his friends, faculty members, former students and trustees. At least 20,000 letters to him and from him from all over the world were available in his files. Issues of the Wheaton yearbook, *The Tower,* from 1936 to 1968 provided pictures and descriptions of his activities, as well as student estimates of him. The files of the Wheaton Record for the same period provided valuable information on his travels for the college, his policies, and relations with the students. Appointment booklets for 1958 to 1963 gave some idea of his daily routine as president. The files of the *Alumni Magazine* supplemented those of the *Record.* Catalogs of the college, faculty minutes, minutes of the executive committee of the board of trustees and of the board itself, and files of correspondence with faculty members who are no longer employed by Wheaton helped to fill in the details of his administration as president and chancellor. The file of dated clippings and pictures maintained during his presidency by the college news bureau gave information on his travels and public relations efforts for Wheaton.

His many writings were also helpful as sources. He wrote more than a score of books and over 200 articles that appeared in the *Bulletin* of the college and in religious magazines, such as *Christianity Today, Moody Monthly,* the *Al-*

liance Witness, Decision, and *Christian Life.* His Ph.D. dissertation and his *The Light in the Dark Ages* are examples of his scholarly writings. Nearly 100 editorials in the *Alliance Witness* from 1965 to 1967 are evidence of his work as an editor. Hundreds of question-and-answer columns in *Christian Life* from 1951 to 1966, as well as those in the student magazine, the *Kodon,* reveal his practical and spiritual outlook in the advice he gave.

His helpfulness as a counselor either orally or in writing was evidenced in thousands of letters to and from him and in many interviews by the author with those whom he counseled. His ministry in the pulpit was documented by loose-leaf leather notebooks for the period from 1923 to 1935, taped copies of his radio, chapel and baccalaureate messages, and several interviews.

The author, a professional historian, was happy to note in the oral and written materials unanimity concerning the facts of Dr. Edman's life. There are at least two independent witnesses for each important fact. Thus it is hoped that this biography of one who lived in the presence of God is as objective as it is possible for subjective man to be.

Notes

Preface
1. A. W. Tozer, *Wingspread* (Harrisburg, Pa.: Christian Pubns., 1943), pp. 7-9.

Chapter 1
1. Phone interview with Walter Hoeppner, May 21, 1969.
2. Letter from John Duff to V. R. Edman, Dec. 26, 1961.
3. Interview with Elner Edman, Dec. 12, 1968.
4. Interview with Mrs. V. R. Edman, Oct. 31, 1968.
5. Interview with David Edman, Nov. 6, 1968.
6. Interview with Mrs. V. R. Edman, Oct. 31, 1968.
7. Hoeppner.
8. Letter from V. R. Edman to the *Geneva Republican*, Sept. 15, 1962.
9. Letter from Mrs. Perry Robinson to author, Jan. 12, 1969.
10. Interview with Mrs. K. B. Tiffany, Mar. 14, 1968.
11. Elner Edman.
12. Hoeppner.
13. V. Raymond Edman, *Storms and Starlight* (Wheaton: Scripture Press, 1951) p. 141.

Chapter 2
1. Phone interview with Walter Hoeppner, May 5, 1969; letter from Hoeppner to author, May 22, 1969.
2. Interview with Mrs. K. B. Tiffany, Mar. 18, 1968.
3. Letter from Vernon E. Midel to author, June 23, 1969.
4. *The Bloom* of 1918, p. 74. (This was the high school year book which he edited.)
5. Ibid., pp. 11, 22, 35, 39, 41, 74.
6. Ibid., p. 60.
7. Ibid., p. 23.
8. Letter from E. L. Boyer to Carey E. Melville, Sept. 24, 1929.
9. Interview with Elner Edman, Dec. 12, 1968.
10. *The Bloom*, p. 68.
11. *Kodon* 4, no. 6 (May 1950): 15.
12. W. Wyeth Willard, *Fire on the Prairie* (Wheaton, Ill.: Van Kampen, 1950), p. 128.
13. Letter from V. R. Edman to Carl M. "Snail" Vining, May 8, 1962.
14. *Wheaton Daily Journal*, Feb. 25, 1947.
15. Letter from Harold M. Metcalf to V. R. Edman, Jan. 5, 1960.

Chapter 3
1. *Contact* 10, no. 51 (Sept. 20, 1964): 2-3.
2. V. Raymond Edman, *Out of My Life* (Grand Rapids: Zondervan, 1961), p. 24.
3. Letter from V. R. Edman to Victorine Stolberg, Aug. 17, 1918.
4. W. Wyeth Willard, *Fire on the Prairie* (Wheaton, Ill.: Van Kampen, 1950), pp. 128-29.
5. Letter from V. R. Edman to Dan Poling, Feb. 1, 1966.
6. Edman, *Out of My Life*, pp. 26-29.
7. Letter from V. R. Edman to Victorine Stolberg, Feb. 9, 1919.
8. Letter from V. R. Edman to Victorine Stolberg, Apr. 11, 1919.
9. Letter from V. R. Edman to James E. Smith, Jr., Nov. 2, 1962.
10. Letter from V. R. Edman to Victorine Stolberg, May 6, 1919.
11. Letter from V. R. Edman to Victorine Stolberg, May 12, 1919.
12. Letter from V. R. Edman to Victorine Stolberg, Aug. 10, 1919.
13. Letter from V. R. Edman to Frederick L. Scoggins, Aug. 4, 1966.
14. *The Illio* of 1922, pp. 424-25.

Chapter 4
1. Interview with David Edman, Nov. 6, 1968.
2. *The Illio*, pp. 227-28.
3. V. R. Edman, *Out of My Life* (Grand Rapids: Zondervan, 1961), pp. 33-35.
4. Letter from V. R. Edman to Robert Quayle, Feb. 5, 1960.
5. Application of V. R. Edman for admission to Nyack, Dec. 9, 1921, and interview with Elner Edman, Dec. 12, 1968.
6. Ibid.
7. Letter from Agnes H. Brown to author, Feb. 27, 1969.
8. Letter from V. R. Edman to A. H. McKibben, Aug. 29, 1955.
9. Letter from Charles Shaw to author, Apr. 8, 1969.
10. Interview with David Edman, Nov. 6, 1968.
11. Letter from Charles Shaw to author, Apr. 8, 1969.
12. Interview with Mrs. V. R. Edman, Oct. 31, 1968.
13. Edman, *Out of My Life*, pp. 38-40.
14. *The Alliance Weekly*, Aug. 9, 1922, p. 359.

Chapter 5
1. Interview with E. Joseph Evans, July 1, 1968.
2. V. R. Edman, *Out of My Life* (Grand Rapids: Zondervan, 1961), pp. 15-17.
3. *Kodon* 6, no. 2 (Dec. 1951): 18.
4. Ibid., 5, no. 2 (Nov. 1950): 15.
5. Ibid., 7, no. 5 (June 1953): 21.

Chapter 6
1. Letter from Agnes Brown to author, Feb. 13, 1969.
2. Letter from Dr. Edman to his brother Elner, Aug. 23, 1923.
3. Diary of H. G. Crisman, Aug. 31 to Sept. 2, 1923.
4. Letter from V. R. Edman to Victorine Stolberg, Sept. 14, 1923.
5. Letter from Grace Morrison to author, Jan. 27, 1969.
6. Letter from Mrs. Clara Carlson to author, Nov. 12, 1969.
7. Letter from V. R. Edman to Victorine Stolberg, Sept. 14, 1923.
8. Letter from V. R. Edman to W. A. Mays, Nov. 23, 1965, and letter from V. R. Edman to the Elner Edmans, Nov. 10, 1923.
9. Letter from V. R. Edman to Mrs. Lucille Turner, Dec. 20, 1962.
10. Letters from V. R. Edman to Victorine Stolberg, Sept. 14, 1923, and to Victorine and Elner Edman, Nov. 10, 1923.

11. Letter from V. R. Edman to Dr. Francis W. Eubank, Feb. 24, 1967.
12. Letter from V. R. Edman to the Elner Edmans, Dec. 15, 1923.
13. *Success Builder,* May 5, 1961.
14. Diary of H. G. Crisman, Dec. 27 and 28, 1923.
15. Letter from Agnes Brown to author, Feb. 13, 1969.
16. Letter from V. R. Edman to Elner Edman, Aug. 23, 1923.
17. Letters from V. R. Edman to Victorine Stolberg, Sept. 14, 1923, and
    to the Elner Edmans, Nov. 10, 1923.
18. Letter from V. R. Edman to the Elner Edmans, Dec. 15, 1923.
19. Interview with Paul Young, Oct. 31, 1968.
20. Letter from H. G. Crisman to author, June 24, 1969.
21. Letters from C. C. Eamigh, Dec. 3, 1968, and H. G. Crisman to
    author, June 24, 1969.
22. Diary of H. G. Crisman, May 9, 1924.
23. Letter from V. R. Edman to the Elner Edmans, Apr. 10, 1924.
24. Letter from Mrs. Carl Carlson to author, Nov. 12, 1969.
25. Diary of H. G. Crisman, May 21, 1924.
26. Letter of C. C. Eamigh to author, Dec. 3, 1968.
27. Letter from V. R. Edman to the Elner Edmans, June 25, 1924.
28. Letter from Grace Morrison to author, Nov. 26, 1968.
29. Diary of H. G. Crisman, June 19 and 20, 1924.
30. *Kodon* 7, no. 5 (June 1953): 21.
31. Interview with Robert Bartel, June 26, 1968.
32. Letter from V. R. Edman to the Elner Edmans, June 25, 1924.
33. Letter from V. R. Edman to the Elner Edmans, Oct. 15, 1924, and
    from Grace Morrison to author, Jan. 27, 1969.
34. Letter from Grace Morrison to author, Dec. 26, 1968.
35. Letter from C. C. Eamigh to author, Dec. 3, 1968.
36. Letter from Etelvina Peto to author, Nov. 24, 1968.
37. V. R. Edman, *Wiser Than They Thought* (Wheaton, Ill.: Scripture
    Press, 1960), pp. 56-61.

Chapter 7
 1. Interview with Mrs. Edman, Oct. 31, 1968.
 2. Letter from George P. Simmonds to author, Jan. 25, 1969.
 3. Letter from Grace Morrison to author, Dec. 26, 1968.
 4. *The Alliance Witness* 101, no. 17 (Aug. 17, 1966): 3.
 5. V. R. Edman, *They Found the Secret* (Grand Rapids: Zondervan,
    1960), pp. 146-47; *K.* 4, no. 6 (May 1950): 15.
 6. Edman, *Out of My Life* (Grand Rapids: Zondervan, 1961), pp. 58-59.
 7. *Success Builder,* Sept. 12, 1960, and letter from Mrs. Arthur Ditt-
    mar to author, May 16, 1968.
 8. Letter from Cora M. Zook to author, Nov. 20, 1968.
 9. Letter from Emanuel Prentice to author, Nov. 9, 1968.
10. Letter from Grace Morrison to author, Dec. 26, 1968.
11. Memo from Reuben Larson to author, 1968.
12. Letter from Emanuel Prentice to author, Nov. 9, 1968.
13. Memo from Reuben Larson to author, 1968.
14. Letter from Homer H. Crisman to author, June 24, 1969, and inter-
    view with Paul Young, June 27, 1968.
15. Letter from José A. Lopez to author, Oct. 17, 1968.
16. Letter from Manuel Orbe to author, Nov. 11, 1968.
17. V. R. Edman's application for aid at Clark University, Sept. 12, 1929.
18. Edman, *Out of My Life,* p. 42.
19. Interview with Mrs. V. R. Edman, Oct. 31, 1968.
20. Letter from Emanuel A. Prentice to author, Nov. 9, 1968.

21. Letter from Gladys Shepherd to author, Jan. 21, 1969.
22. Edman, *Out of My Life,* pp. 42-44.
23. Ibid., pp. 148-51.
24. Letter from V. R. Edman to William Keith, Oct. 6, 1953.

Chapter 8
1. Letter from V. R. Edman to Mr. and Mrs. R. C. Lindborg, July 20, 1960.
2. Letter from V. R. Edman to L. W. Lippert, July 14, 1966.
3. Letter from V. R. Edman to Frank R. Radecki, July 17, 1963.
4. Interview with Guy Burnham, June 29, 1968.
5. Interview with Henri Eckhardt, June 12, 1968.
6. Interview with Mrs. V. R. Edman, Oct. 31, 1968.
7. Letter from Anders Edman to V. R. Edman, Mar. 28, 1935.
8. Edman, *Out of My Life* (Grand Rapids: Zondervan, 1961), pp. 48-54.
9. Interview with Rowena Carr, Oct. 24, 1968.
10. Applications for financal aid from Clark, Sept. 12, 1929, and Feb. 4, 1930.
11. Letter from E. L. Boyer to C. E. Melville, Sept. 24, 1929.
12. Letter from W. M. Trumbull to C. E. Melville, Sept. 26, 1929.
13. Letter from V. R. Edman to department chairman, Clark, Dec. 10, 1930.
14. Application for financial aid from Clark, Feb. 28, 1931.
15. Letter from V. R. Edman to Norman B. Rohrer, Oct. 2, 1959.
16. "How I Found God's Will for My Life," manuscript of proposed article, July 1957.
17. Application for financial aid from Clark, Sept. 26, 1933.
18. *Moody Monthly* 44, no. 11 (July 1944): 612-13; Edman, *Out of My Life,* pp. 55-56.
19. Interview with Guy Burnham, June 29, 1968.
20. *Worcester Daily Telegram,* Apr. 22, 1935.
21. Letter from Anders Edman to V. R. Edman, Mar. 28, 1935.
22. Letter from David J. Fant to V. R. Edman, Apr. 25, 1935.
23. *Worcester Daily Telegram,* May 27, 1935.
24. Ibid., May 29, 1935.
25. "How I Found God's Will for My Life," manuscript by V. R. Edman, July 1957, p. 2.

Chapter 9
1. Letter from V. R. Edman to David H. Dugan, Mar. 28, 1964.
2. Letter from Virginia (Shuman) Hodgkiss to V. R. Edman, May 11, 1967.
3. Letter from John A. Gibbs to author, Oct. 29, 1968.
4. Interview with W. F. Smalley, June 26, 1968.
5. Telephone interview with Earle M. Holt, June 26, 1968.
6. *Record* 76, no. 2 (Feb. 7, 1957): 1.
7. Ibid.
8. Ibid., 50, no. 1 (Jan. 29, 1936): 1.
9. *Wheaton Daily Journal,* Feb. 10, 1936.
10. *Sunday School Times* 78, no. 10 (Mar. 7, 1936): 158-59.

Chapter 10
1. Letter from J. Oliver Buswell, Jr., to V. R. Edman, Mar. 5, 1936.
2. Letter from E. Joseph Evans to V. R. Edman, Mar. 9, 1936.
3. Letter from Clarence Williams to V. R. Edman, Mar. 10, 1936.
4. Letter from V. R. Edman to J. Oliver Buswell, Mar. 10, 1936.
5. *Faculty Minutes,* Mar. 26, 1936.

6. *Minutes* of executive committee of board of trustees, Mar. 26, 1936.
7. Letter from A. C. Snead to V. R. Edman, Mar. 25, 1936.
8. Letter from V. R. Edman to G. Vernon Brown, Apr. 4, 1936.

Chapter 11

1. Letter from V. R. Edman to Eddie Ruch, Oct. 5, 1962.
2. Note from V. R. Edman to Rowena Carr, Apr. 25, 1967.
3. Letter from V. R. Edman to O. E. Tiffany, May 22, 1943.
4. *Daily Journal,* July 29, 1936.
5. *Kodon* 7, no. 4 (May 1953): 4.
6. *Evansville Courier,* Jan. 14, 1955.
7. *Kodon* 5, no. 1 (Oct. 1950): 17.
8. *Bulletin* 3, no. 7 (Oct. 1956): 1.
9. Letter from V. R. Edman to J. D. Morrison, Mar. 8, 1963.
10. *Faculty Bulletin* 5, no. 2 (Oct. 1941): 7.
11. *Kodon* 5, no. 1 (Oct. 1950): 17.
12. *Faculty Bulletin* 5, no. 3 (Feb. 1942): 8.
13. *Kodon* 5, no. 3 (Feb. 1951): 19.
14. Letter from V. R. Edman to Donald Moore, Oct. 11, 1962.
15. Letter from V. R. Edman to Betty Barajas, Nov. 2, 1962.
16. Letter from V. R. Edman to Knute Larson, Sept. 5, 1961.
17. Interview with Hudson T. Armerding, July 23, 1968.
18. Interview with Robert deVette, Apr. 30, 1968.
19. Interview with Billy Graham, Jan. 24, 1969.
20. Interview with Hudson T. Armerding, July 23, 1968.
21. Interview with Mrs. K. B. Tiffany, Mar. 14, 1968.
22. *Faculty Minutes,* June 8, 1937.
23. Ibid., Nov. 2, 1937, and Jan. 11, 1938.
24. Note of V. R. Edman to J. Oliver Buswell Jr., Mar. 9, 1937.
25. *Record* 54, no. 1 (Jan. 23, 1940): 2.
26. *Tower* of 1939, pp. 78-79.
27. Ibid., p. 153.
28. *Faculty Minutes,* Mar. 2, 1937.
29. *Tower* of 1939, p. 113.
30. Ibid.
31. *Record* 51, no. 41 (Oct. 12, 1937): 1.
32. Letter from Thomas Williamson to V. R. Edman, Nov. 22, 1937.
33. *Record* 54, no. 1 (Nov. 23, 1940): 2.
34. Ibid., 52, no. 53 (Dec. 2, 1938): 1.
35. Ibid., 52. no. 56 (Dec. 13, 1938): 5.
36. *Faculty Bulletin* 3, no. 2 (Oct. 1939): 5.
37. *Record* 64, no. 10 (Apr. 20, 1950): 1.
38. Ibid., 54, no. 1 (Jan. 23, 1940): 2.
39. Ibid., 56, no. 3 (Aug. 19, 1942): 1; 55, no. 33 (Sept. 30, 1941): 1.
40. Interview with Billy Graham, Jan. 24, 1969.
41. Manuscript of address by V. R. Edman to TEAM's annual conference, Wheaton, 1936.
42. *Record* 52. no. 59 (Jan. 13, 1939): 1.
43. *Minutes* of Board. Jan. 10, 1939.
44. *Faculty Bulletin* 2, no. 6 (Feb. 1939): 11.

Chapter 12

1. *Minutes* of board, Jan. 10, 1939, and *Minutes* of executive committee of board, Jan. 22, 1936.
2. *Minutes* of the board, June 14, 1941.
3. Interview with Clarence Hale, Nov. 21, 1968.

4. *Record* 53, no. 60 (Jan. 12, 1940): 2.
5. Letter from Donald Hoke to author, Apr. 11, 1969.
6. Ibid.
7. Interview with Edward Cording, Mar. 20, 1969.
8. V. R. Edman, *Out of My Life* (Grand Rapids: Zondervan, 1961) p. 57.
9. Interview with Clarence Hale, Nov. 21, 1968.
10. *Daily Journal*, Jan. 20, 1940.
11. Letter from Don Hoke to author, Apr. 11, 1969.
12. *Minutes* of board, June 8, 1940.
13. Manuscript to David C. Cook, Jan. 21, 1963.
14. Interview with Carter Cody, Feb. 6, 1969.
15. *Tower* of 1941, p. 11.
16. V. R. Edman, *Look Unto the Hills* (Chicago: Moody, 1968), p. 33.
17. *Minutes* of board, Jan. 11, 1941, p. 1.
18. *Alumni News* 7, no. 4 (Jan.-Feb. 1941): 1.
19. Interview with Harvey Chrouser, Sept. 9, 1968.
20. *Daily Journal*, Aug. 15, 1941.
21. *Bulletin* of college (inauguration number), p. 5.
22. *Record* 55, no. 22 (May 6, 1941): 1.
23. Frank Herrick, *College Chimes* (Wheaton: Herrick, 1941), p. 1.
24. *Record* 55, no. 24 (May 13, 1941): 2.
25. *Kodon* 9, no. 4 (Apr. 1955), p. 19; *Record* 55, no. 25 (May 16, 1941): 2.
26. Ibid., 5, no. 4 (Mar. 1951): 17.
27. *His* 1, no. 4 (Summer, 1942): 10-11.
28. *Record* 55, no. 52 (Dec. 9, 1941): 1.
29. Ibid., 57, no. 20 (Apr. 23, 1943): 4; *Bulletin* of faculty 6, no. 4 (May 1943): 2.
30. *Record* 56, no. 12 (Mar. 17, 1942): 1.
31. Note from Edward Coray to V. R. Edman, July 23, 1942.
32. *Minutes* of board, Feb. 13, 1942.
33. Letter from Leland Simcox to author, Nov. 18, 1968.
34. *Alumni News* 10, no. 2 (Jan.-Feb. 1943): 1, 3.
35. *Record* 57, no. 14 (Mar. 23, 1943): 4.
36. *Daily Journal*, July 19, 1943.
37. *Daily Journal*, Oct. 29, 1943.
38. *Minutes* of faculty, Sept. 28, 1943.

Chapter 13
1. Interview with Clyde Kilby, Apr. 25, 1968.
2. *Minutes* of faculty, May 23, 1944.
3. Interview with Lamberta Voget, Mar. 21, 1969.
4. *Alumni News* 11, no. 5 (July-Aug. 1944): 3.
5. *Record* 58, no. 18 (Aug. 18, 1944): 1.
6. *Minutes* of board, June 10, 1944, p. 7.
7. Ibid., Oct. 27-28, 1944, p. 3; interview with Robert Walker, Mar. 26, 1969.
8. *Record* 59, no. 25 (Nov. 1, 1945): 1.
9. Application for U. S. Naval Reserve Commission, Dec. 1, 1944.
10. *Record* 59, no. 8 (Mar. 22, 1945): 4.
11. *Record* 60, no. 8 (Mar. 21, 1946): 3.
12. *Bulletin* of college, 26, no. 1 (Jan. 1949).
13. *Record* 60, no. 11 (Apr. 11, 1946): 3.
14. *Record* 60, no. 19 (Aug. 15, 1946): 1.
15. Ibid., 51, no. 42 (Oct. 19, 1937); cf. ibid., 64, no. 32 (Jan. 11, 1951): 1.

16. Letter from V. R. Edman to H. A. Ironside, Mar. 7, 1947; *Alumni Magazine* 14, no. 5 (Mar. 1947): 1.
17. *Record* 61, nos. 6, 7, 8 and 9 (Mar. 6, 13, 20 and 27, 1947).
18. *Record* 63, no. 12 (May 5, 1949): 1.

Chapter 14
1. *Daily Journal,* Feb. 28, 1947.
2. *Minutes* of board, Feb. 22, 1947.
3. *Bulletin* of college, 24, no. 7 (Oct. 1947): 3.
4. *Newsletter* of college, 24, no. 7 (Oct. 1947): 1-2.
5. Letter from H. M. Shuman to V. R. Edman, Nov. 7, 1947.
6. *Record* 61, no. 25 (Oct. 30, 1947): 1.
7. Ibid., 61, no. 26 (Nov. 26, 1947): 2.
8. Ibid., 62, no. 2 (Feb. 12, 1948): 1.
9. Ibid., 61, no. 34 (Jan. 15, 1948): 1.
10. Interview with Mrs. K. B. Tiffany, Mar. 14, 1968, and Carter Cody, Feb. 6, 1969.
11. Letter from C. C. Brooks to author, Apr. 8, 1969.
12. Letter from Royal Peck to author, Jan. 2, 1969.
13. Letter from Herman Fischer to V. R. Edman, July 5, 1948.
14. Letter from V. R. Edman to Herman Fischer, July 8, 1948.
15. Letter from V. R. Edman to committee of class of 1947, Aug. 3, 1948.
16. Interview with Robert Van Kampen, Mar. 22, 1969.
17. Letter from V. R. Edman to Norman Burns, Oct. 1, 1948.
18. Interview with David Howard, Dec. 7, 1968.
19. Letter from David Howard to Herman Fischer, Sept. 11, 1948.
20. Interview with David Howard, Dec. 7, 1968.
21. Interview with Carter Cody, Feb. 6, 1969.
22. Letter from V. R. Edman to Ralph Mitchell, Sept. 16, 1948.
23. Letter from Charles Edman to author, Nov. 18, 1968.

Chapter 15
1. V. R. Edman's report to the board, Oct. 22-23, 1948.
2. *Minutes* of the faculty, Oct. 26, 1948.
3. Letter from V. R. Edman to Stephen Paine, Aug. 7, 1963, and *Record* 65, no. 2 (Feb. 2, 1951): 3-4.
4. Letter of V. R. Edman to Will R. Elliot, Nov. 11, 1948.
5. *Record* 62, no. 32 (Dec. 16, 1948): 1.
6. Ibid., 63, no. 5 (Mar. 10, 1949): 1.
7. *Record* 63, no. 7 (Sept. 15, 1949): 1.
8. Letter from Cary N. Weisiger, Jr., to V. R. Edman, May 26, 1954, and from V. R. Edman to Cary N. Weisiger, Jr., May 3, 1954.
9. *Record* 64, no. 30 (Dec. 14, 1950): 1.
10. Ibid., 65, no. 33 (Jan. 17, 1952): 1.
11. Interview with David Howard, Dec. 7, 1968.
12. *Record* 63, no. 32 (Jan. 12, 1950): 5.
13. Ibid., 64, no. 2 (Feb. 17, 1950): 1; *Chicago Daily News,* Feb. 10, 1951.
14. Letter from Bud Schaeffer to author, Oct. 31, 1968.
15. *Bulletin* 27, no. 3 (Mar. 1950): 1; Edman, *Out of My Life* (Grand Rapids: Zondervan, 1961), pp. 210-16.
16. Letter from Royal Peck to author, Jan. 2, 1969.
17. *Kodon* 6, no. 4 (Apr. 1952): 21.
18. *Record* 64, no. 17 (Sept. 14, 1950): 1.
19. V. R. Edman report to board, Oct. 20-21, 1950.
20. *Record* 65, no. 13 (Apr. 26, 1951): 1.
21. *Minutes* of executive committee of board, Mar. 14, 1951.

22. *Minutes* of board, June 13, 1952, p. 2.
23. *Alumni Magazine* 19, no. 2 (July 1952).
24. Interview with Robert Van Kampen, Mar. 22, 1969.
25. *DuPage Press*, Dec. 3, 1959.
26. *Record* 67, no. 1 (Feb. 5, 1953): 1; *Out of My Life*, pp. 64-68.
27. *Bulletin* 30, no. 3 (Mar. 1953).
28. *Houston Post*, Mar. 5, 1954.
29. Ibid., 69, no. 3 (Oct. 1, 1953): 1.
30. Interview with Kenneth Gieser, Mar. 3, 1969.
31. Letter from V. R. Edman to David H. Dugan, Jr., Sept. 15, 1953.
32. Letter from V. R. Edman to John W. Bradbury, Dec. 8, 1953.
33. Letter from V. R. Edman to G. W. Johnson, Mar. 23, 1954.
34. *Bulletin* 32, no. 5 (May 1953).
35. *Record* 72, no. 7 (Mar. 17, 1955): 3.
36. Letter from V. R. Edman to Milton Brown, Apr. 29, 1955.
37. Interview with Robert Van Kampen, Mar. 22, 1969; *Kodon* 9, no. 5 (June 1955): 17.

Chapter 16
1. *Tower* of 1955, p. 6.
2. *Record* 65, no. 23 (Oct. 18, 1951): 1.
3. Letter from V. R. Edman to Philip E. Howard, Jan. 13, 1956.
4. *Alumni Magazine* 23, no. 3 (Mar. 1956): 2.
5. Letter from Clyde Taylor to the author, Apr. 17, 1969.
6. *Minutes* of executive committee of board, Feb. 28, 1956.
7. Ibid., Oct. 3, 1957.
8. Report to board, Oct. 28, 1957.
9. *Wheaton Daily Journal* 26, no. 137 (Nov. 14, 1957).
10. Letter from V. R. Edman to Norris Aldeen, June 20, 1958.
11. *Minutes* of faculty, Oct. 14, 1958.
12. Letter from V. R. Edman to Harold Lindsell, Aug. 28, 1958.
13. Letter from V. R. Edman to Walter Knowles, Feb. 4, 1959.
14. Interview with Robert Van Kampen, Mar. 22, 1969.
15. *Christian Life* 21, no. 2 (June 1959): 18-19.
16. Interview with Richard Gerig, Mar. 10, 1969.
17. *Minutes* of faculty, Dec. 16, 1958.
18. *Alumni Magazine* 26, no. 6 (June 1959): 1.
19. Letter from V. R. Edman to Stanley Kresge, Apr. 17, 1962.
20. Letter from V. R. Edman to Paul Brandel, Sept. 26, 1959.
21. Letter from V. R. Edman to Hugo Wurdack, June 11, 1960.
22. *Alumni Magazine* 26, no's. 7-8 (July-Aug. 1959): 4.
23. Ibid., no. 11 (Nov. 1959): 2.
24. *The Alliance Witness*, Apr. 3, 1967, p. 13.
25. Letter from V. R. Edman to Roy LeTourneau, Oct. 5, 1959.
26. Letter from V. R. Edman to R. G. Harris, Jan. 1, 1960.
27. *Alumni Magazine* 27, no's. 7 and 8 (July-Aug. 1960): 15.

Chapter 17
1. *Record* 80, no. 2 (Sept. 24, 1959): 3.
2. Letter from V. R. Edman to Ross Rhoads, Feb. 5, 1960.
3. Letter from V. R. Edman to Stanley S. Kresge, Mar. 12, 1962.
4. Letter from V. R. Edman to Rachel Saint, July 3, 1959.
5. Letter from V. R. Edman to Mrs. Elizabeth Lewis, Oct. 19, 1959.
6. *Success Builder*, July 30, 1959.
7. Letter from V. R. Edman to Mrs. C. H. Thompson, May 13, 1960.
8. Letter from V. R. Edman to Mr. and Mrs. William D. Wheeler, June 7, 1960.

9. Letter from V. R. Edman to Grace B. Holcombe, Aug. 21, 1959.
10. Letter from V. R. Edman to Alan Redpath, Mar. 4, 1960.
11. Letter from V. R. Edman to D. W. Rose, Mar. 21, 1960.
12. Letter from V. R. Edman to Grady Wilson, July 2, 1962.
13. Interview with John H. Fadenrecht, Mar. 7, 1969.
14. Letter from V. R. Edman to Ross Rhoads, Apr. 5, 1960.
15. Letter from V. R. Edman to Mrs. A. G. Cowles, May 5, 1960.
16. Letter from V. R. Edman to David Lindstrom, May 9, 1960.
17. Letter from V. R. Edman to J. Abraham, Oct. 21, 1965.
18. Letter to V. R. Edman from Faye Whitsell, July 16, 1960.
19. *Alumni Magazine* 27, no. 3 (Mar. 1960): 2.
20. Letter from Richard M. Nixon to V. R. Edman, Dec. 8, 1960.
21. *Record* 82, no. 20 (Feb. 23, 1960): 1.
22. Letter from V. R. Edman to Everett R. Rhodes, Oct. 2, 1961.
23. Letter from V. R. Edman to Roy Aldrich, Nov. 8, 1961.
24. *Minutes* of board, Oct. 13, 1961.
25. Letter from V. R. Edman to J. R. Maxfield, Jr., Mar. 1, 1962.
26. Letter from V. R. Edman to Wyeth Willard, Apr. 26, 1962.
27. Letter from V. R. Edman to Gerald Stanton, May 29, 1963.
28. Letter from V. R. Edman to Manly A. Wilson, Mar. 22, 1963.
29. *Record* 85, no. 19 (Feb. 7, 1963): 1.
30. Letter from V. R. Edman to Mrs. Hugo Wurdack, Oct. 2, 1963.
31. *Minutes* of board, Oct. 11, 1963, p. 5.
32. *Minutes* of faculty, Oct. 15, 1963.
33. Letter from Billy Graham to V. R. Edman, Oct. 22, 1963.

Chapter 18
1. Letter from V. R. Edman to Billy Graham, June 30, 1964.
2. Letter from V. R. Edman to Billy Graham, July 10, 1964.
3. *Minutes* of executive committee, July 9, 1964.
4. Interview with E. Joseph Evans, July 1, 1968.
5. *Minutes* of board, Sept. 10, 1964.
6. *Record* 87, no. 1 (Sept. 24, 1964): 1, 3.
7. Letter from V. R. Edman to his sons, Sept. 11, 1964.
8. Letter from Hudson T. Armerding to V. R. Edman, Sept. 12, 1964.
9. Letter from V. R. Edman to Mrs. Nellie E. C. Boyer, Dec. 28, 1964.
10. Letter from Malcolm Cronk to V. R. Edman, Sept. 22, 1964.
11. Letter from Patty and James Hutchens to V. R. Edman, Oct. 10, 1964.
12. *Bulletin* of college, 42, no. 1 (Oct. 1964): 1 ff.
13. V. R. Edman memo to Mrs. Mina Hill, Nov. 9, 1964.
14. Letter from Otto Kerner to V. R. Edman, Dec. 2, 1964.
15. Letter from Howard E. Moffett to V. R. Edman, Dec. 25, 1964.
16. Wheaton College News Bureau release, Jan. 6, 1965.

Chapter 19
1. Letter from V. R. Edman to Walker R. Barndoller, Dec. 4, 1964.
2. Letter from V. R. Edman to Harry J. Williams, Jan. 9, 1965.
3. Letter from H. S. Sutherland to V. R. Edman, Feb. 3, 1965.
4. Letter from V. R. Edman to Charles Schepens, Feb. 2, 1965.
5. Letter from David Howard to V. R. Edman, Jan. 15, 1965.
6. Letter from V. R. Edman to Gerald W. Welbourn, May 24, 1965.
7. Letter from Anita Bailey to author, July 3, 1968.
8. Letter from Jack F. Shepherd to V. R. Edman, June 5, 1965.
9. Letter from Mrs. Homer Crisman to Gladys Shepherd, Dec. 8, 1965.
10. Letter from V. R. Edman to Carol, Nancy, and Susan Edman, Nov. 16, 1965.
11. Letter from Hudson T. Armerding to V. R. Edman, Jan. 26, 1966.

12. Interview with Robert Van Kampen, Mar. 22, 1969.
13. *Alliance Witness* 10, no. 14 (July 6, 1966): 3.
14. Letter from V. R. Edman to Leo C. Lapp, Aug. 10, 1966.
15. Letter from V. R. Edman to Mrs. R. F. Wagner, Dec. 20, 1966.
16. Letter from Rowena Carr to E. M. Blaiklock, Jan. 15, 1967.
17. Letter from V. R. Edman to Rachel Saint, June 7, 1967.
18. Letter from Billy Graham to V. R. Edman, June 7, 1967.
19. Letter from Grady and Wilma Wilson to V. R. Edman, Jan. 9, 1967.
20. Letter from Daniel S. C. Liu to V. R. Edman, Feb. 2, 1967. See *Alumni Magazine* 34, no. 4 (Apr. 1967): 2, 16, for article.
21. Letter from Paul Rees to V. R. Edman, Feb. 27, 1967.
22. Letter from Shannon Vandruff, Feb. 6, 1967.
23. Interview with Nathan Bailey, June 26, 1968.
24. *Record* 90:1, supplement (Sept. 23, 1967): 2.
25. Letter from V. R. Edman to Hudson T. Armerding, Feb. 25, 1966.
26. *Bulletin* of college, 45, no. 2 (Nov. 1967).
27. Letter from Stephanie Ramayah to Dolores Lassen, Oct. 4, 1967.

Chapter 20
1. *Kodon* 8, no. 2 (Dec. 1953): 23.
2. Ibid., 5, no. 2 (Nov. 1950): 15.
3. Letter from Robert J. Richardson to V. R. Edman, Sept. 17, 1961.
4. Letter from Billy Graham to V. R. Edman, Jan. 4, 1958.
5. *Bulletin* of college, 28, no. 7 (Oct. 1951): 3.
6. Letter from V. R. Edman to Stephen F. Burton, Oct. 4, 1961.
7. Letter from V. R. Edman to Philip Howard, Dec. 12, 1951.
8. *Kodon* 7, no. 5 (June 1953), p. 21.
9. *Alumni Magazine* 21, no. 8 (July 1954): 3.
10. Letter from V. R. Edman to Charles Schepens, Apr. 28, 1960.
11. Letter from Madame Chiang Kai-Shek to V. R. Edman, Mar. 25, 1958.
12. Interview with Robert Walker, Mar. 26, 1969.
13. Letter from David Lambert to V. R. Edman, July 13, 1960.
14. Letter from V. R. Edman to Clyde A. Freed, Jr., Mar. 1, 1960.
15. Letter from V. R. Edman to Mrs. Thaddeus P. Bell, Dec. 28, 1961.
16. Letter from V. R. Edman to Mrs. Robert Feltz, May 17, 1963.
17. *Wheaton Leader*, Sept. 28, 1967.
18. *Alliance Witness* 100, no. 13 (June 23, 1965): 2.
19. Ibid., no. 18 (Sept. 1, 1965): 2.
20. Ibid., no. 24 (Nov. 24, 1965): 2.
21. *Kodon* 16, no. 3 (Feb. 1952): 19.
22. Ibid.
23. *Christian Life* 14, no. 2 (June 1957): 104.
24. *Alliance Witness* 14, no. 5 (Sept. 1952): 88.
25. Letter from Rex Jones to the author, Mar. 27, 1968.

Chapter 21
1. Letter from Chester L. Schneider to the Zondervan brothers, Nov. 5, 1961.
2. *Kodon* 6, no. 2 (Dec. 1951): 18.
3. Interview with Kenneth Taylor by phone, Mar. 26, 1969.
4. Letter from V. R. Edman, Sept. 4, 1959.
5. Letter from Philip Lasse to V. R. Edman, May 2, 1961.
6. Letter from David Burnham to V. R. Edman, Aug. 8, 1962.
7. Letter to V. R. Edman, Dec. 18, 1964.
8. Letter from V. R. Edman to Armand R. Haeger, June 13, 1964.
9. Letter from V. R. Edman to Robert Cook, Apr. 5, 1962.
10. Memo from Robert Evans to author, Jan. 17, 1969.

11. Phone interview with Joseph Coughlin, Apr. 21, 1969.
12. *Record* 64, no. 32 (Jan. 11, 1951): 1.
13. Letter from V. R. Edman to Mr. and Mrs. Ray de la Haye, Aug. 30, 1963.
14. Letter from Leighton Ford to V. R. Edman, July 28, 1960.
15. Letter from Leighton Ford to author, Jan. 28, 1969.
16. Interview with Elner Edman, Dec. 12, 1968.
17. Interview with Billy Graham, Jan. 24, 1969.
18. Letter from V. R. Edman to Nelson Bell, Nov. 10, 1952.
19. Letter from V. R. Edman to George M. Wilson, Sept. 30, 1960.
20. Letter from V. R. Edman to Billy Graham, Dec. 22, 1960.
21. Letter from V. R. Edman to Charles M. White, May 6, 1963.
22. Letter from Billy Graham to V. R. Edman, Oct. 6, 1952.
23. Letter from V. R. Edman to Helen Deutsch, Mar. 8, 1963.
24. Interview with Billy Graham, Jan. 24, 1969.
25. Interview wth Kenneth Gieser, Mar. 3, 1969.
26. Letter from Billy Graham to V. R. Edman, Nov. 12, 1964.
27. Letter from Billy Graham to V. R. Edman, July 8, 1964.
28. Letter from Stanley S. Kresge to V. R. Edman, Jan. 25, 1963.
29. Letters from Billy Graham to V. R. Edman, Oct. 28, 1965, and Dec. 27, 1965.
30. Letter from V. R. Edman to Carol Creanza, Nov. 9, 1964.
31. Interview with Robert Noles, Nov. 11, 1968.
32. Interview with David Roberts, July 24, 1968.
33. Letter from Marion Wade to V. R. Edman, Jan. 10, 1963.
34. Letter from V. R. Edman, May 3, 1960.
35. Letter from V. R. Edman to Karen Palm, Mar. 1, 1962.
36. Letter from V. R. Edman to Charles Woodbridge, June 14, 1962.
37. Letter from V. R. Edman to Esther Olmstead, Mar. 3, 1962.
38. Letter from V. R. Edman, Dec. 13, 1966.
39. Letter from V. R Edman to Dorothy G. Wentworth, Mar. 26, 1964.
40. *Record* 90, no. 15 (Feb. 9, 1968): 1; memo from Edwin Hollatz to author, Mar. 13, 1968.
41. Letter from V. R. Edman, Nov. 4, 1959.
42. Letter from V. R. Edman to Lydia Mattar, Jan. 29, 1963.
43. *Now* 21, no. 11 (Nov. 1967): 67.
44. Phone interview with Richard H. LeTourneau, Apr. 17, 1969.
45. Letter from V. R. Edman, Aug. 29, 1955.
46. Phone interview with Robert Walker, Mar. 26, 1969.
47. Letter from Stephen Olford to V. R. Edman, Sept. 16, 1959.

Chapter 22

1. *Christianty Today* 12, no. 1 (Oct. 13, 1969): 31.
2. Letter from V. R. Edman to Joseph S. Maxwell, Apr. 12, 1943.
3. Hudson T. Armerding's memorial address, Sept. 24, 1967.
4. Interview with Carter Cody, Feb. 26, 1969.
5. Interview with Mrs. Edman, Oct. 31, 1968.
6. *Kodon* 5, no. 3 (Feb. 1951): 19.
7. V. R. Edman's *Lessons God Has Taught Me,* pp. 4-5, reprint from *Christian Life* 22, no. 9 (Jan. 1961): 20.
8. Hudson T. Armerding's memorial address, Sept. 24, 1967.
9. Interview with Evan Welsh, Mar. 19, 1969.
10. Interview with Rowena Carr, Oct. 24, 1968.
11. Interview with Carl Armerding, Oct. 18, 1968.
12. Interview with Ray Adkins, May 21, 1968.
13. Interview with Clarence Hyde, Oct. 14, 1968.
14. Interview with Richard Gerig, Mar. 10, 1969.

15. Interview with Mrs. Edman, Oct. 31, 1968.
16. Interview with David Edman, Nov. 6, 1968.
17. Hudson T. Armerding's memorial address, Sept. 24, 1967.
18. Interview with Carl Armerding, Oct. 18, 1968.
19. *Kodon* 6, no. 2 (Dec. 1951), p. 18.
20. Interview with Dolores Lassen, Mar. 12, 1968.
21. Interview with Carter Cody, Feb. 2, 1969.
22. Letter from David Salstrom to the author, Aug. 2, 1968.
23. Letter from Pecos Higgins to V. R. Edman, Feb. 13, 1961.
24. Letter from Nancy Litteral to the author, Aug. 26, 1968.
25. Letter from Rene Padilla to the author, Apr. 21, 1969.
26. Interview with Billy Graham, Jan. 24, 1969.
27. Letter from V. R. Edman to Robert G. Harris Apr. 27, 1955.
28. Letter from V. R. Edman to Morris Nelson, Sept. 30, 1943.
29. Letter from V. R. Edman to Marjorie Glover, Dec. 16, 1953.
30. *Kodon* 5, no. 3 (Feb. 1951): 19.
31. Ibid., 4, no. 5 (Apr. 1950): 17.
32. Letter from V. R. Edman to Mr. and Mrs. Harold Anderson, Feb. 8, 1962.
33. Letter from V. R. Edman to Fred Dienert, Jan. 7, 1960.
34. Letter from V. R. Edman to George Ferguson, Dec. 20, 1962.
35. Letter from V. R. Edman to DeForest W. Abel, Jan. 1, 1961.
36. Letter from V. R. Edman to Dwight Lee, Dec. 12, 1961.
37. Memo from Karyl Louwenaar to author, 1968.
38. Interview with Ray Adkins, May 21, 1968.
39. Letter from Eileen Lum to author, May 21, 1968.
40. Letter from V. R. Edman to Lynne D. Kellaway, Feb. 1, 1962.
41. Letter from V. R. Edman to C. J. Anderson, Dec. 26, 1961.
42. Letter from V. R. Edman to Carol Eaton, Dec. 4, 1964.
43. Letter from V. R. Edman to Joseph S. Maxwell, Dec. 7, 1942.
44. Interview with Dolores Lassen, Mar. 12, 1968.
45. Interview with David Howard, Dec. 7, 1969.
46. Interview with Billy Graham, Jan. 24, 1969.
47. Interview with Harvey Chrouser, Sept. 9, 1968.
48. Interview with Edward Coray, May 7, 1969, and *Bulletin* 28, no. 7 (Oct. 1951): 1-2.
49. Interview with Carter Cody, Feb. 6, 1969.
50. Interview with John Fadenrecht, Mar. 7, 1969.
51. Letter from Jeff Edman to V. R. Edman, Mar., 1963.
52. Letter from Carol Edman to V. R. Edman, Oct., 1962.
53. Letter from Jeff Edman to V. R. Edman, Nov. 30, 1964.
54. *Kodon* 4, no. 6 (May 1950): 15.
55. Letter from V. R. Edman to Carol Ann Edman, June 25, 1962.
56. Letter from Mrs. V. Roland Edman to author, Jan. 25, 1969.
57. V. R. Edman, *Out of My Life* (Grand Rapids: Zondervan, 1961), pp. 90-94.
58. Letter from Carleton Campbell to V. R. Edman, Sept. 20, 1965.